A Biography of Cairine Wilson

FIRST PERSON

Canada's First Woman Senator

Valerie Knowles

Dundurn Press
Toronto & Oxford
1988

Design and Production:Andy Tong
Printing and Binding:Gagné Printing Ltd., Louiseville, Quebec, Canada

The writing of this manuscript and the publication of this book were made possible by support from several sources. The publisher wishes to acknowledge the generous assistance and ongoing support of **The Canada Council, The Book Publishing Industry Development Programme** of the **Department of Communications** and **The Ontario Arts Council.**

Care has been taken to trace the ownership of copyright material used in the text (including the illustrations). The author and publisher welcome any information enabling them to rectify any reference or credit in subsequent editions.

J. Kirk Howard, Publisher

Dundurn Press Limited
2181 Queen Street East
Toronto, Canada
M4E 1E5

Dundurn Distribution Limited
Athol Brose, School Hill,
Wargrave, Reading
England RG10 8DY

Canadian Cataloguing in Publication Data

Knowles, Valerie
    First person: a biography of Cairine Wilson,
Canada's first woman Senator

Bibliography: p.
Includes index.
ISBN 1-55002-029-3 (bound) ISBN 1-55002-030-7 (pbk.)

1. Wilson, Cairine. 2. Canada – Politics and government – 1930-1935.* 3. Canada – Politics and government – 1935-1957.* 4. Women legislators – Canada – Biography. 5. Canada. Parliament. Senate – Biography. 6. Women philanthropists – Canada – Biography. I. Title.

FC581.W54K64 1988   328.71'092'4   C88-093810-2
F1034.W54K64 1988

Senator Cairine Wilson shown at her desk in the Senate Chamber shortly after her appointment.

A Biography of Cairine Wilson

FIRST PERSON

Canada's First Woman Senator

Valerie Knowles

CONTENTS

PREFACE

In the course of the over five years that this book has been in the making many people have given me invaluable support and encouragement. Chief among these has been my husband David who patiently instructed me in the use of a word processor, without which the whole enterprise would have been doomed, and who relieved me of many of the technical chores associated with the preparation of this manuscript. Without his assistance and encouragement I may not have persevered.

To the Honourable George McIlraith goes the credit for encouraging me to embark on this project in the first place. He also lent me important source material, gave generously of his time in interviews and kindly provided an introduction. From his home in Princeton, New Jersey, Dr William Heckscher sent a steady stream of letters replete with useful advice, insights and encouragement. In Ottawa, the late Cairine Wilson, the Senator's daughter and namesake, answered countless queries and located letters and documents that enabled me to plug some of the gaps in my research.

Other members of the Wilson family also furnished much appreciated assistance, notably Angus Wilson, Janet Burns and Norma Davies. A niece of Senator Wilson, Anna Cundill, frequently came to the rescue with information about the Mackay family. Because of the paucity of correspondence in the Cairine Wilson papers in the National Archives, the aid that family members furnished was invaluable.

I am extremely grateful to the many people who granted me interviews and/or supplied information and recollections by letter. I only hope that I expressed the depth of my gratitude adequately by means of footnotes in the book and thanks expressed over the phone or in letters.

I am indebted to Dr Donald Page who provided me with important material for the chapter entitled "Citizen of the World" and made valuable suggestions for its redrafting; to Dr Gerald Dirks who made a number of helpful recommendations for the rewriting of the chapters relating to Cairine Wilson's work with refugees; to the Honourable Eugene Forsey who read various chapters with an eagle eye and made many useful comments; to Mrs Isobel Dobell who contributed useful comments for the rewriting of the chapter on the Mackays; and to my father-in-law, the Reverend Dr E. Clifford Knowles, who tracked down contacts for me and who, along with my mother-in-law, Dorothy, supplied constructive suggestions for the rewriting of some early chapters.

Helping me to find my way through the labyrinth of research were staff at the National Archives, the Library of Parliament, the National Library, the Canadian Jewish Congress, the British Museum, the Department of External Affairs, the Canadian Centre for Architecture and the Ottawa Public Library. Here I would like to extend special thanks to archivists Glen Wright and Maureen Hoogenraad of the National Archives of Canada; Judith Nefsky, Director, National Archives, Canadian Jewish Congress; librarian Marjorie Bull of the Department of External Affairs library, Ottawa; researcher Robert Lemire of the Canadian Centre for Architecture, Montreal; and historian Ted Kelly of the Department of External Affairs.

Finally, I would like to thank the following: Jonathan Williams who edited some of my preliminary chapters before returning to Ireland; Janet Keith and Peggy Blackstock who took over from where he left off and helped me immeasurably; and Jeanne MacDonald of Dundurn Press, who piloted the manuscript through its final stages. And last, but far from least, I would like to thank my agent, Joanne Kellock. She made valuable suggestions for the manuscript's improvement and shared many of my agonies in the trip down to the wire.

Valerie Knowles

Ottawa April, 1988

INTRODUCTION

It is timely and appropriate that a biography of Cairine Wilson is now being published.

Timely because the inspiration that may be drawn from the integrity and character shown by Canada's first woman senator in her persistent and determined efforts to help refugees half a century ago may be relevant today when we are faced once again with the need to act on this question.

Appropriate in that a refreshing revelation of her character as shown in her work in Parliament and her continuing devotion to duty throughout her life will help present-day parliamentarians to summon strength to perform their onerous duties.

It was a pleasure for me both as a private citizen and later as a Member of Parliament to have had the privilege of working with Cairine Wilson in various fields of public endeavour. May the story of her life continue to be an inspiration for all Canadians young and old.

The Honourable George McIlraith, QC, PC

THIS BOOK IS DEDICATED TO
ALL THOSE VOLUNTEERS WHO
HAVE WORKED SO NOBLY
AND TIRELESSLY ON BEHALF OF
REFUGEES, OFTEN WITH LITTLE
OR NO RECOGNITION.

1

A CELEBRATION

Cairine Wilson, Canada's first woman senator, stood beside the white marble sculpture in the Senate antechamber, a slim, slightly stooped woman with widely spaced, deep blue eyes. With just the hint of a smile on her lips, she gazed shyly into the distance, skirting the towering figures of her two companions: John Diefenbaker, Canada's, thirteenth prime minister, and Mark Drouin, the Speaker of the Senate, who took up a position slightly to her left and directly across from the beaming Diefenbaker.

It was a warm, soft evening — 10 June 1960 — and immediately in front of her, crowding the small oak-panelled anteroom, was a host of well-wishers and admirers. From Ottawa, across Canada, and the United States, they had come to watch the formal unveiling of this head-and-shoulders likeness of the Senator and to pay tribute to a remarkable seventy-five-year-old trailblazer.

Among them the Senator could pick out all of her eight children — Olive, the eldest, and then in order of birth: Janet, Cairine, Ralph, Anna, Angus, Robert, and Norma — old friends like Mrs D.C. Coleman and her sister, Mrs John Labatt; five of the six female senators then sitting in the Senate (Senator Mariana Jodoin was kept away by illness); the sculptor Felix de Weldon; colleagues of every political stripe; and dignitaries such as Keiller Mackay, lieutenant-governor of Ontario. The only notable absence was that of her beloved husband, Norman, who had died four years earlier.

Quiet and unassuming, she had dreaded this event, for even after thirty years as a senator, a lifetime of humanitarian service, and countless public appearences, Cairine Wilson disliked being centre stage. That was best left to a combative courtroom lawyer and politician like John Diefenbaker, who stood on the other side of the sculpture. Still, as she later admitted in a letter to a Montreal friend who had been very active in refugee work, Margaret Wherry, the ceremony "passed off much more easily and pleasantly" than she dared hope.[1]

This special event honouring Cairine Wilson might never have taken place at all if it had not been for the determination and organizing genius of two old friends, Kathleen Ryan and Isabel Percival, President of Ketchum Manufacturing of Ottawa, and a dedicated member of the Zonta Club of Ottawa, one of the many service organizations to which the Senator belonged. These two had made it all possible.

The idea for saluting Cairine Wilson in this way originated with Kathleen Ryan, who in 1984 recalled the deep impression that the Senator's appointment had made on her when she was nineteen. A great admirer of Cairine Wilson, Mrs Ryan was vexed that no tangible monu-

National Archives of Canada

Unveiling of commemorative bust of Agnes Macphail, Centre Block, Parliament Buildings, 8 March 1955. Left to right: Margaret Aiken, MP, Charlotte Whitton, Mayor of Ottawa, Senator Cairine Wilson and the Hon. Ellen Fairclough, Secretary of State.

ment had been erected to Canada's first woman senator. Agnes Macphail, Canada's first woman member of Parliament, was commemorated by a bronze bust outside the House of Commons, but in the Senate precincts there was no tangible reminder of Mrs Wilson's many achievements. Kathleen Ryan therefore conceived the idea of installing a monument to Cairine Wilson in the Senate antechamber where, on 11 June 1938, Mackenzie King had unveiled a bronze tablet honouring the five Alberta feminists who had gone all the way to the Imperial Privy Council in London to prove that women were "qualified Persons" and therefore eligible for appointment to the Senate.[2]

As luck would have it, a sculpture that could serve as such a monument already existed. It was a white marble head-and-shoulders study of Cairine Wilson that had been sculpted twenty-one years earlier, in the summer of 1939, by an artist who has since become world famous, Felix de Weldon, (or Felix Weihs, as he called himself before his marriage), the sculptor of the renowned National Marine Memorial near Arlington Cemetery in Washington D.C. The artist, then a young Austrian refugee, had been recommended to the Senator by Miss Macphail, whose own portrait had been executed by the young man (This is the bust that now sits outside the House of Commons.) As Mrs Frazer Punnett, the Senator's secretary at the time, recalls it, Miss Macphail came to the Senator's office one day when Mrs Wilson was out and "left the message that perhaps because of [her] concern about refugees, she might want to give some consideration to a young sculptor from Austria."[3]

It seems that the Senator was initially reluctant to have her portrait sculpted. For, as she confessed to her good friend, Dr Henry Marshall Tory, the noted educator and scientist, "At the time, a bust was the last thing which I desired but I finally agreed, for I had always regretted not having accepted Tait Mackenzie's offer."[4] Evidently Agnes Macphail's example and the Senator's all too human desire to be recorded for posterity were too powerful to be ignored.

The Vienna-born and European-educated sculptor spent the whole summer at Clibrig, the Wilson summer home at St Andrews, New Brunswick, leaving only in mid-September after the outbreak of World War Two. With him went a clay model, which he later reproduced in white marble obtained from the fragment of an old Greek column that he had picked up in a New York antique store.[5] The completed marble version was taken to Ottawa where it was installed in the library of the Manor House, the stately Wilson home in Rockcliffe Park.

Kathleen Ryan, it seems, recalled this impressive sculpture when she began to entertain ideas about honouring her illustrious friend. So did Isabel Percival, who, like Mrs Ryan, was sure that the Wilson family would be glad to donate it for the purpose that they had in mind. The family was approached and after permission was granted, Mrs Ryan and Mrs Percival went to see Ellen Fairclough, Diefenbaker's minister of citizenship and immigration.[6]

Cairine Wilson's portrait bust. Sculpted by Felix de Weldon in 1939, it now sits in the Senate ante chamber.

As a close friend of Isabel Percival and the first woman to be appointed to a federal cabinet, Ellen Fairclough was the logical link with the Conservative government of the day. She was also a fortunate choice because she embraced the idea with enthusiasm, approaching the Prime Minister and the Speaker of the Senate, whose permission was required before the bust could be placed in the Senate antechamber.[7]

The interview with the vivacious, spirited Mrs Fairclough was not without its amusing overtones, because at some point Mrs Ryan raised the question of the bust's low neckline. It appears that the generous expanse of exposed flesh that the sculpture depicted gave her cause for concern. Would it not invite ribald comments from some male observers? When Mrs Fairclough learned of these fears, she burst out laughing, but then rallied with the reply that "certainly everything should be done to make the Senator acceptable to the gentlemen of the Senate."[8]

Eventually everything possible was done to rectify the situation. Felix de Weldon was consulted, and because he weighed much less than the sculpture, it was decided that he would come to Ottawa to make the necessary adjustments to the piece rather than have it delivered to his studio in Washington.[9] In the late winter of 1959-60, therefore, he journeyed to Ottawa where he spent several days modifying the bust by carving the neckline of a dress and giving it some texture. Years later Mrs Ryan would express the view that the sculptor had done "a good job of hoisting Cairine Wilson's dress."

Since 1959-60 was World Refugee Year and because the Senator had long been deeply involved with the refugee cause, her two friends also included a couple of imaginative money-raising projects for the World Refugee Fund in their plans: a Senator Wilson Testimonial Fund and a garden party. A prestigious committee, composed of the two organizers; Senator Olive Irvine; Beatrice Belcourt, a longtime friend; Colonel George Cavey, the former manager of Birks Jewellers and a member of St. Andrew's Presbyterian Church; Mrs Farrar Cochrane, a family friend; Senator Muriel McQueen Fergusson, a colleague and good friend from New Brunswick; Constance Hayward, a close friend who had served as the executive secretary of the Canadian National Committee on Refugees; Mrs A.K. Hugessen, a prominent member of that organization; and Yetty Robertson, wife of the distinguished Under-Secretary of State for External Affairs, Norman Robertson, solicited contributions for the testimonial fund, and the Local Council of Women staged a mammoth garden party in the spacious grounds of the Manor House. Thanks to superb organization and beautiful weather, the garden party was pronounced a huge success, raising $1,600 for the World Refugee Fund.

It had indeed been a memorable week — and an exhausting one. On Monday the Senator had returned from Washington, where she had received an honorary Doctor of Letters from Gaudet College, the only institution in the world for the higher education of the deaf, another cause with which Cairine Wilson had long been identified. Then, on Wednesday, there had been the garden party. Now, here she was in the precincts of the Red Chamber to watch John Diefenbaker, the wild-eyed populist shunned by the eastern establishment, unveil a twenty-one-year-old portrait of her, a leading member of that establishment. Ellen Fairclough opened the proceedings, then presented Mr Diefenbaker, who said in his tribute:

> ...I think of her as one who in the field of social and humanitarian service made a contribution as comprehensive as the numberless organizations in that field. I could name them. To do so would simply mean to name practically all those voluntary organizations which bring about the translation of the concept of brotherhood to those lesser privileged. In that field too Senator Wilson has made a contribution that is recognized throughout the world.[10]

After the Prime Minister had unveiled the portrait, the Senator gave a brief address, concluding her remarks with the observation:

> It has been a great joy and satisfaction to me to know, and to be assured by my colleagues of my own sex that I made the way more easy for them. My husband lived in constant dread that I should do something which would bring the family and my sex into disrepute.
>
> All I can say is, I know that I am unworthy of the tribute you have paid me today.[11]

It was then the turn of Mark Drouin, Speaker of the Senate, to make a few remarks, and he said in part:

> The Honourable Cairine Reay Mackay Wilson completed recently thirty years in the public service of our country. Throughout this long and fruitful career she has won the esteem and admiration of all Canadians for her devotion to the common weal, the maturity of judgment and wisdom of counsel she has constantly displayed in the discussion of affairs of state, her successful initiatives for the relief of suffering and the redress of existing

evils at home and abroad, her effectiveness as an advocate of social justice and security, and her personal qualities of charm, friendliness and dignity. We are grateful to her for her admirable contribution not only to the work of this house but to its reputation and prestige.[12]

John Keiller Mackay, Lieutenant-Governor of Ontario, was caught quite unprepared when asked to bring the proceedings to a close with a few words. Nevertheless, he managed to rise to the occasion with some fulsome praise for his friend and clanswoman, observing, "Her head is crowned not only with silver, but respect, admiration, esteem and love."[13]

It would have been next to impossible for a stranger watching the proceedings to reconcile the subject of all these tributes with the tributes themselves, for Cairine Wilson was not, to use today's overworked expression, a "charismatic" figure — far from it. Nevertheless, she had many qualities that more than made up for this: monumental compassion and loyalty, charm, political acumen, iron determination, an infinite capacity for hard work, a finely tooled feeling for style and propriety, and a certain magic authority. These played an invaluable role in her remarkable career. But so did certain traits that she inherited from her Scots-Canadian forebears. And it was her family's position in Montreal society that allowed the Senator to move freely within the eastern Canadian establishment and to use it to pursue many of her goals.

2

THE MACKAYS

Cairine Wilson was born into a family of wealth. Perhaps even more important, she was born into a Scots-Canadian family that figured prominently in Montreal's English-Scots establishment, an insular society that flourished in Montreal's famous Square Mile, those several blocks in central Montreal where the rich built their mansions in the last half of the nineteenth century and the first years of the twentieth. Until World War 1 thinned the ranks of their youth, they held undisputed sway — a colonial gentry slavishly imitating British social manners and mores and marrying within their own exclusive social circle.

When the future senator was born, in 1885, the British Empire was approaching its zenith and privileged Victorians everywhere basked in opulence and smugness. It was an epochal year for the young dominion of Canada. The financier and politician, Donald Smith, in an act charged with symbolism, drove a plain iron spike into a railway tie at Craigellachie, British Columbia, thereby completing the celebrated Canadian Pacific Railway and welding East to West. In a quite different sequence of events, the messianic Métis leader, Louis Riel, met his end on a jail gallows in Regina after leading his people in the North West Rebellion against the government at Ottawa. With his death he opened up a great rift between French and English-speaking Canadians, because while the former regarded him as a hero and a martyr, English-speaking Canadians denounced him as a rebel and a traitor who richly deserved his fate.

Closely associated with all these developments was Montreal, the metropolis of Canada, a rapidly growing city with an English-French

Cairine Wilson as a young girl.

population of approximately 145,000 and a thriving commercial-manu-facturing sector dominated by English-speaking Canadians. It was a beautiful city with a plethora of gleaming church spires and a tree-covered mountain that sloped gently down to an elegant residential artery, Sher-brooke Street. Before it was expropriated for a public park in 1875, the mountain had been the preserve of private property owners who had dotted it with farms, orchards, gardens and villas. Now, a decade later, its largely unspoilt beauty was enjoyed year-round by all kinds of people, many of them sports enthusiasts who found it a choice location for riding, tobog-ganning and snowshoeing.

In sharp contrast to the peaceful surroundings of Mount Royal was the busy port area which abutted onto the broad St. Lawrence River. The first port in the world to be electrified, Montreal now welcomed the arrival of vessels from some thirteen steamship companies, one of these being the renowned Allan Line. Pre-eminent on the Atlantic, it had been founded in 1854 by a group of friends led by the Scottish-born Montrealer, Hugh Allan, later Sir Hugh Allan.

Just north of the docks and the warehouses, but well within earshot of the shipping sounds and the factory whistles, was the impressive financial and commercial district. Here, clustered on Notre Dame and St. James Streets, could be found an array of fine buildings that had been erected in the economic boom of the 1860s when architects vied with each other to design impressive facades. Reflecting the unabashed pride of their own-ers, these edifices flaunted carved and garlanded walls, pillared porticoes and entrances decorated with a profusion of detail. Now, in the 1880s, they were being eclipsed by larger and even grander buildings, some of which were built to meet a growing demand for rental office space; Montreal was moving into the office age, a phenomenon that continues unabated today.

Despite all the changes that the city had undergone over the years, however, the sharp division that had always existed between French and English-speaking Canadians remained. It expressed itself most visibly in the choice of residential area. For, if one took St. Lawrence Main as a dividing line, nearly all the inhabitants living east of it were French-speaking while virtually all those west of it were English-speaking, whether of English, Scots, Irish or, in rare cases, American origin. Only occasionally did the two groups overlap the conventional barrier.

Commenting on these "two solitudes," a contemporary observer wrote:

> Montreal is a striking exception to the text that a
> house divided against itself cannot stand. Its divisions are
> so fundamental and persistent that they have not dimin-

ished one iota in a century, but rather increased. The two irreconcilable elements are Romanism and Protestantism; the armies are of French and English blood. The outlook for peace is well-nigh hopeless, with two systems of education producing fundamental differences of character, and nourishing religious intolerance, race antipathy, social division, political antagonism, and commercial separation.

Nevertheless, this city of disunion flourishes as the green bay-tree, with a steady if not an amazing growth, which is due chiefly to the separate, not the united, efforts of the races.[1]

In this thriving port and manufacturing centre the Mackay family played an important role, having been established there for over fifty years, thirty of them highly prosperous ones. Cairine Wilson's father, Robert Mackay, was a wealthy man in his own right and one of Canada's leading businessmen. Her mother, Jane Baptist Mackay, had similar bourgeois roots, being the daughter of George Baptist, a successful logging merchant, who had emigrated from Scotland to Canada in 1832 and later created an industrial empire in Quebec's Saint Maurice region.

The first Mackay relative of Cairine Wilson to settle in Canada also emigrated from Scotland to Quebec in 1832. He was her great-uncle, Joseph, the third youngest of ten children born to William and Anne Mackay. The Mackays lived in remote Sutherland, a rugged county of heather-clad moors and precipitous mountains that overlook long dark lochs. Here, in the beautiful strath of Kildonan, William was a small tenant farmer, or crofter, until he and his family were uprooted by the notorious Highland clearances. Today almost forgotten, except in the Highlands, the "clearances" was the name given to the removal of crofters and subtenants from their holdings to permit the conversion of tilled land to pasturage. Actively supported by the law and by the established Church of Scotland, they were widespread in the late eighteenth century and the first half of the nineteenth when sheep farming was introduced by many Highland landlords seeking a better return on their dwindling capital. On the Duchess of Sutherland's estates alone, where the Mackays were tenants, some fifteen thousand crofters were evicted from their crofts between 1811 to 1820, armed force often being used to drive them from their homes.[2]

The first warning of the removals that involved the William Mackay family came in October 1818 when a man roused the Reverend Donald Sage at the manse in Achness to report that the rent for the half-year ending in May 1819 would not be collected because plans were being made to lay the districts of Strathnaver and Upper Kildonan under sheep. The actual evictions took place the following spring when, thirteen days before the May term, an army of burners — sheriff-officers, constables, factors, shepherds and servants from Dunrobin Castle, the Duchess of Sutherland's home, — descended on the townships along the Naver and on Kildonan and torched the victims' homes one by one. In this devastating Clearance, reports Donald Sage in his *Memorabilia*, "The whole inhabitants of Kildonan parish, nearly 2000 souls, were utterly rooted and burned out."[3]

Some of the dispossessed emigrated to Canada and the United States while others accepted small, inferior lots of land on the coast, the theory being that they could maintain themselves by reclaiming waste land and supplementing its produce by collecting and eating edible seaweed. William Mackay eventually settled at Roster in Caithness,[4] that bleak, almost treeless county that occupies the extreme northeast of Scotland. There Joseph spent his days until he left for Canada in 1832, the year of the great cholera epidemic. With him went a fund of heart-breaking stories concerning his family's eviction from Kildonan, lore which would be passed down through succeeding generations of Mackays in Canada and which would eventually help to shape Cairine Wilson's thinking on immigration and refugees.

Twenty-one-year-old Joseph probably sailed from the Highland port of Aberdeen in the late spring or early summer of 1832 on one of the many overloaded emigrant ships that carried half-starved and ailing passengers to North America. Among the sickly passengers would be many who had contracted cholera, either before setting out or on the voyage. However, it appears that the young man was not among them. Nor did he catch the disease after his arrival in Canada, where it was introduced by the *Carrick* when it docked at the quarantine station below Quebec on 8 June 1832. That Joseph did not contract the disease is surprising because Montreal that summer was in the grip of a cholera epidemic. No matter where he went in the demoralized town, Joseph would not have been able to escape the mournful sound of the incessantly tolling death bell or the spectacle of coffin displays and posted advertisements for cheap funerals. He would probably even have come across whole streets that had been depopulated either by death or by the flight of panic-stricken inhabitants to country villages. It was certainly not an auspicious beginning for a stranger in a new land, as his brother, John, realized when he wrote to Joseph from Roster on 20 February 1833:

> I write you these lines in hopes of hearing from you
> and of your state and to let you know of our state. We have

received 2 letters from you the one sent to Aberdeen we
found first which gave us great relief to hear of you being
in life, and health in the place where the Lord cut down so
many by Death, we would write you sooner if not your
father was poorly a long time but he is now getting better,
and myself is still the same, all the rest in good health and
the whole of them lamenting you to be in a wild savage
country, and that you might do well enough near your
own parents besides being among such as you mentioned,
you have left the place where there is hardly any example
and your expence will ballance the outcome of your
trade.[5]

Probably no other letter better illustrates two leitmotivs that run
through the Mackay family history and Cairine Wilson's adult years: a
deep religious faith and an interest in sound business practice. Joseph
himself certainly exemplified these traits. However, unlike his dour
brother, he was of a sunny, optimistic nature. Despite John's forebodings
and entreaties to return to Caithness, Joseph stayed on in the New World,
setting up as a tailor and merchant on Montreal's Notre Dame Street, not
far from the busy harbour. It was to this address that his concerned father,
William, wrote on 24 October 1834:

Dr. [Dear] Child we are something tedious concerning the great expence of your houses and trade and that we
could not fully understand what are you selling out to
make up your expence you know also that our wishes and
desires is not in the least abating for seeing you in this
Country if you would be permitted, but we refair it to your
Makers providence and to your own mind as wishing it to
be guided by him and we trust that yourself hath made up
your mind as considering a measure of both kingdoms.

...P.S. We are regrating that you did not enlarge more
how do you spend the Sabath or is there a sound preacher
among you all.[6]

Clearly, the "Dr. Child" had joined the burgeoning ranks of other
Scots, who were then carving out a commanding position in the economic
life of Canada. Nowhere was the leadership of these men in the Canadian
business world more conspicuous than in Montreal, a city where Scots not
only dominated business but also played a prominent role in the founding
of institutions, the building of churches and the launching of commercial

organizations. Although he could not have known it in 1832, Joseph too would eventually become a prominent member of this group of self-made tycoons.

No doubt impressed by his brother Joseph's rising fortunes, Edward Mackay emigrated to Canada in 1840 and, after spending six months in Kingston, Ontario, settled in Montreal where he became a clerk in Joseph's wholesale drygoods firm. By 1850, he had demonstrated such

Joseph Mackay, Great-Uncle of Cairine Wilson.

industry and business acumen that Joseph took him on as a partner, the firm becoming known in May of that year as Joseph Mackay and Brother. The business grew so quickly that in December 1866 it was reported that the previous year's sales had been well in excess of one million dollars and that the two bachelor brothers were "wealthy."[7]

By then, Joseph had anticipated a trend on the part of the fashionable in Montreal by moving his place of residence from St. Antoine Street, not far from the harbour, north towards the slopes of Mount Royal. There, on Sherbrooke Street at the corner of Redpath, just below the mountain, he had purchased several lots from the estate of the late S.G. Smith and had proceeded in 1857 to build a stone mansion, which he named Kildonan Hall after his birthplace in Sutherlandshire.[8] Before it was razed in 1930 to make way for the Church of St. Andrew and St. Paul, Kildonan, as it was known, was one of the most striking on a wide avenue of impressive mansions. As the historian and journalist, Edgar Andrew Collard, has observed, Joseph Mackay's residence would have been imposing even if it had been situated near the sidewalk. But what really made it stand out was its siting in large shady grounds that resembled those of a magnificent country estate.[9] Near the southeast corner of the property — adjoining a finely worked wrought-iron fence — stood two stone gateposts, which flanked a curving driveway that swept up to a pillared front porch. To the right of the house, as you faced it, was a porte-cochere, to the left, a large conservatory, which featured the prized marble statue, "Diana," one of several legacies that Joseph earmarked for his niece, Henrietta Gordon, who lived with her uncles at Kildonan until she died in 1883, shortly after the death of Edward. Still later, after Senator Robert Mackay's death, the statue would find its way into Cairine Wilson's possession.

Like most large neo-classical houses designed for the very affluent in Victorian Canada, Kildonan had high ceilings and a square floor plan. Opening off the front door was a spacious, but dark, entrance hall graced by a wide, sweeping staircase. Overlooking this — and bearing mute testimony to Joseph's Scottish origins — was an impressive stained glass window depicting Sir Walter Scott's narrative poem, "The Lay of the Last Minstrel."[10]

Kildonan was not only architecturally imposing — with its Italianate touches and large size — it was also richly furnished with art work and heavy furniture, much of which had been purchased by Joseph on his overseas buying trips. The result was an exceedingly gloomy house that bespoke a certain Scottish dourness and fervency of purpose.

Another Montreal landmark closely identified with Joseph Mackay was the Mackay Institution for Protestant Deaf-Mutes, located on the west side of Decarie Road, now Decarie Boulevard. The Montreal merchant first became involved with handicapped children in 1874 when a struggling institution, known as the Protestant Institution for Deaf-Mutes and for the Blind, approached him for financial assistance. A kind man, who was keenly interested in the welfare of the deaf child, Mackay became a governor of the institution and then, in 1876, when larger premises were urgently required, he donated both the property on Decarie Road and a four-storey building where classes could be held. He also assumed the presidency of the school, which in 1878 was renamed the Mackay Institution for Protestant Deaf-Mutes in his honour.[11]

In a speech on the occasion of the laying of the building's cornerstone Joseph Mackay waxed eloquent with the hope that "for years and generations to come the Institution may, through Divine favour, prove a source of manifold blessings to the afflicted classes whose good it seeks, and may never lack warm-hearted and generous friends and wise and godly instructors to carry on the work."[12] The wealthy Montreal merchant would have been gratified to know that members of succeeding generations of Mackays, Cairine Wilson among them, would play a leading role in the school's affairs.

"Kildonan." Mackay family home on Sherbrooke Street West, Montreal. This site is currently occupied by St Andrew's and St Paul's Presbyterian Church. Its church hall is called Kildonan Hall after the original house.

In addition to the role that he played in the Mackay Institution for Protestant Deaf-Mutes, Joseph could also take great satisfaction and pride in the contributions that he was making to his church. A devout Presbyterian, who was deeply conscious of the obligations of God's blessings, Joseph gave generously to the church. He also became actively involved in its work, helping to establish the Presbyterian College of Montreal, which opened in 1867, and serving for a number of years on its board of managers. While travelling on business in the provinces, he kept "his eyes open to the spiritual state of those with whom he came in contact" and when he detected a need for additional Presbyterian ministers, he arranged for Scottish clergymen to come to this country. All told, he brought out ten to twelve ministers of the Free Church of Scotland at his own expense.[13] Following his retirement from business, he became interested in the missionary work of the church and whenever he travelled in Canada or overseas, he made a point of visiting missionaries.[14]

Joseph Mackay died in 1881, but not before sending a last message to his minister. Asked if he had anything he wanted to convey to this pious gentleman, Joseph pondered and then said, "Just this: 'Do good as you have opportunity.'"[15] Two years later Edward died, still a bachelor. By now, however, the flourishing drygoods business had been turned over to the brothers' three nephews, Hugh, James and Robert, sons of their sister Euphemia and her husband, Angus Mackay, of Lybster, Caithness and nearby Roster.

The youngest of the brothers was Robert, Cairine's father. Born in Lybster, Caithness, he had followed Hugh and James to Montreal in 1855 when he was only sixteen. Once arrived in Canada, he had demonstrated his Scots faith in education by taking up bookkeeping and commercial studies. In a letter to a friend in Scotland, written in 1858, he noted that he had begun bookkeeping. Then he went on to observe, "for a time at least I intend to follow commercial pursuits and, if successful, I ultimately hope to return to the land of my fathers and settle down in rural life as a quiet useful farmer."[16] But not alone it seems. In the draft of a letter intended for his cherished friend Catherine Macdonald he enlarges upon this dream, voicing sentiments that hint at some of the qualities that helped to shape his remarkable career:

> I was also glad, for certain reasons, to hear that some of the folk in Newlands have not yet got married as it permits me to hope, that, should my plans for the future be crowned by a kind Providence with success —should I by honest persevering industry and prudent economy gather enough of this world's gear to buy me a snug little farm in dear auld Scotia and enable me to settle down in

quiet independence with the beloved object of my fond affection, I might win her consent to share it with me.[17]

Robert never realized his youthful dream to marry his beloved and to settle down in Scotland as "a quiet useful farmer." But he did fulfill his ambition to succeed in the field of commerce. Shrewd, able and industrious, he personified those traits that enabled the Scots-Canadians of his and his uncles' generations to become the dominant group in the commercial life of Montreal, indeed of Canada. His climb up the ladder of business success was aided, however, by substantial legacies. Along with his brothers Hugh and James, Robert received an equal share of the residue of his Uncle Edward's estate. Then, when James died unmarried in 1889, he inherited, along with Hugh, the remainder of James's estate. Finally, on the death of bachelor Hugh, in 1890, Robert became the sole legatee of that merchant's estate and the proprietor of all the residue of Edward Mackay's succession.

Robert could have frittered away his inheritance, but since he possessed a sound business sense and a marked distaste for frivolity, he invested his legacies providently in an impressive range of stocks, bonds and real estate properties. An editorial that appeared in the *Lethbridge Herald* after the death of his son George illustrates the Senator's prudence (Robert was elevated to the Senate in 1901) and aptitude for business, two qualities that he passed on to his daughter, Cairine, who would have made an excellent businesswoman had she embarked on a business career.

> When the old Senator made a disbursement for the advancement of the business, he was wont to ask George for a memorandum of the requirements, which he would carefully put away, saying, "There should be a record of this for those that come after."

> This methodical manner was an ever-present ideal with the uncles and the fathers in the conduct of their affairs in the important merchandising business that they founded in Montreal and in all their transactions that led to the foundation of a considerable fortune.[18]

In 1893, twenty-six years after becoming a partner in the family firm, and three years after becoming its head, Robert Mackay retired from the drygoods business to devote more time to managing the enormous Mackay estates and to meeting the demands of his wide assortment of business commitments. These multiplied so rapidly that before his death in 1916 he was a director of sixteen companies, including such illustrious institutions as the Bank of Montreal, the City and District Savings Bank, the Dominion Textile Company and the Canadian Pacific Railway. Given his formidable list of directorships and his active participation in the affairs of such companies as the Bell Telephone Company, which he served as vice-president, it is not surprising that he earned the reputation of being the most sought after man in Canada for directorships. In fact, the *Montreal Standard* placed him among the twenty-three titans who were preeminent in the Canadian financial firmament in the opening years of this century.[19]

Notman Collection

Hon. Robert Mackay, father of Cairine Wilson.

When one contemplates the daunting number of directorships and company offices Robert Mackay held, one might conclude that he had little time for anything else. But such was not the case. As befitted a leading member of Montreal's business community, he joined the Board of Trade, becoming president of it in 1900. He was also a member of the Board of Harbour Commissioners, which he served as president from 1896 to 1907. In tribute to his farsighted leadership, a stretch of wharves was named after him as was the tug, "the Robert Mackay." Decades after his death this squat boat could still be seen plying the waters of Montreal harbour, not far from the Harbour Commissioners building and the richly furnished third-floor boardroom where the Senator and his fellow commissioners met weekly to manage the port and plan its future. Cairine Wilson's father also played a leading role in preserving the traditions of his native Scotland, serving at one time as president of the local St. Andrew's Society and as honorary lieutenant colonel of the 5th Regiment, Royal Highlanders of Canada. His abiding love of tradition and history would be inherited by his daughter, Cairine, who, in her adult years, would amass scrapbooks crowded with clippings relating to her family and things Scottish.

When it came to business acumen and moral earnestness, Robert Mackay resembled Joseph and Edward. But unlike his "kindly uncles," as he once referred to them, and his brothers, Hugh and James, he abandoned celibacy for marriage and the role of paterfamilias. On 10 May 1871, at the home of the bride's father, in Trois Rivières, Quebec, which in those days was called Three Rivers, he married Jane, the twenty-one-year-old daughter of George and Isabella Baptist.

A self-made lumber baron, George Baptist had begun his career as a sawmill employee in Dorchester County, Quebec in the 1830s. From these humble beginnings he had gone on to become a member of the "brotherhood of the Saint-Maurice barons," a group of powerful logging entrepreneurs that exploited the enormous timber wealth of the Saint-Maurice region of Quebec. By the time that Robert Mackay became his son-in-law, this transplanted Scot had created an industrial empire that produced between 25 to 30 million feet of lumber each year. He had also succeeded in becoming an outstanding member of Trois-Rivières' growing bourgeoisie. Of his eight children, five were daughters, Jane, or Jeannie, as she signed herself in her letters to her husband, being the youngest. Like Jane, the older girls all married businessmen. Phyllis married James Dean, a Quebec City merchant; the other daughters married local men: Isabella, George Baillie Houliston, a lawyer, banker and broker; Margaret, William Charles Pentland, an accountant; and Helen, Thomas McDougall, a metallurgist.[20]

Robert, the up-and-coming merchant and financier, was thirty-two when he married Jane Baptist in her family home in Trois Rivières. From a Notman photograph taken in 1878, we can see that the young Mrs Mackay was, if not exactly pretty, at least tall and handsome, with a high forehead and fair hair that was parted in the middle and then pulled straight back. Resplendent in a dark dress whose severity is relieved by a border of brocade, she stands beside a draped table and stares pensively at the camera. Even more impressive in appearance is her sombre husband: a strikingly good-looking man with deeply chiselled features, a high intellectual brow and a short cropped beard. In later photos, taken when he was in his fifties, the beard appears more luxuriant, the face fuller and the expression, if anything, sterner.

The somewhat hazy picture that emerges of Jane Mackay is of a kind woman who was dominated by her husband and plagued by ill health. A family story, perhaps apocryphal, claims that Robert Mackay would dole out some money to his wife for groceries each month and then pocket any that she left on the hall table after she had made up her monthly accounts. Certainly she was no bold, high-spirited chatelaine, as this rather pathetic excerpt from a letter written in 1879 indicates:

> ...I regret dear Robert that home is not more happy for you. I know that you feel that you have more to bear with than a great many, but you must not forget that I have my own little troubles & I know I am not able to bear up the way I ought to. I will try in the future to keep these little things to myself & not trouble you more than I can help.[21]

Just what she meant by these "little troubles" is not known. But no doubt the reference alludes, in part, at least, to assorted ailments that afflicted her during her lifetime and to the demands made upon her far from robust constitution by frequent and debilitating child-bearing. The first child, a daughter, Louisa, had arrived during the first year of marriage and had died shortly thereafter. Then, in rapid succession, had come Angus Robert (1872), George Baptist (1874), Hugh (1875), Euphemia (1876) and Isabel Oliver (1878). At the time that she penned her rueful observations in a fine copperplate hand to Robert, she was pregnant with her seventh child, Anna Henrietta, who would enter the world on 25 December 1879. Mercifully for Jane, there would be a six-year interlude until Cairine arrived in 1885. Edward, the last of the children, would be born in 1887.

Cairine Mackay was born in February 1885, a month that would later prove to be a portentous one for Montreal. For it was in February that a Pullman porter from the Chicago train was admitted to the Hotel Dieu hospital with a slight skin eruption that was later diagnosed as smallpox. The disease quickly spread to other patients and before long a major epidemic was in progress. Goaded into drastic action by a public outcry for sterner measures, the city finally introduced compulsory vaccination that fall and soon the epidemic petered out, but not before some three thousand lives had been claimed and thousands of French Canadians had rioted in the streets to protest the new measure.[22]

Interestingly enough, the day that Cairine Mackay appeared on the scene — Wednesday 4 February — a notice appeared in the *The* [Montreal] *Gazette* advertising the sale by auction of her father's semi-detached stone house on Edgehill Avenue off Dorchester Street West. According to the ad, this most comfortable of family residences boasted bay windows and a wide verandah in the rear as well as a "faultlessly laid out" interior and "light and cheerful" rooms. Even allowing for some descriptive license on the part of the copy writer, it must have been an inviting house, not gloomy and depressing like Kildonan. However, it was at Kildonan that Cairine Mackay was born and it was here that she would pass her impressionable years before her marriage in 1909.

Robert Mackay had moved his family into the Sherbrooke Street mansion shortly before the birth of his youngest daughter and not long after the death of his cousin, Henrietta Gordon, who, by the terms of Joseph's will, was allowed to occupy Kildonan for a period of five years after her uncle's death. For the next forty-five years, until its demolition in 1930, the house would be owned exclusively by Mackays or by the Robert Mackay estate.

The child born to Jane and Robert Mackay on 4 February was christened Cairine (Gaelic for Catherine, the name of Robert's older, unmarried sister and of his beloved cousin, Catherine Gordon) and Reay (after the chief of the Mackay clan) on 23 June 1885 by the Reverend A. B. Mackay at Crescent Street Church. With this ceremonial sprinkling of water, she was formally initiated into the Presbyterian church, one of her great-uncles' preoccupations and destined to be a major force in her own life.

The details of Cairine Wilson's childhood are sketchy because she seldom referred to it in conversations with her own children. We do know, though, that her gruff, demanding father exercised a powerful influence and that relations between the parents and their children were punctilious, so formal as to perhaps move the wistful daughter to say in an interview granted in 1930:

> I earnestly believe that parents and children both gain
> more by establishing a close comradeship than by the
> parents standing aloof and accepting the position of
> judge, disciplinarian and critic of their children. There is
> no reason why parents should not be pals of their children

and still have respect and reverence and obedience from them. In fact I think they are more likely to possess these from children who feel that their parents are understandingly one with them, than are the parents who insist on implicit obedience and rigid respect without having first won the loving confidence of their children.[23]

The stiff relations between parents and children could not detract, however, from the basically warm, kind nature of Jane Mackay. To her children in distress, she was the embodiment of sympathy and loving attention, as young Cairine realized all too well when, on a trip to Europe, she was taken ill and longed for her mother.[24]

Notman Collection

Mrs Robert Mackay, mother of Cairine Wilson.

We can assume that as the child of a wealthy family that had just become part of the elite of this young country, Cairine was raised according to the essentially bourgeois standards of her class. These called for ladies to speak softly, to not appear intellectual and to strive at all times to be decorative. Instead of sipping madeira or port at the table after dinner, as did the men, it was their lot to withdraw to spacious drawing rooms to chat about children, servants and fashion and to indulge in the latest society gossip. In 1892, in Montreal, this would probably have been dominated by revelations concerning "the most sensational elopement" the city had ever known, that of Jack, the eldest son of Andrew Allan, one of the millionaire partners in the Allan Royal Mail Steamship Line, and the wife of a bank inspector named Hebden.[25]

But if the latest doings in society were welcome topics of conversation, some subjects — money and sex — were taboo. Indeed, ladies were not even supposed to think about them. Probably the greatest taboo, however, was feeling. Not only did a member in good standing of the bourgeosie, especially the Scots-Canadian middle class, not express emotion, he or she did not even mention it. People whose work owed its existence to feeling — writers, artists, actors — were as declassé as tradesmen. Equally horrendous was marriage outside this bourgeoisie unless it was to someone from the British gentry or aristocracy. Anna Mackay upset her father merely by marrying an American. Robert Loring might be charming and well educated, but nevertheless he was an American and that alone placed him beyond the pale!

Like most heads of Scottish-Canadian families, Robert Mackay was a strict disciplinarian who actively supported a "spare the rod and spoil the child" regime. Since he was also a devout Presbyterian, he insisted that his children be raised according to the dictates of Scottish Presbyterianism. One of the driving forces of the Scottish character, it emphasized the duty of each Christian to manifest God's will in everything he did or, as the more lyrical phrase has it, "to glorify God and enjoy him forever." Not surprisingly, this translated into a divine calling to work (the Protestant work ethic) and a God-given responsibility to demonstrate initiative, risk-taking and foresight. Yet, contrary to what many people think, it did not result merely in a desire to accumulate material riches. Along with it went the concept of stewardship, the belief that individuals should use their talents and any wealth that they had to benefit their fellow brothers and sisters.[26]

These and other Calvinistic positions — for Presbyterianism was deeply rooted in Calvinism — were incorporated in the faith's standard catechisms: the very detailed Larger Catechism and the less formidable manual of instruction, the Shorter Catechism ("for such as are of weaker capacity"). Coming as they did from a staunch Presbyterian home, Cairine and her siblings were instructed in the Shorter Catechism, which has 107 questions and answers, the first of which reads: "What is man's chief end? Man's chief end is to glorify God and enjoy him forever."

Luxury for the Mackay children was therefore tempered not only by a very strict upbringing but also by the teachings of their church. Perhaps because of this, the boys, with the notable exception of the painfully shy and abstemious Edward, earned a reputation for being rather wild in their youth. In fact, one of their chief delights was to down a few drinks and then career around the top of Mount Royal on horseback.

Young Cairine, however, never rebelled overtly against her puritanical upbringing or against the earnest self-denial and self-discipline that Scots Calvinism implies. Nevertheless, all these influences made for a very shy, reserved woman who found it difficult to express emotion and who was seldom demonstrative, even with members of her own family and friends. Those who came to know her well, though, would discover that beneath the reserve was an abundance of warmth and compassion, qualities that perhaps were inherited from her mother and then nurtured by circumstances. Much more obvious were superb organizing skills and her talent for righting misunderstandings with tact and diplomacy. These were developed as early as the age of twelve when her mother began saying, in the event of any domestic difficulty, "Cairine will settle it."[27]

For those privileged to live in Montreal's large ornate houses in the late Victorian period, life had a lot to offer. Still, the early childhood years that Cairine spent at Kildonan were not particularly happy ones. As her mother was frequently ill and Kildonan was a large household, she had a lot of responsibility thrust on her shoulders, including the care of her younger brother, Edward, to whom she was very close before her marriage. Far removed from her daily orbit, because of their age differences, were her older brothers, Angus, George and Hugh. Yet Cairine greatly admired the eldest, Angus, perhaps because he was more widely read than the others and she had developed a taste for books and learning. She had to do most of her admiring from afar, however, because Angus went off to Boston to study engineering at the Massachusetts Institute of Technology and after his graduation, in 1894, settled in North Dakota where he supervised some of his father's mining interests. George, the second eldest, also left Montreal, to attend M I T briefly and then, after a short stint as a bank clerk in Montreal, to serve in the Boer War. After the conclusion of hostilities, in 1902, he struck out west, and put down roots in Alberta, eventually becoming one of Lethbridge's best known and most public-spirited citizens. Hugh remained in Montreal, where he graduated in law from McGill University in 1900 and went on to become one of the city's most prominent corporation lawyers and company directors.

In her early childhood years, Cairine would have seen more of Edward and her three sisters, Euphemia (Effie), Isabel and Anna than her older brothers. For this reason the early deaths of the older sisters, Euphemia and Isabel, were especially poignant. Both succumbed to that great scourge of Victorian times, tuberculosis, Isabel dying in 1894 when she was sixteen, and Effie in 1897 at age twenty-one. Isabel's illness and subsequent death perhaps accounts, in part at least, for the sad expression that is so evident in an undated photograph of Cairine. Taken when she was around eight or nine years of age, it shows a very solemn youngster clasping a single-stemmed rose as she poses in a white dress. What is most striking is not the dress, the long, gently flowing, dark hair, or the somewhat heavy features, but the eyes. Deep set and widely spaced, they have an inescapable look of sadness.

The Montreal that Cairine came to know between 1890 and 1909, when she married and went to live in Rockland, Ontario, was only a fraction of the city — indeed, only a portion of the district inhabited by English-speaking Montrealers, who, for the most part, lived west of St. Lawrence Boulevard. Geographically it encompassed the area bounded by University Street to the east, Guy Street and Côte des Neiges to the west, Dorchester Street to the south and Cedar and Pine Avenues to the north. Here, in what would later be labelled "the Square Mile," flourished an English-speaking society that boasted some of Canada's wealthiest tycoons, many of them self-made men, who, for the first time in their lives, had money to squander. And, in imitation of the great fur trading barons at the end of the eighteenth century and the beginning of the nineteenth, many of them did.

The streets of the Square Mile were filled with the residences of magnates: Sir Hugh Allan (shipping), Lord Strathcona (CPR), Lord Mount Stephen (CPR), Lord Atholstan (*Montreal Star*), Sir William Collis Meredith (law and banking), Sir William Van Horne (CPR), Sir William Macdonald (tobacco), Greenshields (law, wholesale dry goods and stockbroking), Dawes (brewing), Birks (jewellery), Morgan (department store), Ogilvie (flour), and Molson (brewing), to name but a few.[28] But although every street in the Square Mile was considered fashionable (and in actual fact some of the most impressive homes, those belonging to Lords Strathcona and Shaughnessy, were located on Dorchester west of Guy) not one was more fashionable than the mile-length section of Sherbrooke Street that ran between University and Guy.

An elegant residential stretch, rivalled only by Dorchester Street, it abounded in mansions built of handsome limestone obtained from local quarries. The architecture of these varied greatly, some being formal and rather austere like Kildonan, others Scotch baronial like the "grandly artistic house" built by Sir George Drummond at the southeast corner of Sherbrooke and Metcalfe Streets. No matter what its architecture, though, every house invariably had three dining rooms: the main dining room, the children's, and the servants' hall. There was also a formal drawing room and a spacious conservatory, often supported by a large greenhouse which grew not only an abundance of flowers, but sometimes fruits, such as nectarines, grapes and peaches.[29] Most households had a staff comprising a coachman, groom, chauffeur (after the advent of the automobile), butler, cook, kitchen maid, housemaid, tablemaid and a permanent charwoman. A few establishments had many more than nine servants.

Sherbrooke Street was the aristocratic street of Montreal before commercialization began to make itself felt in the late 1920s. Indeed, this artery of success created such an awesome impression on late Victorian observers that the authors of an article on Montreal in 1882 stated emphatically, "Sherbrooke Street is scarcely surpassed by the Fifth Avenue of New York in the magnificence of its buildings."[30]

Four or five blocks east of Kildonan, on Sherbrooke Street, was one of these magnificent edifices, the massive stone residence of Sir William Van Horne, a friend and business associate of Cairine's father. In this impressive, 52-room home could be found one of the largest collections of Japanese porcelain in North America as well as a mammoth art collection, both assembled with the same spirit and energy that this huge Renaissance man had brought to the laying of the Canadian Pacific Railway's tracks when he was in charge of the railway's construction.

Across from the Van Horne mansion, on the south side of the street, just west of Peel, at number 916, was the "young ladies' school" where Cairine Mackay obtained her early education, for, unlike children from many other wealthy families, she was not educated by a governess and tutor at home. Known by the delightfully old world name of "Misses Symmers and Smith's," it frequently enjoined its pupils — who were always referred to as "young ladies" — to cultivate that most desirable of attributes, the soft, low voice of woman. It also appears that Miss Smith was fond of quoting the verse in Ecclesiastes that reads, "Whatsoever thy hand findeth to do, do it with thy might." This, at any rate, was the injunction that above all others made a deep impression on Cairine Mackay because in later life whenever she was tempted to skimp on a job, she would recall these words and then strive to do her best.[31]

Her final school years, 1899-1902, were spent at Trafalgar Institute, which opened in 1887 in a red sandstone house on Upper Simpson Street, just a short walk from Kildonan. At this most exclusive of ladies' finishing schools, Cairine Mackay was deeply influenced by the headmistress, Grace Fairley, a remarkable woman, who demonstrated by word and deed her firmly held conviction that "It is much better to sacrifice all in defence of country or ideals, even though one knows at the outset that there is no hope, than it is to take the easy way out."[32] This maxim, like the verse from Ecclesiastes, made a lasting impression on Cairine Mackay and became an infallible guide in the years that lay ahead.

Her firmly held principles, notwithstanding, Miss Fairley does not fit our stereotyped image of the Victorian headmistress. Far from being intimidating, she was an approachable person who stood at the head of the school stairs and personally welcomed each pupil at the start of the school day. She also expressed a great love of flowers, children and small animals and tried to inculcate in her students an understanding and appreciation of each season and its particular beauties. Moreover, where another teacher might insist on adhering to a rigid timetable and a prescribed format, this gifted classics scholar was not above encouraging her pupils to close their books and to air their thoughts on topics quite removed from the lesson at hand.

Such is the stuff of which fond school memories are made, at least for Cairine Wilson, who thirty years after graduating from her alma mater, recorded them in a tribute to Grace Fairley, who had died a few months earlier.[33] Still later, beginning in the 1950s, and continuing until her death, the Senator donated a special award, named the Fairley Prize, to a member of the graduating class at Trafalgar who had made an outstanding contribution to school life. Since Cairine Wilson's death the prize has been donated annually by the Trafalgar Old Girls' Association " in memory of Miss Fairley and the Hon. Senator Cairine Wilson."[34]

Cairine enjoyed studying, her favourite subjects being history and mathematics. No doubt to the delight of her education-conscious father, she earned good marks, ranking second in Form IV, third in Form V and first in her graduation year, by which time the school body had grown to seventy-eight boarders and day pupils and a separate day school wing had been added to the original house.[35] At Trafalgar she learned French, which would prove an invaluable asset in later years, and developed close friendships with Elsie Macfarlane McDougall, Louise Hays Grier, Winnifred Stanley Hampson and Pauline Hanson Davidson. No matter what the years would bring in the way of vicissitudes and changing circumstances, they would remain "best friends," corresponding, telephoning each other, and exchanging gifts at Christmas and on birthdays. And when it came time to draw up her will, Cairine Wilson would remember Elsie McDougall's children just as if they were members of her own family.[36]

However, although she was a good student and would probably have benefited a great deal from a university education, Cairine Mackay never went on to higher learning. Probably she, like most other women raised in the Anglo-Celtic tradition, regarded the life of the mind as essentially a male preserve. McGill could take the bold step of admitting women for the first time in 1884, but in Cairine Mackay's circle in 1902, it was still unthinkable for a woman to enrol in a university program — unthinkable, that is, for everybody but precocious Marion Creelman Savage. Born in Toronto, she studied at the prestigious American women's college, Bryn Mawr, Queen's College, London, and McGill University, from which she obtained a bachelor of arts degree in 1908. It was probably while she was enrolled at McGill that she came to know Cairine Mackay who became a lifelong friend.

Although school and church were important influences in Cairine Mackay's life, social functions and sports were not neglected. For young ladies from her set winter sports had a special attraction, and none more so than tobogganning which had come into its own in the early 1880s. It was the most exciting sport in nineteenth century Montreal because nothing could equal it in speed, skiing not entering the picture until the closing years of the 1890s. To hurtle down steep hills like Ontario Avenue (now Avenue du Musée) or the daunting five-lane toboggan slide that was conveniently situated just across Sherbrooke Street from Kildonan was to ride with the wind and experience thrill after thrill. Even more exhilarating was to race down one of the gaily festooned slides that shot over the ice of the St. Lawrence River during Winter Carnival week, a week which also offered such attractions as driving in a tandem on snowy streets to swirling around the ice at a fancy dress skating ball.

Year round, on Mount Royal, there was riding, the sport that above all captured Cairine's fancy. That she prided herself on her horsemanship and love of horses is evident in this excerpt from the one diary of hers that survives. Describing a tour that she made of the Scottish border country in 1904, she observes in her large bold hand:

> On the way back [from Roslin] Janet and I managed to get box seats much to my delight. Our driver had a very jolly face & although he said little interested me very much I was very pleased when he turned to me and asked if I did not know something about horses. He said he just thought I must.[37]

Sewing was another great love. Indeed, she became so proficient with the needle that she taught ladies how to sew, and they in appreciation gave her a gold thimble for a wedding gift. Before long, though, sewing would take second place to knitting, the great diversion of her adult years.

In her teenage years, there were the inevitable winter season balls, some of which were staged at the sumptuous Windsor Hotel, where visiting royalty, heads of state, and celebrities, such as Lillie Langtry, usually stayed when they were in Montreal. Others, however, were held in the stately mansions of the Square Mile, one of these being Kildonan, where scores of young people attended Cairine's own debutante party in 1905. Given her extreme shyness, it was probably a painful initiation.

The *Sunday Sun*, a faithful chronicler of news in the fashionable set of English-speaking Montreal, informed its readers on 5 February 1905:

> During the past week things have been more or less at a social standstill, Mrs Robert Mackay's dance being the only big private function of the week. It took place on Friday evening and everything possible was done to make it a success. The popular debutante, Miss Cairine Mackay, in whose honour the dance was given, looked exceptionally well in a yellow gown, a charming touch of colour being given by her bouquet of deep tinted roses. She received with Senator and Mrs Mackay, the latter quite recovered from her recent severe cold, looking well in black and white. The charming married daughter of the house, Mrs Robert Loring, was present as well as a large number of the younger married set. Indeed, it was quite a big dance and the rooms were taxed to their utmost capacity. The decoratitions [*sic*] while simple were pretty.

"The charming married daughter of the house" was, of course, warm, vivacious Anna, six years Cairine's senior. She had married Robert Loring in the autumn of 1903, following a flurry of entertainments that included teas and dinner dances, all packed into a few short weeks "owing to the illness of Mrs Mackay."[38] After their marriage, Anna and her husband, a Boston native and an M I T graduate, installed themselves in the George Smithers house, on Sherbrooke Street, a couple of blocks west of Kildonan. With Anna's departure from the family nest, Cairine became the only daughter still at home. And it was perhaps partly to compensate her for some of the loneliness that she undoubtedly experienced that her father gave her a trip to Europe and the United Kingdom in the summer of 1904.

Cairine embarked on her trip at the height of what the French would later call "la belle époque," that period of remarkable stability that ran from the turn of the century until the outbreak of World War 1. The phrase itself conjures up a host of nostalgic spectacles: elegantly attired gentlemen and expensively gowned ladies walzing in ornate ballrooms to the music of Franz Lehar; women wearing long, flowing dresses and hats with artificial fruits and plumes, waists tightly corseted; bearded men sporting dark clothes and bowler hats in the winter, white linen and Panama hats in the warm weather; leisurely boating on the Seine, and throughout Western

Europe generally an air of optimism and extravagance.[39] Even in Britain it was a time of worldliness for three years earlier Queen Victoria had died and had been succeeded by her bearded, portly son Albert as Edward VII. With the accession of the champagne-and-fun-loving monarch to the throne, the Victorian age was over and Victorianism as a state of mind and as a mode of behaviour became a thing of the past.

In the company of her life-long friend, Elsie Macfarlane McDougall, and three other girls — Mary Clark, Janet Anderson and J. Alice Gingras — plus three chaperones, Cairine sailed from New York on 25 May on the "S.S. Ryndam," bound for Rotterdam. After four whirlwind months on the Continent and in Britain, they sailed from Naples for Boston and the final leg of the trip to Montreal.

The diary that she kept of the trip reveals a keen appreciation of art and old world architecture, both of which are described in loving detail. Noticeably lacking, however, is any enthusiasm for the International Congress of Women that was held that June in Berlin. For Miss Hill, a tour chaperone, this Congress was the tour's *raison d' être*, but for Cairine Mackay it was a boring event whose social functions and working sessions were to be avoided if at all possible. In diary entries that hint at a latent contempt for aggressive feminism, she wrote:

> **June 8:** "Much to our disgust we were taken after break-fast to the Congress of Women from all parts of the world. Routine business was discussed and after a short time we left, Miss Hill having been elected President's Proxy for Canada." **June 9:** "Reception in honour of the delegates to the Congress of Women." **June 11:** In the evening the others went to a reception given by Mrs May Wright Sewell President of the International Congress of Women, but I escaped."[40]

A meeting in Berlin with Susan Brownell Anthony, the pioneer leader of the women's suffrage movement in the United States, failed to rate a mention in the diary. Not until she had become a reluctant trailblazer herself would Cairine Mackay refer to the encounter.[41]

At the Old Ship Hotel, in the seaside resort of Brighton, Cairine just missed seeing Rudyard Kipling, who had left minutes earlier in his car and, in Scotland, she found herself captivated by the beauty of Sir Walter Scott's country and intoxicated with joy, riding in a horse-drawn coach:

> We reached Aberfoyle about 11:45 and after we had eaten our bread on the gallery above the entrance, where

our party must have presented an amusing spectacle, we went for a short walk until the coach started. We stood for a few minutes on the bridge mentioned in Rob Roy as the one over which the Baillie and Frank Osbaldestone went. We then got on the coach and had a fine drive from Aberfoyle to Loch Katrine. The scenery was magnificent particularly near the Trossachs and I felt as if I could spend my life driving, indeed to wear a red coat and handle 4 horses was the height of my ambition. The boat Sir Walter Scott was waiting for us so as soon as the passengers were on it started across the lake, which looked beautiful shut in by the mountains, although there was no sun to lighten it. Until I saw the country, however, I had never realized the beauty of Scott's descriptions.[42]

Before her marriage, Cairine Mackay made at least two trips to Europe and travelled extensively in Quebec. She also came to know St Andrews-by-the-Sea, New Brunswick, where her father built a summer home, Clibrig, in 1905, after sending his family to various watering spots on the lower St Lawrence River in previous summers. But, with one exception, the rest of Canada was by and large foreign to her. That one exception was Ottawa.

Cairine Mackay's introduction to this raw, parochial capital came through her father, a Liberal Party stalwart and a friend of its leader, Sir Wilfrid Laurier. Robert Mackay, in fact, had been one of four affluent Liberals — the others were Newell Bate and William Hutchison of Ottawa and William Cameron Edwards of Rockland, Ontario and later Ottawa — who signed an agreement calling for the Liberal Party to purchase an Ottawa residence for its chief and then to vest the property in the names of the cosignatories as joint tenants.[43] Lady Laurier later bequeathed the residence to William Lyon Mackenzie King, stating in her will, "The house having been given us by political friends of my husband, I am of the opinion that it should revert to the Liberal Party represented by its chief WLM King for the purpose of being his official residence."[44]

Robert Mackay did not confine himself to supporting the party financially and to assisting in the purchase of a house for its somewhat impecunious leader. He also lobbied vigorously on behalf of defeated election candidates and operated as a de facto riding worker in Montreal, sniffing out developments of possible interest to his fellow Liberals and firing off letters bristling with wise counsel. After the election of 1896, for instance, he reported to Laurier:

I had the pleasure of meeting today Dr Innes (whom I knew before) who was the member for S. Wellington for so many years & one of your most earnest admirers and supporters while you were both in the cold shades of opposition. He was signally unfortunate in losing his re-election at this particular time, & his friends feel it would be a gracefull [*sic*] recognition of his services to the Liberal Party for over 40 years if the Government could see its way to present him with the Senatorship now vacant for Ontario. I make this suggestion with all due regard to the many considerations which must enter into the giving of this appointment.

I am sorry to have to trouble you so much, but I feel I would be neglectfull [*sic*] of my duties to our Party did I not warn you of a growing feeling of discontent among your English speaking Protestant supporters in this district. They are being threatened with the filling of any vacancies that may arise in positions now held by their class by our French Canadian friends. Needless to state that these reports come principally from our opponents, & it will be, if justified by events, made the most of to the detriment of the Government, & I have therefore felt it right (not sharing in the feeling myself) to send you a friendly word of warning regarding any appointment to such vacancies.[45]

That same election of 1896 also saw Cairine's father enter the political fray for the first time. After "accepting the call of the leading representatives of the mercantile, manufacturing, and industrial classes of Montreal," he contested St Antoine division for the Liberals, but lost to his Conservative opponent. He did succeed, however, in reducing the adverse majority in this long-held Tory riding from 3,706 to 157.[46]

Four years later, he again tried his luck in St Antoine division, but once more he went down to defeat. The following year, on 21 January, just as the old Queen's life was ebbing away, he was appointed a Liberal senator for the division of Alma in the province of Quebec. His commission as senator was the last one signed under Victoria's reign.

Once appointed to the Senate, the family patriarch began making regular trips to Ottawa to attend sessions of parliament. He was frequently accompanied by Cairine, who, alone of the Mackay children, appears to have taken an interest in politics at an early age. Perhaps it was the long passages that her father read from the works of Gladstone, Fox, Morley and Bright to his assembled family that fired her imagination, or maybe it was the heated political discussions that, along with the comings and goings of politicians, were so much a feature of life at Kildonan. But more likely it was the magnetic presence of the tall, graceful Sir Wilfrid himself, who with his high starched collar and shock of grey-tinged chestnut hair epitomized a late Victorian prime minister. A frequent visitor to Kildonan, Sir Wilfrid would pat young Cairine's black head and tell her that one day she would be the wife of a great politician.[47] Like so many other admirers, she quickly succumbed to the prime minister's charm and one day when she was brushing the hair of eight-year-old Edward she groaned, " You will never make a Sir Wilfrid Laurier!"

In Ottawa, Cairine often stayed at the Laurier home, the large brick house in Ottawa's Sandy Hill area that is now known as Laurier House. Long would she remember the happy mornings that she spent there: breakfasting with Sir Wilfrid, who taught her how to eat oatmeal in true Scottish fashion — with salt — and later watching her idol depart for his office, wearing impeccably creased striped trousers and a dignified Prince Albert coat with, no doubt, the horseshoe stickpin that was his signature in the lapel.[48]

Still later in the day there might be visits to the Senate Chamber, then, as now, found at the east end of the "House of Commons Building," and to the Commons Chamber itself, a square-shaped room, located not in the extreme west of the Centre Block, as today, but in the middle of the building. Then, in the evening, there might be a social function to attend. One, in fact, stands out above all the others. This was the ball at Government House at which Cairine met her future husband.

3

YOUTH AND MARRIAGE

Cairine Wilson once recalled that it was a quadrille which first brought Norman Wilson into her life. Whether this is correct — at the time of the interview she was not sure that her memory was all that reliable on this point — the fact remains that she met her husband at a State ball at Government House, the rambling Regency-style villa built in 1838 by a fellow member of the Clan Mackay, Rideau Canal contractor, Thomas MacKay.[1] It was May 1905, and Cairine Mackay was making her first visit to the Lauriers in Ottawa. She had come to the capital to see her father, who was then attending sessions of the Senate. In the absence of her ailing mother, she accompanied the Senator to the gala function at Rideau Hall, one of a host of "entertainments" staged annually by the newly arrived governor general, Lord Grey, and his wife, Alice. Had she tried, Cairine Mackay could not have chosen a more romantic setting in which to meet her future husband: a brilliantly lit ballroom in which massive oil portraits looked down on swirling dancers, some of whom were resplendent in gold-braided Windsor uniforms. Nor could she have hoped for a more fitting person to make the necessary introductions on that memorable May eighteenth evening: Lady Laurier.

Formidably plump Zoë Laurier, who was then emerging as a political personality in her own right, had no children of her own. However, she loved the company of young people, especially women. So, not surprisingly, she took a liking to shy Cairine Mackay and, eager to make her feel at ease, presented her to one of the capital's most eligible bachelors, Norman Wilson. To the end of her life, Lady Laurier would claim

Norman Wilson c 1925.

responsibility for initiating the resulting match and would take a keen interest in the six Wilsons who were born before her death.[2]

At the time of the introduction, Cairine was twenty years old, five feet, six inches in height, slender, and, although reserved and serious, not without a quiet sense of humour and a sparkle in her deep blue eyes. No doubt it was this sparkle and her warm smile that attracted her to Norman Frank Wilson, who, at age twenty-nine, was the second youngest member of the House of Commons (George Parent, a friend and fellow Liberal in the House, was three years his junior.)[3] A newspaper photograph of the time reveals a youthful-looking, clean-shaven Norman, with dark hair parted in the middle and a rather handsome face. Like Cairine's father, he had high cheekbones and a deep forehead, but unlike the gruff, intimidating senator, he was sunny and cheerful. To add to his appeal, he was a Liberal and a Presbyterian, who came from an exemplary bourgeois family that had been headed by a dynamic entrepreneur of Scottish origin, William Wilson.

Norman's father, who died in 1891, was a native of Edinburgh, who had emigrated to Montreal with his parents as a young boy. He launched his working career by serving as a Crown Timber agent in Buckingham, Quebec (known as Canada East in those days). Then he settled in nearby Cumberland where he had purchased a property in 1845. Once established in this small eastern Ontario community, he proceeded to forge a leading role for himself as a farmer, storekeeper, sawmill operator, flour mill owner, township reeve and justice of the peace. With his wife, Mary McElroy, he also raised a large family.

The first child, Catherine Margaret, was born in 1859, the youngest, Norman Frank, in 1876. Of thirteen children born to William and Mary Wilson, nine survived to adulthood, among whom was Catherine or Kate, as she was called.[4] In 1885, she married William Cameron Edwards, an Ottawa Valley lumber tycoon, who became Liberal MP for Russell in 1887 and, then, in 1903, a Senator. As a member of the Upper House he became a good friend of Cairine's father because not only did the two millionaires occupy adjoining seats in the Senate for a time, they also joined forces to bankroll the Liberal Party when it was in a chronic state of bankruptcy. Another sister of Norman's, Ida Francis, also married a prominent Ottawa lumberman: John A. Cameron, son of the late John A. Cameron, who had been a partner with W. C. Edwards in the lumber business which eventually became the W. C. Edwards and Company.

Norman Wilson, in other words, was well-connected and he was able to benefit from his connections. After attending public school in Cumberland, he continued his studies at the elite Toronto boys' school, Upper Canada College, thanks to the generosity of his brother-in-law and guardian, W. C. Edwards, who also assisted in the education of Norman's brother, Reginald (Reggie), born in 1875. From Upper Canada College, Norman went to the Ontario College of Agriculture at Guelph, where he obtained a bachelor of science in agriculture. Equipped with his degree, he returned to Cumberland to work the family farm and to become a vice-president of the Russell County Agricultural Society and president of Cumberland Township Agricultural Society.

However, Norman was not content to be just a working farmer and a self-described member of that "class of toilers who are the greatest wealth-producers of Canada." As befitted a protégé of W. C. Edwards and the son of a township reeve, he entertained political ambitions. In 1904, thanks in large part to Edwards's influence and the prominence of the Wilson family, the young farmer became the unanimous choice of Russell County Liberals for their standard-bearer in that year's general election. Having won the nomination by acclamation, he then went on to defeat his Conservative opponent, J. E. Askwith, in the election, by nearly a thousand votes. When Cairine Mackay first met him, he had served one year in Parliament and would have another three to go, after which he would become manager of the W. C. Edwards and Company mills at Rockland, Ontario.

If young Cairine had any plans for her future when she first met Norman Wilson, they were those of most starry-eyed girls of her generation and circumstances: a handsome lover, a blissful courtship and marriage, and the raising of children in a happy home.[5] At this point in her

National Archives of Canada C 12150

The W.C. Edwards' sawmill, Rockland, Ontario c 1908.

life, she could not conceive of playing a role of any consequence outside the home and a traditional marriage. Still, she did not rush into matrimony. Not until some three years later, in 1908, did she become engaged to Norman, who then swept her off to Quebec to participate in that city's tercentennial celebrations and to meet the stocky bachelor who shared a desk with him in the House of Commons in 1908, William Lyon Mackenzie King.[6]

The marriage took place the following year, on 23 February, Cairine Mackay's birthday month and later the month of her elevation to the Senate. It was held at nine in the evening at gloomy Kildonan, transformed for the occasion into a bower of spring flowers, palms and laurel. The ceremony, reported the *Montreal Herald*, was performed under a large white floral bell in the inner drawing room by the Reverend Dr R. W. Dickie, the tall, striking minister of Crescent Street Church. Cairine appeared in an Empire gown of ivory duchess satin with a panel skirt embroidered in silk and pearls. Her veil, which had been worn by her mother at her marriage thirty-seven years earlier, was of silk embroidered net. For a bouquet she carried lilies of the valley and white orchids. Orchids, in fact, would figure in Cairine's later social life because whenever they dined out or entertained, Norman would present her with an orchid corsage.[7]

Members of the bridal party included Cairine's sister, Anna Loring, as matron of honour, Isett Baptist, a cousin from Trois Rivières, and friends Elsie Macfarlane and Mabel Murray-Smith. The groom was attended by best man, Senator Edwards, and the ushers were George Parent, Harry Christie of Ottawa, and Edward Mackay, Cairine's youngest brother.

The ceremony was followed by a supper served in the large dining room that overlooked the back garden and the slopes of Mount Royal. Later, Cairine and Norman left for Montreal's Place Viger Hotel, the bride muffled in ermine furs and wearing a dark blue broadcloth dress, trimmed with a collar and cuffs of white embroidered silk. After a short stay at the Place Viger Hotel, the couple journeyed to New York, where they had first class accommodation on the S S "Baltic," a "twin screw steamer" that sailed for Liverpool on 27 February.[8] Their wedding trip would take them to London and the Continent before their return to Canada and a radical change in life-style for the new Mrs Wilson.

Twenty-two years after her mother's death, Janet Burns would observe that her father was "a most devoted husband" and that her parents enjoyed a good relationship. It is a sentiment echoed by other close observers of the couple, but at the time of their marriage there must have been those who wondered if the match could be a durable, happy one. Cairine, after all, was quiet and introverted with an interest in reading and stimulating conversation. Her husband, although basically shy, was outgoing and gregarious with family and friends, not given to deep reflection, and, certainly not by any stretch of the imagination, intellectually inclined. Norman, however, had the best of dispositions and a strong sense of his own identity and self-worth. These qualities, plus the couple's mutual devotion would make for a rewarding relationship and eventually allow Cairine to pursue a career of her own outside the home, something almost unheard of in the conservative, upper class circles from which she came.

The first decade or so of married life, however, epitomized the life-style decreed for a woman of her circumstances: raising children and acting as chatelaine of a large home. Only the setting struck an incongruous note because after her marriage to Norman, the physical contours of Cairine Wilson's world changed dramatically. Leaving behind the enchanting city of Montreal with its busy harbour, glinting church spires and Mount Royal, she went to live in a small eastern Ontario mill town, situated some twenty miles east of Ottawa, in gently rolling country beside the Ottawa River. No longer would one of the most elegant avenues in North America — mansion-lined Sherbrooke Street — be the centre of her physical universe. For the next nine years it would be replaced by a three-storey, red-brick house and its immediate surroundings in Rockland.

When Cairine Wilson arrived in Rockland, in April 1909, it was a town of almost four thousand, the overwhelming majority of whom were French Canadians, many descendants of settlers who had left overpopulated Quebec parishes in the last quarter of the nineteenth century to work in the W. C. Edwards and Company lumber mills. In a recital of bald facts, the 1908 edition of *Lovell's Gazetteer of the Dominion of Canada* reveals that the town boasted three churches, twenty stores, three hotels, one flour mill, one sash and door factory, two lumber mills, one mica factory, a bank and telegraph and express offices.

The English-speaking population numbered only three or four hundred people in the years that the Wilsons made Rockland their home. Nevertheless, this small minority held a commanding influence in the town's affairs, occupying the top positions in the W. C. Edwards and Company and in the civic administration. A tightly knit community, they developed their own institutions — two Protestant churches, a public and a secondary school — and indulged a passion for such organized sports as hockey and curling. Curling was especially favoured by company officials, who built their own curling hall and mounted a winning team against rivals from Ottawa, Thurso, Cumberland and Buckingham.[9] One of the company skips was Norman Wilson, who, after the family's move to Ottawa, became a leading force in the Rideau Curling Club, serving as its president from 1928 until 1942.[10]

For her part, Cairine Wilson would have little time for recreational activities, organized or unorganized, during this period in her life. On the rare occasions when she did, she would drive the pair of Roan ponies that she had received from the Edwards for a wedding present or help the family gardener to tend the large vegetable and flower gardens on the Rockland property.

Work, of course, dominated the lives of all the townspeople in these years for most worked long hours six days a week. The largest employer was the W. C. Edwards and Company whose two lumber mills at Rockland were managed by Norman Wilson. The largest of these was built in 1875 to replace an earlier and more modest mill constructed in 1868. That was the year when W. C. Edwards, then a young man of twenty-four, embarked at Thurso, Quebec on the steamer "Caroline" of the Ottawa Forwarding Company, his former employer, and disembarked at what is now Rockland to dig and prepare the foundation for the first of many sawmills in what would become a lumbering empire. With forwarding merchant, James Wood, Edwards formed the firm of W. C. Edwards and Company and then proceeded to work side by side with his employees in all departments of the mill's operations, from the cutting and hauling of logs to the driving of the steam engines and the shipping of the lumber. A man of great zeal and energy, who routinely worked fourteen to sixteen hours a day, Edwards built the business into a flourishing enterprise that spawned a second mill in Rockland and then expanded to Ottawa. Here, the lumber magnate acquired several industrial properties on both sides of the Rideau Falls, which he proceeded to convert into an impressive wood manufacturing complex consisting of a planing mill, a sash and door factory, and a mill for shaping hardwood lumber. When these buildings were destroyed by a spectacular fire in 1907, the Senator took the insurance money, added to it, and built one of the most modern fireproof sawmills in Canada.

The W. C. Edwards and Company, therefore, was one of the largest and most prosperous lumbering manufacturing firms in the country when Norman Wilson stepped down from Parliament in 1908 and became manager of the large mill on Edwards Street and the smaller one on Woods Street. The town that became his second home and to which he brought his bride in 1909 owed its existence and prosperity largely to these sawmills. From six in the morning to six at night, six days a week, they screeched away, relentlessly cutting Ottawa Valley lumber into lengths that were sorted and then pulled by horse-drawn trolleys on rails to vast lumberyards for storage. Most of this lumber, along with such secondary products as boards, slats and shingles, was shipped across Canada and out of the country. Some, however, was sold at nominal cost to company employees to encourage them to build their own homes. Still more wood was used in the construction of company houses that were rented for three to four dollars a month to employees. Rockland was nothing if not the quintessential company town. W. C. Edwards even served as the town's mayor from the time of its incorporation in 1908 until the next year when he and his wife Catherine moved to Ottawa and into the large, picturesque stone house, which in 1949 would be designated the official residence of the prime minister of Canada.

The large red-brick residence with the impressive facade and circular driveway that became Cairine Wilson's new home and that was occupied rent-free by the family belonged to Senator Edwards. Three storeys high, with a verandah that opened off the second floor and a palpable air of prosperity, it stood beside a clump of pine trees on a hill that overlooked the sprawling white mills and huge piles of drying white and red pine and spruce that stretched as far as the eye could see. Nearby on the grassy slope were the homes of other members of the Edwards' entourage and their families — the Binks, the Murrays and the Reeces.

In keeping with the estate of a lumber king, there were stables, where Cairine could keep her pair of Roan ponies, a garage for the family's Franklin car, and large vegetable and flower gardens. But, apart from these features and a contingent of servants, there was little to remind her of the life-style that she had left behind her in Montreal, except perhaps the visits of family members and Montreal friends. Among the first arrivals was sister Anna who visited her sister and brother-in-law in August 1909. Then that autumn Cairine's parents came to pay their respects and find out how their daughter was faring. Brother Edward arrived in May 1910 as did a close childhood friend of Cairine's, Mildred Forbes. Mildred would pay several visits to the Wilsons when they lived in Rockland, and when she served overseas as a nurse during the First World War Cairine would arrange for numerous food parcels to be dispatched to her.[11]

Family members and old Montreal friends were not the only visitors to find their way to Rockland from larger, more sophisticated urban centres. During their years in this out-of -the-way town the Wilsons also drew visitors from New York, Liverpool, Washington, D.C., Tokyo, The Hague, Glasgow, London, San Francisco, Kansas City, Chicago and Montevideo.[12]

No sooner had she settled into her new home than Cairine found herself pregnant. On 16 January of the following year, the first of the Wilsons' five daughters, Olive Mackay, was born at Kildonan where Cairine had returned for the birth, for in those days a baby invariably entered the world in the family home rather than in a sterilized hospital maternity ward. Less than a year later, on 13 November, Janet Mary was born at the Rockland home[13] Then, the following September, an event occurred which was to sadden Mrs Wilson and alter the tenor of life at Rockland. Her gentle mother died at St Andrews, New Brunswick following an "attack of paralysis." The end came suddenly during an illness that occurred when Cairine was at Clibrig. News of the death was emblazoned across the front page of the 21 September issue of the *Montreal Star*, which noted that the late Mrs Mackay had always been interested in "private benefactions" and had been associated with several charitable institutions, including the Mackay Institute for the Protestant Deaf-Mutes and the Women's National Emigration Society. At the age of sixty-two, Jane Mackay's not too robust constitution had finally caught up with her. At her death, though, she was still a handsome woman with the golden hair of her youth.

Photo by D. Will. McKay, St. Andrews, N.B.

Cairine Wilson with Rebecca and Rowena c 1909-1910.

After her mother's death, life became more complicated and taxing for the young Mrs Wilson because now that her father was a widower she felt obliged to make frequent trips to Montreal to supervise Kildonan. In fact, her strong sense of duty goaded her into spending the next four winters at the old family home, overseeing the servants and attending to the needs of her aging father and her taciturn brother, Edward. Her daughter, Janet Burns, who was only a toddler when her grandmother died, recalls with affection the sleigh ride across the Ottawa River to catch the train for Montreal, a journey that was not without its diversions because one horse loved to lie down in the snow! For her mother, though, the memories would have been less rosy because she was attempting to juggle two very different lifestyles, run three large households (at Rockland, Montreal and St Andrews, New Brunswick), and raise a growing family, often with inexperienced help. Life at Rockland was further complicated by Senator Edwards' predilection for looming up, unannounced, for lunch with his business associates. When the small, dapper figure in the dark suit appeared on the front steps about mid-day he was not always a cause for rejoicing, especially after a particularly hectic morning. Fortunately Cairine Wilson was genuinely fond of the endearing senator. "Uncle Willie," as he was called, also had a warm affection for his young sister-in-law whose energy and vitality made a deep impression on him. Later he would be one of the small coterie of male admirers who encouraged her to become involved with politics.

However, if life was difficult in these years, it was not without its bright spots. One was the birth of an eagerly awaited son, Ralph, on 15 March 1915 at Kildonan. From England, where the Lorings then lived, sister Anna wrote in her large, bold hand:

> I was simply delighted at the news contained in the cable which came today, and I hasten to offer you our heartiest congratulations on the arrival of a son. I have not dared mention Norman jr all these months in case it might have a bad effect, but now I rejoice with you in the glad tidings. May your boy grow up to be a great comfort and blessing to you. I do hope everything went well and that you did not have too hard a time. How thankful I am that it is over! I have been thinking of you so much lately, especially after receiving yr. letter of the 2nd for things seemed to be made so difficult for you.[14]

As married women, Cairine Wilson and Anna Loring became very close, so it was a matter of no small regret that her older sister lived so far away when Cairine desperately needed her understanding and support.

For female companionship she had to turn to Rockland's English-speaking community, where she found her confidantes among the wives of company officials, Julia Binks being one who became a lifelong friend. It was almost as if Cairine Wilson had left one insular society for another, but with this difference: Rockland's English-speaking elite, unlike the residents of Montreal's Square Mile, made a practice of learning and speaking French. This increased opportunity to practise her French would pay big dividends when Mrs Wilson entered the political arena.

In Rockland, however, politics had to take second place to other considerations. With the birth of her namesake, Cairine Reay, on 18 October 1913, followed by that of Ralph in 1915, and her long sojourns in Montreal, Cairine Wilson had little opportunity to pursue outside interests. Part of what little time she did have was devoted to working for the small Presbyterian church (now St Andrew's United Church) erected on Marston Road (now la rue St-Jean) near the corner of Rockland's principal artery, Laurier. Further opportunities to broaden her horizons arose in World War 1 when she set about recruiting and organizing neighbourhood women for a knitting war. Under her direction, countless socks and sweaters were produced for the local Red Cross Society, which then distributed them to the Armed Forces. Her Red Cross work and the administration of the Rockland, Clibrig and Kildonan households absorbed most of the organizing ability that she had demonstrated as a young girl and that she would later put to such remarkable use in politics.

* * * *

As 1916 drew to a close, Cairine Wilson watched the life ebb away in her father, the quiet, intimidating figure who had played such a formidable role in her early development. On 19 December, following a brief illness, the Senator died at Kildonan. He was seventy-six. In an obituary the next day, the *Montreal Star* informed its readers:

> On June 14 last, Senator Mackay had a narrow escape
> from death when an electric car crashed into and ditched
> his motor car. He suffered serious injuries and for a time
> his life hung in the balance. He recovered, however, and
> had apparently regained his old-time health and vigor.
> Less than a week ago he was taken ill and did not again
> leave the house.

The funeral cortege, as had so many before it, wound its way from Kildonan to Crescent Street Church, where a service was conducted on the afternoon of 21 December. Afterwards, family members and a large number of friends and dignitaries assembled on the frozen slopes of Mount Royal to participate in a graveside ceremony at the Mackay family plot. Here, sixty-one years after leaving his beloved Caithness, the Senator was buried beside his wife, Jane, and his "friendly" uncles, Joseph and Edward.

Robert Mackay left an estate valued at $8,200,180.07, a sum that translates roughly into $80 million in today's dollars. After legacies had been made to a wide variety of institutions and to old family retainers like the coachman, John Scott, a residue of $7,753,542.84 remained. It was left to the Senator's six surviving children: Cairine, Anna, lawyer Hugh, Edward, an engineer with the Bell Telephone Company in Montreal, George, a hardware merchant in Lethbridge, Alberta, and the second engineer in the family, Angus, who lived in Wickenburg, Arizona.

According to the will, which became a model of its kind, the residue was divided into two equal parts:

> One part which was divided into equal shares among the surviving children;

> The second part which, in the words of the will, "shall be held, administered and managed by my Executors who shall hold it in trust for such of my children as may be alive at my death and the issue of any deceased child as representing their parent so that each living child shall have no share and the issue of a deceased child collectively one share.

> "My executors shall administer the whole of this half of my Estate or whatever may remain of it in their hands as one mass, dividing the net income therefrom among the beneficiaries entitled thereto according to their respective rights.

> My executors shall pay to each child of mine who may survive me, during his or her lifetime, his or her share of the net income corresponding with his or her share of the principal."[15]

So that each heir would have a share equal in value to the shares held by each sibling, the will provided that every child, in rotation, would choose the household effects that he or she desired. Those who selected more than they were entitled to were to be charged for the excess value of their shares. It all sounds straightforward enough, but because of the size of the estate and the number and personalities of the beneficiaries, it took years to wind up the proceedings. Hugh Mackay was even writing to his sister, Cairine, about the distribution of effects at Kildonan as late as 1922. All the haggling aside, the chief significance of the estate settlement is that it left Cairine Wilson a wealthy woman, who could well afford to make generous contributions to causes of her choice, the Liberal Party being one of these.

While the estate was being settled, a family crisis erupted. Although potentially very serious, it was not without its amusing and ironic over-tones, although Cairine Wilson would probably have failed to recognize these at the time. As the years progressed, however, she would develop a worldly wise sense of humour that allowed her to laugh gently at the world's flaws and people's imperfections while at the same time maintaining an awareness of her own weaknesses and strengths. The crisis involved Angus, the revered older brother who, in her eyes, could do no wrong. Aimiable, paunchy Angus, who had a penchant for alcohol, went on a bender during a stopover in Buffalo while en route from Montreal to Arizona in January 1918. Picked up by the police, he was taken to their headquarters, where he was searched and found to have a valuable diamond brooch and diamond studs on his person. When questioned about this, he told a disconnected story about being a man of influence in Montreal and heir to a large estate. Not surprisingly, this disclosure was received with skepticism, if not incredulity, by his interrogators, who then wired the police in Montreal for information about their subject. On learning of Angus's plight, his brother, Hugh, contacted a Colonel E.R. Carrington, in Ottawa, who instructed a Toronto detective agency to dispatch two "operatives" to Buffalo to locate Angus and report on his condition. The men left immediately for the border city where they learned that five husky policemen had been required to handle the inebriated engineer.[16] Cairine Wilson, Hugh, Edward, George and Anna also paid a hurried visit to Buffalo where they saw their brother in the General Receiving Hospital and learned for the first time of the existence of his commmon-law wife, Grace. After leaving hospital, Angus appeared before a magistrate and was formally discharged. Five months later, in June, he died in Oakland, California.

Cairine received the devastating news of Angus's death when she was pregnant with her sixth child, Anna Margaret, who would be born on 9 December 1918, following the family's move to Ottawa. This took place in the fall of 1918 hard on the heels of the purchase of the Rockland mills by the Riordan Paper Company and the formation of a new lumber merchants' partnership comprising Norman Wilson, Gordon C. Edwards, W. Humphry, John Cameron and E. Bremner.

The five partners carried on a wholesale lumber operation in Ottawa which, before being sold to another Ottawa lumberman Edgar Boyle, carried on the W.C. Edwards name. Although a part-owner, Norman never devoted much time to the business. On weekdays he customarily spent an hour or so at his office in the Victoria Chambers on Wellington Street and then devoted the rest of the day to other pursuits. After lunch at the nearby Rideau Club, for instance, he often spent the afternoon curling or golfing, depending on the season. Two or three times a week he drove to Cumberland to oversee operations on the Wilson family farm, which was run by a manager before it was turned over to Angus Wilson, Cairine and Norman Wilson's son. Norman, in other words, effectively retired from active business at age forty-two.

Less than three years after the Wilsons' move to Ottawa, their kindly benefactor and friend, W.C. Edwards died. With his death, on 17 September 1921, a central figure passed from their lives, leaving a fund of cherished memories that included frequent visits to the Wilson home with birthday and other anniversary gifts for the children. As evidence of his respect and fondness for Norman Wilson, the Senator had made Cairine Wilson's husband an executor and beneficiary of his large estate.[17] The following year his wife, Norman's sister, Aunt Kate, died, without leaving a cent to her brother. Catherine's will had originally provided for a legacy of five thousand dollars to her brother, but before her death, this entry was crossed out and initialled by the three executors.[18] To add further insult to injury, Catherine had ensured that Norman and Cairine Wilson would never own the Edwards' beautiful family home at 80 Sussex Street, now known as 24 Sussex Drive. In line with Catherine's will's instructions, Edith Wilson, her sister, was given possession of the house for one year, after which it was deeded to Catherine's nephew, Gordon Cameron Edwards, the son of her husband's older brother, John.

Cairine and Norman Wilson had been led to believe that they would eventually inherit the stone mansion that stands on the edge of a cliff overlooking the Ottawa River and the Gatineau hills. However, because Senator Edwards had transferred ownership of the house to his wife in 1916, the Wilsons would never occupy this celebrated landmark. Always very jealous of her energetic, able sister-in-law, Catherine had seen to it that neither Norman nor Cairine would be among her beneficiaries. Anna Loring wrote immediately to her sister when she learned of the will's contents.

> I was just sick when I read about Mrs Edwards' will, for although I was not altogether surprised at its contents, I am naturally terribly disappointed for Norman & you. Of course, I really blame the Senator, for knowing the feelings of his wife, he ought to have guarded against this contingency. You have both been fed on promises all

your lives, & it does tend to shatter your faith in human
nature. I don't wonder that Norman feels hurt & the
hardest part is to keep up a bold front & face the world as
if nothing had happened... [19]

When Anna Loring wrote this letter she was still reeling from the death
of her beloved husband, Rob, who had died in Asheville, North Carolina
in April. Shortly after Cairine had visited her there, Anna wrote a moving
testimony of the sisters' love for each other.

How kind everyone has been to me in this sad time,
and you especially my dear sister. I can never forget it —
your coming to me without a moment's notice, & leaving
all those little children behind. I did not say much but you
must know how deeply I appreciated your attention. I feel
too that there is a perfect understanding existing between
us and that there never will be any change. Rob was so
fond of you and so disappointed that you were not able to
come to Asheville this winter...[20]

* * * *

When the Wilsons took up residence in Ottawa, it was a small,
parochial capital with a population of approximately 110,000. Long gone
were the days when it was a lusty, brawling lumbertown. All too visible,
however, were such reminders of its lumbering heritage as the screeching
sawmills and giant piles of wood that dotted the LeBreton Flats area, just
west of Parliament Hill, and the hodgepodge of mills that straggled across
nearby Victoria Island and the bank of the Ottawa River. Further east, the
skyline was dominated by the copper-sheaved towers and turrets of the
East Block and the famous Chateau Laurier Hotel, which had opened for
business in 1912. Parliament Hill, far from being a scene of order and
beauty, was strewn with men, building materials and equipment as work
proceeded on the rebuilding of the Centre Block, razed by fire on the night
of 3 February 1916.

Nineteen-eighteen was a noteworthy year not only for Cairine Wilson
but also for her fellow Ottawans. That autumn the worldwide influenza
epidemic swept through the city, forcing the closure of schools, churches,
theatres, pool halls and laundries. At the height of the outbreak — the last
week of September and the first half of October — 520 residents died of
influenza and pneumonia. No sooner had the epidemic abated than news
of Kaiser Wilhelm's abdication reached the city. As soon as the power
companies conveyed the glad tidings to the local citizenry by a pre-

arranged signal, people rushed into the streets, clutching flags and noise-makers. Two days later, on the 11 November, the capital became the first city in Canada to learn of the Armistice and once again joyful crowds poured into the streets, this time to form into parades where they blew horns and surged around gaily decorated cars.[21]

Notwithstanding these developments, Ottawa was normally a quiet, sedate capital with the feel and atmosphere of an Ontario town. Although the Great War had resulted in an expansion of the civil service, the business of government had yet to engulf the community's basic forest industry. Lumber magnates and their descendants were well represented in the tiny Ottawa establishment, where everybody knew everybody else and much time was devoted to the assiduous study of relationships among the top members. What counted most in this hothouse society was not money but family pedigree and occupation. Like Montreal's English-speaking estab-lishment, Ottawa society was highly stratified, with a social pecking order that ranked doctors above dentists and placed retail merchants and men engaged in trade — unless they were well educated and wealthy — on the lower rungs of the social ladder. For the Wilsons and other members of this aristocracy, life was gracious living par excellence with a surfeit of thé dansants, intimate dinner parties in private homes, dances at the exclusive Country Club and the Royal Ottawa Golf Glub, afternoon teas and receptions and functions at Government House. For debutantes, there was also the opportunity to be presented to the viceregal couple of the day at one of the Drawing Rooms, held in the ornate red and gold Senate Chamber.[22] Such was the "Old Ottawa" that the Wilsons came to know well after they left Rockland.

Before moving into the Manor House in 1930, the family lived in Ottawa's Sandy Hill, then a prestigious residential district, noted for its large stately houses, many of which had adjoining stables and generous gardens. One of the most impressive of these was the home that Cairine and Norman Wilson rented in 1918 from Sir Charles Fitzpatrick, Chief Justice of the Supreme Court of Canada before he was appointed Lieuten-ant-Governor of Quebec in the autumn of 1918. A handsome, two-storey building with graceful lines and a gothic roof, it stood at 240 Daly, near the corner of Friel and just a few blocks east of Laurier House.

The family lived at 240 Daly for two years, during which time not only was Anna Margaret born, but also Angus Mackay named after Cairine Wilson's favourite brother (16 March 1920). Children continued to arrive after the family's move to 192 Daly, which the Wilsons bought in 1920. On 11 November 1922, Robert Loring was born, followed by Norma Francis on 1 August 1925. With Norma's arrival, at Clibrig, the family was at last complete. Cairine Wilson's cherished dream of having several children had been amply fufilled. In an ironic twist of fate, however, she would spend less time with her offspring, particularly the "second family," as she called it (the four youngest children) than her warm, fun-loving husband. Indeed, because of their mother's increasing involvement with the community, the younger Wilsons saw very little of her when they were growing up. Because of this and her great reserve, they never came to know her well, at least not until they were adults, and in some cases parents. As a result, this thoughtful, compassionate, but undemonstrative, woman sometimes elicited feelings of intimidation rather than love. Norma Davies, for example, recalls that when she was twelve she was "terrified" by the prospect of having to converse at length with her mother on a long train trip to St Andrews-by-the-Sea.[23]

However, if she intimidated some of her children, such as Norma and Olive, she earned only respect and affection from four long-serving family retainers. These appeared on the scene in the 1920s when the Wilsons lived in the large red-brick house at 192 Daly. Central to the household was Martha Hemsley, the cook, who arrived in Canada with the Governor-General and Viscountess Willingdon. Except for a seven-year absence, she served Mrs Wilson until the Senator's death in 1962. Another key figure was George Betts, the butler, who arrived in 1922 from the United Kingdom where he had been trained as a footman. Amusing and loyal, he had a reputation for being the best diplomat in Ottawa. Before Cairine Wilson went out to a luncheon one day, Betts intoned, "Nobody else will have the courage to tell you, but you have a run in your stocking, Ma'am."[24] Equally indispensable was the chauffeur, Clifford Dazé, noted for his good humour and accommodating ways. There was also the English nanny, Eva Baker, who raised Norma. She entered the household in 1924 and died in 1971 while still serving the family.

* * * *

When the Wilsons moved to Ottawa in 1918, Cairine Wilson was in her thirties, for many people a significant period of passage and redefinition of goals. These years were no less decisive for Mrs Wilson, who, at some point in her early thirties, was jolted into the jarring realization that, for her, at any rate, life should involve more than marriage and raising children. She alluded to this when she wrote in the *Canadian Home Journal* in 1931:

> To many modern women who claim the right of self-expression and desire to lead their own lives, my early experiences would not appeal. Almost last of a large family, I was accustomed to being suppressed through my childhood and young womanhood which did not help to overcome a great natural timidity.

My marriage brought great happiness, but deprived
me of practically all outside companionship and for ten
years I devoted myself so exclusively to the management
of three houses and the care of my children that a blunt
doctor finally brought me up with a start. Never had he
seen a person deteriorate mentally as I had, he told me,
and from an intelligent girl I had become a most uninter-
esting individual. I have been grateful since that date for
his frank words, for it caused me to realize that the work
which I had always considered was my duty was not
sufficient. At once I made a determined effort not to merit
such a consideration and have endeavoured to keep
alert.[25]

Since no clues are given to the doctor's identity, we can only speculate
that he might have been the family doctor in Montreal, Dr. Evans, or his
Rockland counterpart, Dr Tweedie. But that is not important. What is
significant is that Cairine Wilson was so stung by the physician's remarks
that she began seriously to question her role in life and the conventional
wisdom about that role. Was she content to be merely a jewel in her
husband's crown, a gracious, well-dressed chatelaine, who directed the
running of a large household, raised her children, and discharged the
prescribed social obligations? Or did she want something more —
something that she could not yet define but which was beginning to create
a gnawing sense of restlessness? Apparently she answered yes to the
second question because when the family lived at 240 Daly Avenue, she
enrolled in a mind and memory course offered by the Canadian Correspondence College in Toronto.[26] With this conscious decision to hone her
mental skills and broaden her horizons, Cairine Wilson set out to become
something more than just a society matron. That something turned out to
be a conscientious worker for a large number of community and national
organizations and a zealous Liberal whose organizing genius and quiet air
of authority inspired hundreds of women and led to the founding of two
key Liberal Party associations: The National Federation of Liberal Women
of Canada and the Twentieth Century Liberal Association.
Given her family's involvement and her own longstanding interest in
politics, it was almost inevitable that Cairine Wilson would choose this
field in which to carve out a special niche for herself. She took the plunge
during the federal election campaign of 1921 when she suddenly found
herself called upon to speak in public, something that she had hitherto
considered quite beyond her powers.[27] It is not known who asked her to
give that address, but it is possible that it was that charming neighbour

from across the street, Henry Herbert Horsey. A dedicated Liberal, who had been defeated at the polls in 1917, he was very active in the Eastern Ontario Liberal Association, where he became a good friend and political mentor of Mrs Wilson. Such was Cairine Wilson's gratitude to Horsey that she made a pitch to Mackenzie King, in December 1927, to have her mentor, who had been defeated in two more elections by then, summoned to the Senate. With characteristic diffidence, she wrote, "My small entry into political life was brought about by Mr H. H. Horsey and naturally we should be pleased to see him appointed to the Senate."[28] On 14 December 1928 Henry Herbert Horsey was called to the Red Chamber where he became one of its most popular members. Whether or not his good friend's lobbying was instrumental in getting him appointed is open to conjecture, however.

With Horsey's and Uncle Willie's support and encouragement, Cairine Wilson ventured into politics, taking on the sort of jobs that had hitherto been the preserve of men. Unlike most other women of her time and class, she was not content merely to adorn political banquets and pour tea at election gatherings. Shunning the role of dilettante, for which she had little but contempt, she waded right into the arena of political combat, tackling the routine of organization and rubbing shoulders with other workers. The first political office that she took on was that of joint president of the Eastern Ontario Liberal Association (The other president was Gordon C. Edwards, lumber merchant nephew of Senator Edwards), which supervised organization in twenty-three constituencies adjacent to Ottawa. She accepted the post in June 1921, at a time when the newly formed Progressive party, under Thomas Crerar, the Conservatives, led by Arthur Meighen, and the Liberals, headed by Mackenzie King, were gearing up for an election campaign that would culminate in the return of the Liberals to power.

Wily Mackenzie King, who would lead the Liberals to victory on 6 December 1921, was a good friend of Norman Wilson and a party chief who attracted the unflagging loyalty and friendship of Mrs Wilson, no matter how much he disappointed her by the stand that he took on some of the issues closest to her heart. This consummate political strategist and tactician was born in Berlin (Kitchener), Ontario in 1874, the son of John King, a lawyer, and Isabel Grace Mackenzie, the daughter of William Lyon Mackenzie, pre-Confederation Canada's most colourful radical. Raised on tales of his grandfather's exploits, King early felt himself destined for a great career, in which thinking he was constantly encouraged by his possessive mother whom he worshipped.

When the future prime minister was still a child, his debt-ridden father moved his young family to Toronto, where the shy, introverted son later attended the University of Toronto. Following graduation, Mackenzie

King spent a year doing social work at the University of Chicago. He then completed his studies at Harvard University and returned to Canada in 1900 to become the first deputy minister of the fledgling federal Department of Labour. In 1908, he entered the House of Commons as a Liberal and the following year he became the Minister of Labour in Laurier's government.

After this dazzling beginning, King lost his seat in the election of 1911 that routed Laurier and the Liberals from office and brought Robert Borden and the Conservatives to power. For the next few years the plump bachelor with three university degrees and an ingratiating personality divided his time between serving as a labour negotiator for the Rockefeller family in the United States and working for the Liberal Party and the furtherance of his own political ambitions. Engaged by the Rockefeller Foundation in 1914 to undertake a study of capital-labour relations, he wrote *Industry and Humanity: A study in the Principles Underlying Reconstruction* which earned him an enviable reputation as a progressive authority on labour-management relations. His political future, however, was always uppermost in his mind, so when Borden called an election in 1917 King returned to Canada to participate in the bitterly fought campaign, a contest which was enlivened and embittered by that most contentious of issues, compulsory military service. Two years later, in 1919, he won the leadership of the Liberal Party when four-fifths of the convention delegates from Quebec voted for him instead of W.S. Fielding, who had deserted Laurier over conscription.

Convinced that the hand of destiny was upon him, the new leader set out to transform a faction-ridden party that had been reduced to eighty-two seats in Parliament in the 1917 election into an harmonious political alliance. Fortunately for the party's survival and well-being, King had the single-minded vision and political shrewdness to realize this goal, but the task would take many years to achieve. Along the way he would receive generous assistance from Cairine Wilson, who realized full well the invaluable contribution that educated women could make to Liberalism and the Liberal Party, both of which she identified with the good of Canada.

It is significant that Mrs Wilson took on her first political office in 1921 because that year marked the first time that all Canadian women were eligible to vote in a federal election. However, although she was to play a significant role in the campaign preceding this election, Cairine Wilson could not claim that she had made any contribution to the women's suffrage movement and the breakthrough developments that finally culminated in 1918 in voting equality at the federal level. As a shy housewife she had been far removed from the struggle. Nevertheless, in the years ahead she would devote enormous amounts of time and energy to organizing women into an effective political force, albeit one designed to advance the interests of an established party.

She took an important step in this direction when, as chairwoman of a fifty-member committee, she played the leading role in founding the Ottawa Women's Liberal Club, of which she served as president for three years. Shortly after its launching with seventy members in February 1922, Cairine Wilson wrote to Mackenzie King:

> In a reckless moment you once suggested that we might take the stump together. I have no intention of inflicting such an ordeal upon you, but it would give me and all the other members of the newly formed Ottawa Women's Liberal Club immense gratification if you could consent to speak at our inaugural luncheon on March 11th.
>
> Our corresponding Secretary has already written to you officially, but I wish to add a personal appeal. In some way I seem to have attained undue prominence for I do not feel gratified to act as chairwoman upon such an occasion.[29]

Certainly the last thing that she felt was gratified because Cairine Wilson dreaded public appearances. Even after she had chalked up an impressive record of them, she felt unsure of herself when it came to presiding in a public capacity. This point is driven home in a letter to Mackenzie King in which she noted poignantly, "Your endorsation means much for I am afraid there are times when, without the never failing interest and encouragement of our late legal adviser and constant friend, I am inclined to hesitate and seriously doubt my own abllility to proceed."[30]

The phrase "our late legal adviser and constant friend" is a reference to the noted Ontario Liberal Party organizer, Alex Smith. Smith was one of those rare male political workers: a man who never aspired to political office, but who gave unselfishly of his energy and talents to the cause of his party. At a time when Liberal fortunes were dismal, he worked tirelessly to perfect the machinery of the Eastern Ontario Liberal Association and to recruit new members for it. The association's female members owed him a special debt of gratitude because it was his advice and encouragement that persuaded many of them to enter politics. Cairine Wilson was obviously one of his devoted admirers. In fact, one wonders whether she would have taken on her first political jobs without the encouragement of men like Horsey and Smith, raised as she had been in circles where women were expected to defer to men's opinions and look to male figures for support and wisdom. It is indeed fortunate that these two political mentors recognized her organizing genius and capacity for hard work and were prepared to provide her with continuing injections of self-confidence.

In the new role that she was forging for herself Cairine Wilson would never become one of those radical feminists, who often attacked the churches, capitalism and bourgeois society in general. From time to time she would take unpopular positions on controversial questions and even oppose stances adopted by the Liberal Party, her "dear chief" and friend, Mackenzie King, and members of the establishment. But strident militancy was quite foreign to her nature. Throughout her life in politics she would become an exponent of what has been called "maternal feminism" — the belief that women have special qualities, virtues and interests that they should employ in making the world a better place in which to live. Some of this thinking is hinted at in the following selection that she wrote in 1922 for a preface to a booklet on Liberal clubs. In all likelihood she was asked to compose this introduction by Alex Smith.

Until recently the great mass of women have been regarded as children whose activities must be limited. We women wish to develop the political strength that comes from organized association and discussion and the spirit that arises from activity.

For generations men have had wide political opportunities and are therefore more experienced to speak upon a great many subjects, but there are topics to which women bring a more intimate personal knowledge as well as a greater degree of interest.

As women we wish to use our powers to redress existing evils and in every respect to promote legislation which will benefit the greatest number. With the mothers and children we are primarily concerned and we hope that no mother will in the future be forced through poverty to be separated from her children. These little ones are the Nation's greatest asset and if we are able to teach the boys and girls a love of country and to take a sane, responsible interest in public affairs, we may leave Canada in safe hands.

There are also the older people to be considered and those who have laboured and sacrificed must not be forgotten when their period of active work is past...[31]

While she was at the helm of the Ottawa Women's Liberal Club, Cairine Wilson assisted Norman in his campaign to get reelected to the House of Commons. After seventeen years out of active politics, he ran in Ottawa's Capital Ward in the federal election of 29 October 1925. The timing was not fortuitous. On the morrow of the nation-wide Conservative landslide, the Wilsons discovered that Norman had polled fourth among four contestants and that two Conservatives had been elected in the two-member constituency. This would be Norman Wilson's last attempt to get reelected. In the future he would confine his politicking to trying to influence Liberal Party nominations and to aiding the campaigns of friends such as George McIlraith.

Having led the movement to found the Ottawa Women's Liberal Club, Cairine Wilson became the driving force behind the establishment of a district federation of women's Liberal clubs and the National Federation of Liberal Women of Canada, a country-wide federation of women's Liberal clubs. Thanks to the intervention of two federal elections — in 1925 and 1926 — the nationwide federation took five years to organize and place on a permanent footing. Cairine Wilson embarked on this most ambitious of undertakings in the spring of 1923 when she convened a meeting of the wives and daughters of Liberal MPs to discuss plans for a national organization of Liberal women. At this gathering, it was decided to establish a nationwide federation and Mrs Wilson, as chairman of a provisional committee, began spearheading arrangements for a mammoth meeting of Liberal women to be staged at the Chateau Laurier Hotel on 17 and 18 April 1928.[32]

When the inaugural assembly was held it was Mrs Charles H. Thorburn, an Ottawa Liberal powerhouse, rather than the Federation's founder-organizer, who chaired the proceedings. From the first day of that momentous gathering, Mrs Thorburn had her work cut out for her as she attempted to bring order to oftentimes heated discussions. Once the meeting almost broke down when the number of speeches forced her to try to cut off discussion. Among the most controversial issues dealt with that day was the advisability of segregating men and women in different political organizations. Mrs Mary MacCallum, a Saskatchewan delegate, anticipated arguments that led to the Federation's dissolution in 1947 when she opined, "Personally I do not think it is the best thing for men and women to be segregated into political organizations for the different sexes. If there is one place where men and women should work together it is in politics. Politics that are for the benefit of men are without exception for the benefit of women and vice-versa." Her views were echoed by other western delegates, who urged cooperation between the sexes, especially in local committees.[33]

Overshadowing this issue, however, was the design that the organization's constitution should take. It proved so contentious that each item in the document had to be voted on clause by clause. As finally defined, the objects of the federation were: To encourage the organization of Liberal women throughout Canada; to uphold the cause of Liberalism; to raise the status and advance the political education of women; to aid in securing and maintaining good government and to encourage a broad spirit of Canadian nationality within the British Empire.[34]

After the close of official business, Cairine Wilson, in her capacity as banquet chairwoman, introduced Mackenzie King at a sell-out dinner at the Chateau Laurier. Nearly one thousand women greeted the Prime Minister with repeated cheers and the singing of "For He's a Jolly Good Fellow" before order could be restored and Mrs Wilson could make the necessary introductions. In her remarks she said in part:

> We are gathered here not to seek high places, but to create a healthy interest in the study of political affairs and in the Liberal policy, which we think is the best for Canada. The man-made civilization of the East has failed and we hope in this newer land to build a better one in which we may all work together. We do not expect to dictate, but we wish to learn and to make the best use of the powers which God has given to us and there are some problems to which women bring a more intimate knowledge than men.[35]

"Eloquent" is the last word that can be used to describe this excerpt. Indeed, rarely, if ever, did Mrs Wilson rise to heights of oratorical brilliance, for public speaking was not one of her strong points. Scintillating oratory, distinguished by originality of thought and ease of delivery, was the last thing that was expected of her. Even when she became a seasoned political figure and competent speaker, she had to fight to overcome her nervousness when speaking in public. Nevertheless, this excerpt is significant because it encapsulates Cairine Wilson's approach to politics. The ideas it expresses helped to motivate her entry into politics and provided the philosophical underpinning for much of her political action. In all likelihood, though, these thoughts were far from her mind as she listened to King's high-pitched, southern Ontario voice ramble on about his party's faith. With the conference fast drawing to a close, she probably snatched moments to reflect on its evident success. Although only Ontario and Nova Scotia boasted women's Liberal organizations when it convened, well over five hundred women from across Canada had attended. Delegates from the other provinces had organized into committees so that additional provincial associations could be established at a later date. A constitution had been approved and a name for the new federation had been selected. A president had also been chosen, Mary Ellen Smith, a member of the British Columbia cabinet since 1921. Wanting to remain in the background, Cairine Wilson had allowed herself to be made only an honorary president. But that was as it should be because now she wanted to get another project off the ground.

With the National Federation of Liberal Women of Canada off and running, Mrs Wilson turned her attention to another cherished interest of hers: the political education of Canada's young people. She had just led the way in establishing an organization that would inform women about the issues of the day and, it was hoped, pave the way for their smooth entry into political careers. Now she proposed to mastermind the setting up of an association that would attract young Canadians and introduce them to the world of politics.

The first steps along this road were taken at the inaugural assembly of the women's federation when a committee was formed under Cairine Wilson's leadership to establish a "League of Youth."[36] Two years later, in the winter of 1930, just before her appointment to the Senate, the Twentieth Century Liberal Association of Canada came into being. To mark its launching, seven hundred young people from across Canada assembled at the Chateau Laurier for a memorable banquet featuring an address by Mackenzie King and the presentation of a draft constitution for individual Twentieth Century Liberal clubs. Young people's Liberal clubs were not, of course, a new phenomenon; they had been active across the country for years. What made this association so different was that it represented an attempt to coordinate the activities of the clubs already in existence, to establish new ones where none operated, and to bring all clubs together under one organizational roof. It also had an imaginative and evocative name, one clearly designed to appeal to its potential membership — Liberals born in the twentieth century.

In any event, the idea certainly fired the imagination of young people. Watching the spectacle of new Twentieth Century Liberal clubs blossom across the Canadian landscape, one enthusiastic witness rhapsodized:

> One of the greatest innovations of the twentieth century, a century full of wonders and innovations is the organization of the Twentieth Century Liberal Clubs. In Ontario the Provincial Association covers a vast territory extending from Kenora to Ottawa, and along the border to Windsor. From a small beginning and in a very short

time, the Twentieth Century Liberal clubs are springing up apparently overnight and are composed of the younger set, every member having been born in the twentieth century.[37]

The first club was established in Ottawa by Odette Lapointe Ouimet, daughter of Ernest Lapointe, a good friend of Cairine Wilson's and at the time Mackenzie King's minister of justice. George Higgerty, reporting to the association's first national convention, in June 1933, observed, "To Miss Odette Lapointe we should all pay homage for having started the Twentieth Century movement."[38] In the sense that Odette Lapointe called together a group of young women in the winter of 1929 and launched the first club, then homage is due her. But both she and lawyer Sadie Lieff, another early member, have insisted that the idea for the movement originated with Cairine Wilson.

Mrs Wilson paid the rent for the association's headquarters, a suite of two rooms on the seventh floor of Hope Chambers on Sparks Street. Here it shared space with the National Federation of Liberal Women of Canada, whose dedicated executive secretary, Helen Doherty, ran what has been described as "a national propaganda office." Her assistant was Helen Campbell, who handled correspondence for the Twentieth Century Liberal Association and newsletters for the women's federation. One of the most useful tools for this purpose was a Gestetner machine, which churned out thousands of newsletters for distribution across the country. "We became familiar with names in every hamlet across the country," recalled Mrs Campbell. She also had vivid memories of Mrs Wilson's organizing genius. "She was very persuasive. If she told you to stand on your head in the corner, you'd do it."[39] Another association member who could vouch for this was Ida Low. When Mrs Low was eight months pregnant, Cairine Wilson asked her to give a paper at the Chateau. The mother-to-be protested, whereupon Mrs Wilson replied, "Sure you can, just wear a cape." Mrs Low wore a cape and gave the paper.

In Ottawa, members of the local Twentieth Century Liberal Club met four or five times a year wherever they could scrounge space, sometimes in a senator's office. This meant that young men and women might find themselves sitting on the floor and leaning against a wall.[40] Kathleen Ryan recalled that outside of national conventions, men and women in Toronto met separately. Unless there was an election, each group convened seven times a year to hear a speaker, discuss issues of the day and take care of business matters. During election campaigns the members addressed envelopes, answered phones and canvassed for candidates by phone. "Because of Cairine Wilson, the association had members with some standing in the community. In Toronto, for example, sixty percent of the women's branch were Junior Leaguers," reported Mrs Ryan. According to the one-time journalist, there was nobody to give young women leadership and direction before Cairine Wilson came to Toronto on Twentieth Century Liberal Association business. Mrs Wilson provided that inspiration. "We had such confidence in her. Here was a woman who didn't need to do this, but she did. She took everything in her stride," observed Mrs Ryan.[41].

With the founding of the young Liberals' association, Cairine Wilson could look back on a decade of outstanding achievement. Her eldest child, shy Olive, was now twenty and a leading light in that organization. The other children, with the exception of four-year-old Norma, were all enrolled in school, the girls at exclusive Elmwood School for girls, the boys at Ashbury College. Life had been, indeed, full. Little did she know, though, just how eventful it would become in the months ahead.

4

TO THE RED CHAMBER

Cairine Wilson's entrance onto the centre stage of Canadian politics occurred on 15 February 1930 when her "dear chief" and friend, Mackenzie King, appointed her Canada's first woman senator. In a sense, all the work that she had done in the political arena since 1921 had been preparation for this new and unsought appointment, an honour that followed some four months after the winning of the *Persons* case.

Today, it is difficult to imagine that learned counsels would be called upon to debate the meaning of the phrase "qualified Persons" as found in section 24 of the British North America Act. Yet this is what happened back in the 1920s when a band of determined Alberta feminists, led by Judge Emily Murphy of Edmonton, set out to prove that the Act's reference to "qualified Persons" applied to both men and women and that, as a consequence, women could be summoned to the Senate, the upper house of Canada's parliament. The disputed section reads:

> The Governor General shall from Time to Time, in the Queen's Name, by Instrument under the Great Seal of Canada, summon qualified Persons to the Senate; and, subject to the Provisions of this Act, every Person so summoned shall become and be a Member of the Senate and a Senator.

Since only the masculine pronoun is employed in section 23 to describe the qualifications of a senator, the question arose whether "qualified Persons," as described in section 24, included both men and women.

The so-called *Persons* case came before the Supreme Court of Canada in 1928, but only after an indomitable struggle whose roots reached back to 1916. In June of that year the progressive Sifton government of Alberta decided to demonstrate its faith in women by appointing Emily Murphy magistrate of the newly established Women's Court in Edmonton. Friends and feminists applauded the move, but not so some of the magistrate's male colleagues. In fact, the new appointee soon discovered that the honour of becoming the British Empire's first woman police magistrate was not without its drawbacks; on the first day that she presided over her court, an enraged counsel informed "Her Honour" that she was not a "person" under the BNA Act of 1867 and that therefore she had no right to be holding court.[1]

Similar objections were raised in the months that followed, but always the judge held her peace, thinking that the provincial government could prove, if necessary, that she was a "person." The question finally came to a head after Mrs Alice Jamieson was appointed a Calgary police magistrate in December 1916 and one of her cases was appealed on the ground that a woman could not qualify for the position of magistrate. The case was taken to Alberta's Supreme Court where Mr Justice Scott ruled: "...there is at common law no legal disqualification for holding public office in the Government of this country arising from any distinction of sex..." [2]

And there the matter might have rested but for Emily Murphy. Not content with having the issue settled for Alberta, she began to ponder the whole question of the position of women under the BNA Act and the Act's implications for their eligibility for appointment to the Senate.

In 1919, at the first conference of the Federated Women's Institutes of Canada, Magistrate Murphy, by now the president of the FWIC, spearheaded a unanimous resolution requesting the Canadian government to appoint a woman to the Senate. The request was soon taken up by many other women's organizations, including the powerful National Council of Women.

Two years later the Montreal Women's Club, under the presidency of a resolute feminist, Mrs Isabella Scott, threw vagueness to the winds and asked Prime Minister Arthur Meighen point-blank to name Mrs Murphy to the Senate. Meighen turned down the request. Nevertheless, he was sufficiently impressed by the Club's petition to promise during the 1921 election campaign to appoint a woman to the Senate if he was re-elected. The promise was unredeemed, however, when the Conservative Party went down to defeat.[3]

Despite such setbacks the issue did not die. Throughout the 1920s, Canadian women's organizations continued to lobby the Government to appoint a woman to the Senate, but to no avail. Then, in 1927, an aroused Emily Murphy embarked on a new course of action. After consulting with her brother, Mr Justice Ferguson of the Supreme Court of Ontario, she decided to take advantage of Section 60 of the Supreme Court Act, which allows for any five interested persons to petition the Government for an order-in-council directing the Court to rule on a constitutional point in the BNA Act. Mrs Murphy applied to the Government for leave to present such a petition and was successful.[4] Indeed, the Government considered the subject of the petition so important that it decided to defray all legal expenses associated with it.

National Archives of Canada PA 138909

Senator Wilson flanked by her two sponsors on the opening day of Parliament, 20 February 1930. Left to right: Hon. Raoul Dandurand, Cairine Wilson and the Right Hon. George Graham.

Then Emily Murphy found four "interested persons" to sign the petition with her. Her first choice was a friend and colleague, Nellie McClung, novelist, temperance worker and suffragist. The next person selected was Louise McKinney, a leading Women's Christian Temperance Union organizer and an ex-member of the Alberta legislature. One of the two remaining appellants was English-born Irene Parlby, who served as Minister without Portfolio in Alberta for fourteen years. The other was Henrietta Muir Edwards, a prominent feminist, who in 1908 compiled a summary of Canadian laws relating to women and children and later wrote two books pertaining to the legal status of women.

Since the Government was assuming their legal expenses, Mrs Murphy and her fellow petitioners chose a well-known Toronto lawyer, Newton Wesley Rowell, to present their case in Ottawa and subsequently in London. To add to his already impeccable credentials, Rowell had demonstrated his strong support of woman suffrage in 1916 and 1917 when he was leader of the Liberal Opposition in the Ontario legislature.

The petition was forwarded to Ottawa in August 1927 and the following March the case reached the Supreme Court. After weeks of deliberation and despite Rowell's well-sustained arguments, the five Supreme Court justices decided that the BNA Act must be interpreted in the light of what was intended when it was drawn up and because women did not hold public office of any kind in Canada in 1867, they were not eligible for elevation to the Senate in 1928.

All five Supreme Court judges ruled that women were ineligible, but for different reasons. Chief Justice Anglin and three other judges adopted a medieval approach to the question, invoking a common law rule that barred women from exercising any public function because historically only men had fought in battle and had been considered fit to govern. For his part, Lyman Duff, the fifth judge, rejected the proposition that section 24 of the BNA Act contained "a general presumption against the eligibility of women for public office." In language chosen with the utmost care, he wrote:

> It might be suggested, I cannot help thinking, with some plausibility, that there would be something incongruous in a parliamentary system professedly conceived and fashioned on this principle, if persons fully qualified to be members of the House of Commons were by an iron rule of the constitution, a rule beyond the reach of Parliament, excluded from the Cabinet or the Government; if a class of persons who might reach any position of political influence, power or leadership in the House of Commons, were permanently, by an organic rule, excluded from the Government.[5]

And he noted that:

> ...the Constitution in its Executive Branch was intended to be capable of adaptation to whatever changes (permissible under the Act) in the law and practice relating to the Election Branch might be progressively required by changes in public opinion.[6]

Having said all this, however, Duff still could not rule in favour of the women. Instead, he concluded that "there is much to point to an intention that the constitution of the Senate should follow the lines of the Constitution of the old Legislative Council under the Acts of 1791 and 1840," from which women had always been excluded. In other words, according to a strict reading of section 24, only male persons qualified for appointment to the Senate.[7] This argument would later be struck down by the Judicial Committee of the Privy Council in Great Britain which, in so doing, would pave the way for the appointment of the first woman to the Canadian Senate. That woman was, of course, Cairine Wilson, who, ironically, was a great friend of Lyman Poore Duff, a future Chief Justice of the Supreme Court. Equally ironic, Cairine Wilson herself would cling to the mistaken belief that Duff had broken ranks with his colleagues on the bench and ruled in favour of the appellants.[8] But all this lay in the future.

On the same day that Chief Justice Anglin delivered the Supreme Court judgment — 24 April 1928 — Mackenzie King's Minister of Justice, Ernest Lapointe, announced in the House of Commons that the Government would act immediately to have the BNA Act amended to permit the appointment of women to the Senate. When a year later no steps had been taken to implement Lapointe's promise, the "five persons" requested an order-in-council allowing them to appeal to His Majesty's Privy Council in London. The request was granted and Mr Lapointe's department agreed to defray the costs of the action. Decades later, in the midst of tense leadership balloting at the 1958 Ontario leadership convention, Cairine Wilson would refer to her old friend Ernest Lapointe's role in the case. With perhaps unconscious humour, she observed, "My unmerited distinction in being the first woman named to the Senate was due to the interest the Right Honourable Ernest Lapointe, minister of justice, took in women." Not surprisingly, this remark brought down the house.[9]

Certainly the Gilbertian overtones of five learned British judges deliberating the meaning of the words "qualified Persons" as found in section 24 of the BNA Act did not escape the notice of one observer. In a Canadian Press account describing the arguing of the *Persons* case by the Judicial Committee of the Privy Council in July 1929, Lukin Johnston wrote:

In a quiet room at Number One, Downing Street, five great judges, with the Lord Chancellor of England at their head, and a battery of bewigged lawyers from Canada and from England, are wrestling with a question, propounded on behalf of their sex, by five Alberta women.... Deep and intricate questions of constitutional law are debated back and forth. The exact shade of meaning to be placed on certain words is argued to the finest point.... . And so it goes on, and probably will continue to go on for several days. At the end of all these endless speeches, lessons on Canadian history, and questions by five great judges of England, it will be decided, if one may hazard a guess, that women undoubtedly are Persons. Which one may say, without exaggeration, most of us know already![10]

Lukin Johnston was prescient. For, on 18 October 1929, Lord Sankey, the Lord Chancellor, delivered a judgment reversing the decision of Canada's Supreme Court. The crux of that judgment read:

Their Lordships have come to the conclusion that the word *persons* includes members of the male and female sex and that therefore the question propounded by the Governor-General must be answered in the affirmative; and that women are eligible to be summoned and become members of the Senate of Canada.[11]

Upon learning of the Privy Council ruling, the *Ottawa Evening Journal* rhapsodized:

We knew all along we were right. When our Supreme Court last year said that women weren't "persons" we got into a towering rage. We said that in our judgment a woman was not only a person but a personage... . The Privy Council, of course, doesn't mention us... probably the reason he [Lord Sankey] didn't name us right out there in court was that he didn't want to create hard feelings, or sort of rub the thing in. Some people, and especially some judges are terribly touchy.[12]

Whether there were many women who coveted a Senate seat is unimportant. The real significance of this decision lay in the fact that Canadian women had at last become persons in the eyes of the law and that a formidable psychological barrier to political equality had been removed.

Emily Murphy's friends and supporters naturally expected the doughty crusader to be appointed Canada's first woman senator. Instead, the Alberta judge, a Conservative, saw the first female appointment go to a dedicated Liberal, who had never been a militant feminist and who had never evinced the remotest interest in receiving a summons to the Red Chamber. However, although she was bitterly disappointed with and deeply hurt by this turn of events, Mrs Murphy refused to parade her feelings in public; she made no public statement whatsoever on Cairine Wilson's appointment.

Emily Murphy could have been appointed the following year when the Conservatives were in office and the death of an Edmonton senator, the Hon. E.P. Lessard, created a suitable vacancy. But because the Bennett government wanted to replace him with another Roman Catholic and Mrs Murphy was an Anglican, it selected a Roman Catholic male senator instead. Two years later, in 1933, Judge Murphy died, her cherished dream unfulfilled.

Cairine Wilson's appointment was made on 15 February 1930, some six months before Mackenzie King's government was tossed out of office by R.B. Bennett's Conservatives and eight years and a day from the date on which Mrs Wilson had founded the Ottawa Women's Liberal Club. When she was catapulted onto the national stage, Cairine Wilson was forty-five, but still a remarkably young-looking, slender woman. Only one child was living away from home and that was eighteen-year-old Janet, the second oldest daughter, and she was studying in Paris. "Baby Norma," the youngest member of the family, was only four. Although she had been very active in the Ottawa community for almost a decade and had given freely of her time and her money to the Liberal Party, Cairine Wilson professed to being surprised by Mackenzie King's summons. Her name had been bandied about in connection with the existing Senate vacancies and even Janet in Paris had heard a rumour that her mother might be appointed to the Senate. Still, Cairine Wilson informed an interviewer that the summons was "something of a shock." Later she would concede that she had told King, "You are going to make me the most hated woman in Canada."

According to gossip of the day, Alex Smith, the Ontario Liberal Party organizer, suggested Cairine Wilson's name for this trailblazing appointment on the grounds that Mrs Wilson was a successful spoke in the Party wheel.[13] Whether or not he started the ball rolling, it appears that the power brokers settled on Cairine Wilson's name on 11 February. As Mackenzie King noted in his diary for that date:

I went to the office at noon and discussed Senate appointments with Ontario colleagues & Haydon.[14] None cared particularly about Percy Parker, & we got down finally to three names, Mr. Raymond, Mr. Oakes, & Sinclair. The latter wd. be my choice. We came to agreement on Mrs Norman Wilson as first woman Senator to be appointed. She has taken a leading part among the women — speaks English & French & is in a position to help the party & will. Was a close friend of Lady Laurier's, is a lady & there will be less jealousy of her than of any other person.

King might have added that he felt comfortable with this choice for other reasons, one being his longstanding friendship with the Wilsons, who had entertained him in Ottawa and at their summer home in St. Andrews. Perhaps even more important, Cairine Wilson was a woman of wealth with high ideals and a social conscience — attributes that the pious prime minister always found attractive in the female sex. She was also, like King, a Presbyterian and a faithful member of St. Andrew's Presbyterian Church in Ottawa.

As so often happens in such cases, the decision to name Cairine Wilson to the Senate was reported in the press before the appointment was made official, in fact, even before the Prime Minister had approached the recipient about it. "Mrs Norman Wilson likely for Senate" proclaimed the *Ottawa Evening Journal* in a subhead emblazoned across its front page on 14 February. Accompanying this bold announcement was a photograph showing an extremely youthful-looking profile of Mrs Wilson and an article which reported:

> The appointment of Canada's first woman Senator is likely to go to Ottawa. It was being forecast today in well-informed political circles that Mrs Norman Wilson, wife of Norman F. Wilson, ex-M.P. for Russell County, is to receive the vacancy in the Upper House created by the death of the late Hon.(Dr) J.D. Reid.

> It is likely the matter will be decided by the Government at this afternoon's meeting of Cabinet Council. It was stated this morning that until the appointment of Mrs Wilson is made there is an element of uncertainty as great pressure is being brought to bear on behalf of other candidates. However it is quite probable Mrs Wilson will be named. Mrs Wilson has all the qualifications for the post and if she accepts she will enjoy an honour held by her father, the late Senator Robert MacKay.(*sic*)

Just who leaked news of the government's intentions is not known.
Mackenzie King speculated in his diary that it was either his Secretary of
State, Fernand Rinfret, or P.J. Veniot, a former premier of New Brunswick
who served as Postmaster General. It could also have been Rinfret in
collusion with James Malcolm, the Minister of Trade and Commerce. In
any event, when the diffident bachelor went to the Wilson home that
evening he was greeted by a highly embarrassed Cairine Wilson.[15]
According to letters written by the Wilsons and to jottings in King's diary,
the Prime Minister discovered a very reluctant recipient.

The famous diary reports:

> Mrs Wilson seemed confused, said she was flattered
> to be asked but felt she could do more out, said others
> would be jealous, suggested Mrs Thorburn's name [16] etc.
> I told her we were agreed a woman should be appointed,
> also from Ont. rather than Quebec, of Ont. she was the
> unanimous choice & Cabinet today had all approved. I
> wd. put thro appointments tomorrow.[17]

King put through Cairine Wilson's appointment the next day, Saturday 15 February. However, before the Governor General, Viscount
Willingdon, signed the commission, various roadblocks had to be overcome. One of these was Norman Wilson. The product of a conventional
upbringing, he subscribed to the then widely held belief that a married
woman belonged in the home and not in the paid work force, and certainly
not in the limelight. So it is not surprising that he informed the Governor
General that the couple "did not wish" the appointment. His Excellency
thereupon phoned King, who in turn phoned Cairine Wilson. She reported
that the appointment "might mean a divorce but that she wd. accept." The
Prime Minister then asked if Norman Wilson would really object and she
ventured the opinion that he "would be all right."[18] Fortunately the
prediction proved correct. Norman Wilson would not only accept the
situation, he would become immensely proud of his wife in her new role.
There is no doubt, though, that Cairine Wilson spent many hours in
anguished soul-searching, wondering if she had let events stampede her
into a disastrous move. Some of her inner turmoil is alluded to in a letter
she wrote to her daughter, Janet. Writing from a secluded Gatineau
farmhouse, owned by her brother-in-law, Jack Cameron, the new senator
reported:

> On Sunday I was so miserable that I missed writing
> and yesterday Dad and I beat a retreat here. Long before

you receive my letter you will probably have heard what has befallen me and I am still wondering how I walked into such a difficulty. Friday evening the newspapers came out with headlines of my appointment as Senator and at eight or later the Prime Minister arrived. I was overwhelmed and scarcely knew how to refuse for I knew that Dad would not be pleased. However I was over persuaded (*sic*) the order was signed by the Governor General the following afternoon.[19]

Once the news leaked out, 192 Daly Avenue was besieged by reporters and inundated with telegrams, letters and telephone calls. In a desperate attempt to escape the furore, Cairine Wilson remained in bed Sunday morning and "kept hidden" during the afternoon. Then, early Monday morning, she and Norman left by train for her brother-in-law's farmhouse at Six Portages in the Gatineau Hills, not far from Blue Sea Lake. There, after a midday meal, they skied for an hour-and-a-half in bitterly cold, but exhilarating, temperatures. Not until Wednesday afternoon did they reluctantly take the return train to Ottawa and then only because they had to attend an evening performance of the Minto Skating Club's annual carnival.[20]

With her elevation to the Senate, Mrs Wilson became the subject of countless newspaper articles and editorials across the country. Her name even travelled to the outer reaches of the British Empire — to Australia. Typical of the sentiments expressed by many editorial writers are the following which appeared in the *Ottawa Journal* of 17 February 1930.

When it comes to making a virtue out of a political necessity, Mr King is always dependable. Thus, driven into a position where the appointment of a woman senator was inescapable, Mr King met the correspondents on Saturday afternoon and told of Mrs Wilson's selection for the Upper House with the air of one who had at last achieved the greatest desire of his heart. The stage certainly lost out when our Premier took to politics.

As for the appointment itself, it is an excellent one. Mrs Wilson is the very antithesis of the short-haired woman "reformer," is the exact opposite of that unlovely female type which talks of Freud and complexes and the latest novel and poses as being intellectual. She is of the much more appealing and competent kind who make a success of their job of taking care of a home and rearing a family before meddling with and trying to make a success of everything else. There are few women in Ottawa, and very few anywhere, who have taken a more informed and useful interest in worth-while social effort; few whose activities have been less concerned with a personal liking for the limelight.

Although one just man would have saved Sodom and Gomorrha, one good woman will hardly save our Senate. But while we need not expect the Millennium from what has now come, it is at least possible to expect that the fresh viewpoint of a woman, to be reinforced shortly, let us hope, by the viewpoints of other women, will do the Senate some good. THE JOURNAL, at all events, permits itself to be optimistic.

Although Cairine Wilson's appointment was lauded across Canada, there was justified opposition to it, especially on the part of some westerners who, not surprisingly, felt that either Emily Murphy or one of the other four appellants should have been the first woman appointed to the Canadian Senate. An editorial in the *Regina Star* of 7 March 1930 summarized these views as follows:

"Unto him that hath shall be given." It is a piece of irony that the first senatorship to be given to a woman — and possibly the last under the King government — has been given to one who never raised a finger in the fight to win for women the right to sit in the red chamber at Ottawa. So often the plums fall into the laps of those who stand idly by, while others do the work.

The fight was waged by five western women, any of whom together with Mrs Mary Ellen Smith, former M.L.A. and cabinet minister of Vancouver, would have been most eligible for the honour. So the honour was given to an eastern lady who has never taken any part in public life.

On the other hand, it may be a gentle hint from the bachelor premier that the ladies who find favour in his sight are those who leave public affairs to their men folk, and devote themselves at home to the raising of large families.

... Possibly the chief qualification in his eyes was that Madam Senator Wilson is a daughter of Quebec and made her introductory speech in the Senate in Quebec French.

However, much satisfaction the appointment may give to Quebec, to the great multitude of women who have given public service in Canada — and who are much too good sports to complain — the appointment must be a subject of dissatisfaction.

If the appointment pleased some Quebeckers, it certainly riled others. One of these was Azilda Dumas, a member of the Canadian Alliance for the Quebec Women's Vote. On 17 February, in the white heat of fury, she fired off a letter to Mackenzie King that stated in part:

Allow me to express to you, how deeply you have grieved a great many women of this Province, by choosing for *your first senatrix in Canada*, a woman from Ontario!

Have you forgotten that Canada has been French for many years — hard years of trouble and sacrifices, etc., before it passed under the British Flag? Only the loyalty of our forefathers has kept this country to the English crown; but it is still *our home* where every other nation has been welcomed and treated with justice and fair-play.

On this important question of a first woman being appointed to the Senate, this honour was due to the French Canadian woman; the "priority" of the Province of Quebec should not have been overlooked to elect instead, a woman, who has done comparatively nothing towards obtaining the eligibility of the woman to the Senate. It is the greatest injustice one could inflict on the Quebec women! [21]

And then there was opposition of quite another kind — the petty opposition of self-righteous observers who expressed the view that no wife and mother, let alone one with *eight children*, should take on the role of senator! To their way of thinking, only the most brazen woman would openly dispute the adage that her place was in the home. Even union organizers condemned married women who worked outside the home and this despite the fact that thousands earned paychecks as school teachers, telephone operators, store clerks, house-keepers, garment and other factory workers.

More significant was the criticism of some members of Parliament. In public they attacked the appointment on the grounds that women were not qualified to study legislation dealing with public questions and the law. But in private, among themselves, they probably gave vent to their true feelings — resentment that another male bastion was being invaded by women. Cairine Wilson would always contend that she had been well received by her fellow senators and that the all-male Senate had never displayed any resentment to her appointment.[22] Be that as it may, there was undoubtedly some resistance — at least initially to her presence.

But fortunately this opposition in no way recalled that which greeted Agnes Macphail when she first entered the House of Commons as Canada's first woman MP. The searing memory of being constantly under observation and of being continually subject to criticism once led Miss Macphail to tell Cairine Wilson that "she would not like to see any other woman go through what she had to go through when she first came into the House of Commons."[23]

In addition to all the attention heaped on her by the press, friends, and the public, Cairine Wilson had to face a major ordeal before the week was out: the opening of the fourth session of Canada's sixteenth Parliament on Thursday and her swearing in as Canada's first woman senator. For many neophyte MPs, who had rehearsed in fantasy the exciting events that unfold on such an occasion, this was an event to be welcomed and cherished. However, for Cairine Wilson, who disliked the prospect of being a cynosure and who had never sought a Senate appointment, it was an event to be dreaded.

Since the British House of Lords and the upper houses of North American provincial and state legislatures had no women among their members, there was no obvious precedent regarding what the new celebrity should wear for her induction to office. The prevailing dress code dictated that women on the floor and in the balcony of the Canadian Senate wear formal evening dress, but whether the code applied to a woman senator was, of course, debatable.

True to form, the Canadian press poured out columns of advice. One faction claimed that Mrs Wilson should don tailored clothes, so as to be inconspicuous among her fellow senators, while another urged her to wear full evening dress to dramatize the shattering of tradition that her appointment created. Indeed, some papers got carried away by the dress question. One notable exception was the *Toronto Telegram* of 18 February 1970, which attempted to place things in perspective:

> Some people seem to be more concerned as to what Canada's first woman Senator will wear at Ottawa's Parliamentary opening than about any of her other problems.

> But surely in this season of ensembles nothing could be easier than for a woman to sit among Senators who are wearing day clothes and yet attend a reception afterward in evening dress as are the other feminine guests.

As it turned out, this was finally the course adopted, but not without some detours along the way. Knowing that all the other ladies present would be in evening dress, Cairine Wilson initially opted for a black evening gown, but after consulting with Raoul Dandurand, government leader in the Senate, she decided that a dark green and black afternoon dress would be more in keeping with the business suits of her "fellow members of the Senate." Before making her grand entry, however, she changed her mind once again, this time settling the dress question once and for all by choosing a powder blue lace afternoon dress with long sleeves and matching shoes.

The switch was reported by various papers the following day along with a comment suggesting that she was a "normal" woman, i.e., fickle. For those papers that went to press before the opening of Parliament actually took place, however, Mrs Wilson's frequent changes of mind posed problems. Because it was the practice of female guests to submit detailed descriptions of what they would wear for such an occasion, several papers mistakenly reported that Cairine Wilson made her debut as a senator wearing a black and green printed crepe afternoon frock. Be that as it may, at no other time would the Senator be so preoccupied with such inconsequential concerns. As a matter of fact, when shopping for clothes at the Chateau Modiste and Beauty Shop, her favourite dress store in Ottawa, she invariably had her mind on other things.[24]

Thursday 20 February ushered in balmy, unseasonably warm weather for Parliament's opening. An immensely proud Anna Loring came from Montreal for the occasion and, after an early lunch at the Wilson home, set off for the Senate to watch her sister's swearing-in. She left shortly before 1:30 p.m. for Parliament Hill, followed later by her niece, Olive and still later by the Senator-designate. Why members of the family had to leave at different times is not explained. Certainly Olive, then aged 20, found the staggered departure times ridiculous and said so in a letter to her sister Janet.[25]

Although Canada's years of prosperity had come to an abrupt end with the the Crash in the autumn of 1929 and plummeting wheat sales, the opening pageantry was just as lavish and colourful as any in the history of the Canadian parliament. This year, however, it was probably witnessed by more women than ever before, judging from a photograph of the day which shows a long queue of bobbed ladies in ankle or calf-length gowns framed in the arch of the Senate lobby. In fact, so many people wanted to attend this historic ceremony that large numbers had to be denied invitations. Nevertheless, despite space limitations, there was, in the words of *Saturday Night*, a "representative gathering of the citizens of Canada from coast to coast as well as many distinguished visitors from other lands."[26]

The tone of the ceremony was set by the Viscountess Willingdon, who arrived on Parliament Hill wearing a tiara and a stunning gown, whose heavy train was carried by two young pages dressed in white satin and black velvet with gold braid. Mackenzie King, resplendent in the gold braided uniform of the privy councillor, met Lady Willingdon at the entrance to the Senate and from there escorted her to a dais on the left side of the throne. Not far behind was her husband, the Governor General, a striking white-haired gentleman, who resembled a Spanish grandee, but a grandee attired in full court dress with cocked hat, white breeches and stockings.

As the clock tower boomed out three o'clock, Lord Willingdon entered the main door of the Centre Block and then passed through an honour guard comprising officers and associate members of the Defence Council. Stepping into Confederation Hall, that magnificent rotunda at the main entrance, he was met by the Prime Minister and Senator Raoul Dandurand. Accompanied by these two dignitaries and other distinguished officials, including the Gentleman Usher of the Black Rod, he proceeded to the Senate where he joined his wife.

Once their Excellencies were seated, Black Rod began enacting the time-honoured ritual that requires him to summon members of the House of Commons to the Red Chamber to hear the Governor General read the Speech from the Throne. Everything went as choreographed. Then, the reading finished, the procession to His Excellency reformed and escorted him to the exit. Thereupon the members of the House of Commons returned to their chamber. However, not a person moved who was not obliged to for everyone was eagerly awaiting the entry of Cairine Wilson, then nervously pacing the floor of the robing room, Norman at her side.

After a short interval, the business of the Senate resumed. In accordance with tradition, the Senate's "pro forma" Bill No. 1, "a bill relating to railways," was read.[27] Having thus signalled the immemorial right of the Upper House to attend to its own business before considering that of the Crown, the Speaker proceeded to read and then to table the Throne Speech. These preliminaries out of the way, he intoned the message that everybody had been waiting for: the announcement that two new senators, Cairine

Wilson and the Hon. Robert Forke, the former minister of immigration, would be installed. Forke, from Pipestone, Manitoba, who had been appointed before Mrs Wilson, was the first to be introduced and sworn into office.

Then it was Cairine Wilson's turn. Escorted by Senator Raoul Dandurand, in a privy councillor uniform, and her good friend, the Rt Hon George P. Graham, journalist and former Liberal cabinet minister, she stepped into the chamber, a slim figure with closely cropped dark hair and a composed demeanor. As she made her entrance, several gallant senators rose instinctively to their feet, but, then realizing that their example was not being emulated, reseated themselves. Seemingly unperturbed by this diversion, Cairine Wilson and her sponsors continued up the red carpeted aisle of the Senate past rows of senators attired in sombre morning coats and towards the quaint-looking figures of the Supreme Court justices huddled on the woolsack in their scarlet and ermine robes. Applause rippled across the audience, inspired in part, no doubt, by the new senator's natural carriage and poise. Then, before the trio reached the Clerk's table where Cairine Wilson was to take her oath, an impulsive senator rose and shouted, "Three cheers for our first lady member!"[28] Unfortunately for Senator Peter Martin, but fortunately for the dignity of the Senate, nobody responded. So, without further interruption, Mrs Wilson proceeded to the table, recited her oath in a clear, firm voice and signed the roll. As she did so a surpressed titter ran through the chamber for at some point the gold braid of Senator Dandurand's uniform had become entangled in the blue lace of her dress.[29] In any event, after signing the roll, Mrs Wilson then went to the dais, shook the white gloved hand of the Speaker, turned, and took a seat on the government side of the chamber.[30] With the completion of these formalities, Cairine Wilson became a fully-fledged senator entitled to occupy a Senate seat for life. As payment for her services, she would receive a sessional allowance of $4,000 for every session of Parliament that extended over a period of sixty-five days. Only if she chalked up less than fifty days' attendance in one particular session would she forfeit her right to the full amount, in which case she would be paid $25.00 for each day's attendance. She would hold her seat for life unless she failed to attend two consecutive sessions of the Senate; ceased to be a citizen; was adjudged bankrupt or insolvent; was tainted by treason or convicted of "felony or of any infamous crime" or no longer qualified in respect of property or residence.[31]

From all accounts, she had succeeded admirably in suppressing her nervousness and in conveying the impression that she was her usual serene self. The realization pleased her as no doubt did the realization that she was regarded first and foremost as a wife and mother, not as a militant politician like Agnes Macphail, the hard-working, sharp-tongued pioneer, who had become Canada"s first female MP in 1921. As one reporter observed, when referring to the new senator's swearing in, "Perhaps one of the interesting sidelights on her demeanour was that throughout it all she was predominantly Mrs Wilson."[32]

That men and women alike regarded Cairine Wilson primarily as a wife and mother is vividly illustrated by an anecdote related in "The Homemaker" column of the *Toronto Globe* on 29 November 1930:

> "I don't know," said a man whose name would be familiar to many of you, but who might blush to find it inscribed on a page so largely devoted to women's interests, "I don't know why you don't write something about our one woman Senator."

> I felt rather pleased that he had followed the page closely enough to notice the omission, so I smiled encouragingly, and he went on:

> "I'm on the other side of politics, but I do think she is so — so womanly."

> I had seen him among the many who listened eagerly to Senator Cairine Wilson's words at the dinner of the Women's Teachers' Association last week. And I had noticed that all the other men agreed with him. "Womanly" was the word that came most easily to their lips, but there were other qualities that made her so attractive to women, there was the delightful twinkle in her eye which told of an unquenchable flicker of humor, and this was part of the unfailing responsiveness each speaker felt as she addressed herself to the guest of the evening.

In any case, the day after her swearing in, Cairine Wilson plunged back into her normal routine, rising early for breakfast and getting her youngest children off to school. After disposing of a number of household tasks, she conferred with the cook, then set off to do some family shopping. Later in the day she fitted in a business appointment, a board meeting and an appearance at the Governor General's Drawing Room. Except for the latter, this was a typical day in the life of Cairine Wilson, or was until she began spending a good deal of her time on Parliament Hill.

The Drawing Room — an annual event that loomed large in the social life of the capital up until World War II — was staged by Their Excellencies in the ornate red and gold Senate chamber, which had been cleared of desks for the occasion. For magnificence and quiet dignity, probably no other location in provincial Ottawa could rival the Red Chamber as a setting for a formal function which was "de rigueur" for society matrons, debutantes, Members of Parliament, top military officers, deputy ministers, church dignitaries and members of the diplomatic corps. Accompanied by Norman and Olive, Cairine Wilson entered the Chamber with fellow members of the Senate and made her bows to Their Excellencies who were standing on a dais halfway down the room. Olive, displaying her customary resourcefulness, collected two friends, Odette Lapointe (Ernest Lapointe's daughter), and Kiki Roy, and pushed her way up to the rope in front of the Willingdons. From this superb vantage point, she watched some 1,200 guests bow to the viceregal party, observing that some of the bows were "very funny."[33]

Mackenzie King took a somewhat more jaundiced view of the occasion. In one of his periodic attacks against High Society, he confided to his diary:

> Another function over this evening. The Drawing Room is to me a very tiresome sort of business, it is painful rather than beautiful there are so many evidences of vanity, so many evidences of striving for effect in dress & manners — such obsequiousness in some of the bows, women putting their whole souls into their (word illegible) to place and power & pomp.[34]

There is no record of how Cairine Wilson felt about such functions, but we do know that Norman Wilson, once reconciled to the Senate appointment, became ecstatic about developments. In prose as elegant and as carefully constructed as King's, he reported to Janet:

> The greatest event in British history as far as women are concerned is now passed. Mother is a full fledged Senator taken the oath her seat in the Red Chamber, made her bow to their Exs at their Drawing Room and with it all is the same good mother that she has always been really it was a great sight. I was & she was opposed to her accepting the great honor but now that it is passed & the Government was bound to elect a woman I feel that Mother was the best possible to be the first lady in the Red Chamber.

...Your mother is first in History of the British Empire.*
So you see how suddenly you have become famous. No
joking Janet one can hardly realize what an honor it is to
one who did not seek it & was reluctant in accepting it fact
turned it down but it appeared in the papers & she could
not any longer refuse. His Ex. wrote her a very nice note
everyone seems pleased.[35]

On 25 February Cairine Wilson passed another nerve-wracking test
with flying colours — her maiden speech in the Senate. The day began
innocuously enough with an early morning call from her political mentor,
Henry Herbert Horsey. Later there was a session with her French teacher,
Mademoiselle Mortureux, who listened to the Senator read a revised
version of the French portion of her address.[36] Then there was what can
only be described as a memorable mid-morning interview with Senator
Dandurand.

The septuagenarian with the bristling white beard was, despite his
years, a devoted friend of the feminist movement. In 1909, he had presided
with Dr Grace Ritchie-England, a medical doctor and a resolute feminist,
over a suffrage meeting in Montreal and, in 1918, he had delivered a
gallant speech in favour of the women's Franchise Bill. So it was not
because he underrated women's abilities that he took a highly embarrassed
Cairine Wilson into the Senate Chamber, locked the door and insisted that
she rehearse her French "speech." After this ordeal, confessed the Senator,
she was not the least bit nervous about the prospect of delivering her
maiden address in the Senate that afternoon.[37]

The all-important speech was given shortly after the Senate convened
at 3 o'clock. With Norman, Olive and young Cairine looking on from the
gallery, Mrs Wilson seconded the reply to the Speech from the Throne.
When she rose to give her address, her fellow senators tendered her a
rousing ovation. Then, steeled by the morning's rehearsals, she plunged
into fluent French. With becoming modesty, she noted that she had not
sought the great honour of representing Canadian women in the Upper
House; she was there because her services had been requisitioned. The
new senator then paid tribute to Judge Emily Murphy and the four other
appellants who had taken the *Persons* case all the way to His Majesty's
Privy Council.

---

* Norman Wilson, like many newspapers, was incorrect on this point because four
women sat in the first senate of the Irish Free State, then a member of the British
Empire. The four female senators who took their places on 11 December 1922 were
Eileen Costello, Ellen Desart, Alice Stopford-Green, and Mrs Wyse-Power.

Still speaking in French, Cairine Wilson observed that she had always been interested in public affairs, having been raised in a family where politics was the chief source of conversation.

> Being a firm believer in the doctrines of Gladstone, Edward Blake, and Laurier, it was quite natural that I should give my support to a cause that was dear to me, without, however, forgetting my domestic duties. I say this because I desire to remove the misapprehension that a woman cannot engage in public affairs without deserting the home and neglecting the duties that motherhood imposes upon her. Sometimes I am amused to hear this argument on the lips of certain fathers who are utterly indifferent to the upbringing of their sons and leave that solemn obligation to the mother alone.

> A man is supposed to devote his time to the material needs of his family. No one disputes his right to participate in public affairs. But does such activity relieve him of his duties towards his children? Yet we constantly hear mothers complain of the husband's indifference about the supervision and guidance of his sons.

> I trust the future will show that while engaged in public affairs, the woman, the mother of a family, by reason of her maternal instinct and her sense of responsibility, will remain the faithful guardian of the home.[38]

Before concluding her French "speech," Mrs Wilson referred to the province of Quebec where she had been born and raised:

> I cherish tender recollections of my native province, the old French province of Quebec, where it is good to live, because of the broad spirit of tolerance that animates its people. In this connection I recall a thought that the honourable leader of the Government in this House [Hon Mr Dandurand] expressed at the Assembly of the League of Nations in Geneva. Speaking of the problems of minorities in Europe, he asked that they be treated not merely with justice, but with generosity. "Let us deal with them," he said, "in such a way as to make them forget that they are minorities." I avail myself of this opportunity to declare with pride that the English and Protestant minor-

ity in Quebec has never been made to feel itself a minority
in that province. I desire to pay this tribute to my native
province and cite it as an example for the whole of
Canada.[39]

In the English portion of her address, the Senator repeated many of the
themes that she had raised earlier. When alluding to a woman's duties,
however, she called upon members of her sex to use the vote responsibly
and to work for peace in the world.

She evidently acquitted herself satisfactorily because after the Senate
adjourned, staid members crowded around her to extend congratulations.
Afterwards, the Senator wrote to Janet, "From all accounts I managed
fairly well and felt relieved when the ordeal was over for everybody was
filled with curiosity."[40]

Norman Wilson, not surprisingly, was less reserved in his assessment
of her performance. In a news bulletin, destined for Janet, he reported,
"Mother made her first speech in the Senate yesterday & I am pleased to
say she did exceedingly well."[41] The day after this newsworthy speech,
Cairine and Norman Wilson attended a dinner given by close friends, the
Ken Greenes, then went on to a reception at Government House. More
recognition came the following day, 27 February, when Mrs George
Graham, the wife of Senator Graham, gave a lunch in Mrs Wilson's honour
at the Country Club. That evening Club members rose to the occasion with
a magnificent banquet. Sir George Perley, local lumber merchant and
Conservative member of Parliament, chaired the evening, and Hamnet
Hill, the Senator's lawyer and a long-time friend, delivered a witty toast.
Norman Wilson pronounced the event, which was attended by almost 120
people, "the finest thing that [he had] ever been at."[42]

Cairine Wilson's use of French in her maiden speech in the Senate did
not go unnoticed by editorial writers and writers of letters to the editor.
Incensed by the *Mail and Empire's* comments on the subject, an irate L.N.
Haynes of St Catharines dispatched the following letter to the Toronto
paper:

> In the Saturday issue of the Mail and Empire, Feb. 22,
> on page 15, there appeared an editorial written by one of
> your staff in which the following sentence appeared:
> "While the new senator is thus sacrificing herself to aid
> her party" [by making a speech in the French language]
> "how much are the Conservative women of this province
> doing to aid the premier in his efforts to remove from the
> vast majority of Ontario folk the disgrace of unilingual-
> ism in a bilingual country?" I do not wish to comment on

the manifest absurdity of the Cairine McKay [sic] Wilson sacrificing herself by making a speech in a language with which we are told she has been familiar since childhood, but I speak for some millions of Canadians when I say it is no disgrace to be unilingual in any Canadian province that has but one official language, the language spoken by the great mass of its people — the English language.[43]

The frantic pace continued almost without let-up. Saturday evening: dinner at the home of friends, the Fred Bronsons; Monday evening: dinner at 192 Daly with the Rev Mr W.H. Leatham, minister of St. Andrew's Presbyterian Church, and Mrs Leatham, Senator Robert Forke and Mrs. Forke, Senator Hewitt Bostock and Mrs. Bostock, and the O.D. Skeltons.[44] And so it went. It is no wonder that Norman Wilson informed Janet, on 28 February, that "Mother" had lost six pounds over the last few days and that he was planning to take her to an undisclosed location for a ten-day rest.

Besides fitting in a plethora of social engagements and Senate sittings, Mrs Wilson had to organize her Senate office, acknowledge about 400 congratulatory letters and 350 telegrams, supervise the running of her household and attend meetings of various organizations to which she belonged. She also had to grant interviews to assorted journalists, one of whom, Norma Phillips Muir, asked Cairine Wilson what she hoped would be achieved by the admission of women to the Senate. In reply the new senator said:

I think that there will be a keener and growing appreciation of women's problems grow out of the appointment of a woman to the Senate... and of the admission of women to the lower house too. I hope it will mean the taking of steps to definitely better conditions for women, and to finally and completely end our tolerance of a double standard of morals. To me it is a dreadful thing that women should not only bear the physical agony of child bearing as a result of sin or weakness, but should bear a stigma of shame all through life when the men, the partners in their degradation, [are] not only allowed to go 'scot free' but [are] socially accepted in the circles from which the women are outcasts.[45]

In addition to coping with all these responsibilties, Cairine Wilson also had to find time to look after a myriad of details concerning the Manor House. Since 1962 the official residence of the Papal Pro-nuncio, this graceful, French-styled chateau was occupied by the Wilson family in the late spring of 1930. At the time it gave every appearance of being a completely new residence, but in fact its roots went back to 1835 when Duncan MacNab began constructing a picturesque freestone cottage on a piece of land in what is now the village of Rockliffe Park. After his death, in 1837, his widow supervised the completion of "Rockcliffe House," so called for its location on a rocky escarpment overlooking a broad sweep of the Ottawa River. In 1868, Thomas Coltrin Keefer, the distinguished civil engineer, purchased the property for his mother-in-law, the widow of the Hon Thomas McKay (no relation to Cairine Mackay Wilson) when her house, "Rideau Hall," was sold to the Government as a residence for Canada's first governor general. Mr Keefer transformed Rockcliffe House into a Victorian gothic residence and then occupied it himself in 1888. However, to avoid confusion with the newly created Rockcliffe Park, the civil engineer renamed his new home the "Manor House." He died there in 1915, but his descendants remained in possession of the property until 1928, when they sold it to Cairine and Norman Wilson.[46] The sale completed, Cairine Wilson commissioned an acquaintance from the summer colony at St Andrews to draw up plans for renovating the residence: the well-known Boston architect, John W. Ames.

The Wilsons had expected to retain the basic fabric of the house. However, when structural problems were uncovered, they undertook a major rebuilding program, using for a major part of the financing the profits from a highly lucrative stock market transaction that Norman had made. By the time that they moved into their new home — on 29 May 1930 — only the original dining room, now the library, survived. In short, because its occupancy had to be delayed, the Manor House demanded a lot of Cairine Wilson's attention at a period in her life when events were threatening to overwhelm her. Never a person to shirk time-consuming detail, she became immersed in all the minutiae associated with a major renovation project. Typical is the letter that she wrote to Ames on 13 February 1930:

> The hardware man cannot give you the lger. knobs without long delay, because he has no castings of them and he is moreover strongly of the opinion that the smaller ones are more stylish. I have ordered these, with the key hole escutcheons and the wardrobe door knobs of the smaller size. The price for the knobs is $4. a pair: the key hole escutcheons are 50¢ apiece and the wardrobe knobs will be somewhat less than $2. apiece, but he does not know exactly how much. Now if you feel strongly that you want the 2" knobs, you had better telegraph me on

receipt of this, because, as I say, I have placed the order
& it should be countermanded within a day or two if not
satisfactory...[47]

March and April were equally frenzied months as a host of organizations rushed to fete her. Chief among these were various women's groups
such as the local Council of Women (Ottawa), and The Montreal Central
Women's Liberal Club. The Local Council of Women's reception, which
was staged in the Chateau Laurier's mammoth ballroom, elicited " one of
the most spontaneous tributes of admiration ever accorded a woman in
Ottawa." Practically every women's organization in the capital was represented at this function, which not only honoured Cairine Wilson, but also
celebrated the recognition of Canadian women as "persons" and their
eligibility for appointment to the Senate. On accepting a beautifully
illumininated scroll from Mrs Robert Forke, president of the Local
Council, a visibly moved Cairine Wilson said, "You could never expect
a Scottish woman to express all I feel. I know my great-grandchildren are
going to grow tired hearing about this day. You see I am expecting to live
a long time in the Senate."[48]

But impressive as this reception was, it was upstaged by the luncheon
held for Mrs Wilson on 11 April by Montreal's Liberal women. The
Ottawa Evening Journal of 13 April 1930 reached for superlatives when
describing this tribute:

> Such homage as probably never before had been paid
> a woman in Montreal marked the welcome to Senator
> Cairine Wilson on Saturday at the luncheon organized for
> her by the Montreal Central Women's Liberal Club.
> Many distinguished women have received full meed of
> acclaim here but the simple, dignified tribute conveyed
> when the vast audience that attended the function rose as
> salute (*sic*) and stood for a moment in silence after a
> ringing outburst of applause was almost unique.
>
> For a full minute, they remained standing, a company
> of 800, facing Canada's first woman Senator, who had
> risen to speak. That Senator Wilson was deeply moved by
> this spontaneous gesture was evident. She looked out
> over and around the room, then bent her head for a
> moment.

It was revealing of her humanitarian interests that Cairine Wilson
chose on this occasion, her first public address outside the Senate, to speak

on a government-sponsored bill dealing with veterans' allowances. Eschewing the opportunity to speak in platitudes, she launched immediately into an able and concise description of the provisions that the bill made for veterans' pensions and hospital care. In so doing, she demonstrated a clearer grasp of the issues covered by the bill than many members of the House of Commons who had spoken on it.

It was, indeed, a remarkable performance, a performance that boded well for the new role that Mrs Wilson had assumed. Her Senate seat might be "soft and seductive," but it was obvious that she was not going to treat it as such. Furthermore, to commemorate the day that she was appointed a senator and perhaps also to remind herself of the high hopes invested in her by the women of Canada, she would send a plant to Mackenzie King every February fifteenth for the rest of his life, choosing as her first such gift pots of flowering tulips and hyacinths.[49]

5

THE SENATOR AT WORK, 1930-1950

When Cairine Wilson was invested as a senator on 20 February 1930, she experienced the awe and excitement that other newly summoned senators have felt on crossing the threshold of the Red Chamber; feelings evoked not only by the moving pomp and circumstance of the induction ceremony itself but also by the physical setting in which the proceedings unfold. For the Senate chamber is a architectural jewel with its red carpeting and rich ornamentation. Everything combines to impress, from the intricately carved main oak doors to the soaring ornate ceiling and the wood-carved walls above which are large murals depicting Canada's role in World War I.

In addition to its imposing setting, the Senate boasts the ambience of an elite private club which goes out of its way to pamper its members. Staff members, from the Clerk of the Senate to the messengers and commissionaires, act as if it were a privilege and a pleasure to serve the members of this appointed upper house, which Agnes Macphail once described as "House of Refuge." The guards at the entrance to the Senate block know the names of all the senators, salute them when they pass, and open doors. And as they do now so did they when Cairine Wilson was a member of the Upper House. She, in fact, was a particular favourite of the ever-friendly Senate doormen who showed genuine admiration and respect for her.

In her time, as now, the Senate membership was composed overwhelmingly of older men, many of them lawyers, corporate directors and one-time federal cabinet ministers — the bulwarks of society that the Fathers of Confederation had in mind when they designed the Canadian senate to protect the country against radical or revolutionary legislation. They were the sort of men that Cairine Wilson would ordinarily have felt most comfortable with, but on becoming a senator she entered a clubby, male world where initially she felt lost and lonely. Not until Muriel McQueen Fergusson and Nancy Hodges, two prominent Liberals, arrived on the scene in 1953 would she strike up close friendships with female colleagues in the Red Chamber. Although fourteen years her junior, Mrs Fergusson, a Fredericton lawyer, would become Cairine Wilson's best woman friend among the small number of female senators appointed during her tenure.

Fortunately there was one colleague in the early days who was prepared to take her under his wing — the personable Lethbridge, Alberta publisher, William Buchanan. Billy, as he was known by friends, had been a neighbour of the Wilsons when they lived on Daly Avenue. He had also been a friend of Cairine Wilson's brother George, who had been one of Lethbridge's most public spirited and best loved citizens before his death in 1924. It was undoubtedly these connections plus Cairine Wilson's admiration for Buchanan's quiet effectiveness that brought the two together. The 54-year-old journalist became her earliest and best friend in the Senate. When paying tribute to him in January 1955, some six months after his death, she said, "I was always happiest when I could have his counsel and advice. Of his unselfishness and his devotion to duty, I can speak most highly, and I should like everyone here to know that he was a very fine man."[1]

Her colleagues' patronizing gallantry and Billy Buchanan's friendship aside, there must have been many a time early in her Senate career when Cairine Wilson felt that she was on the stage and that if she made a mistake or faux pas her fellow senators would say, "Oh, just like a woman!" She hinted at this dilemma when on 20 March 1930 she wrote to Mackenzie King, "Soon I fear that I shall lose my head entirely for to take an inoffensive woman from comparative obscurity and give her the full glare of publicity is somewhat overwhelming." Then, alluding to a banquet held the previous evening to launch the Twentieth Century Liberal Association, she continued, "I should like to thank you for your very kind words last evening and I appreciate your kindness in letting the public know that I did not clamour for the position. Your speech was a triumph and made me wish that I could join the 20th Century Club [sic] in place of the 'Home of the Immortals'."[2]

The reference to her Senate appointment relates to a passage in King's one and a quarter hour address in which he described his attempts to persuade Cairine Wilson to accept a summons to the Senate. According to

King, when the Governor General was just about to sign the order-in-council ratifying her appointment, Cairine Wilson exercised a woman's ancient prerogative and changed her mind about accepting the honour. As a result, the Prime Minister had to hurry back to Mrs Wilson's home and plead the cause again. This time he met with success and the appointment was ratified.[3]

Some six months after that King banquet speech, when she was still becoming acclimatized to her new role, Cairine Wilson again gave voice to her diffidence when she wrote somewhat coyly to the Prime Minister:

> You will observe from the enclosed letters in what a conspicuous position you have placed me. Probably better than anybody else you are aware of my limitations and I should be most grateful if you would let me know what you would prefer me to do. The invitations to speak continue to pour in, but the letter from Mr Phillips makes this request a little more difficult to refuse.[4]

National Archives of Canada C 13266

William Lyon Mackenzie King. Taken in 1936.

The invitations to speak certainly did pour in that year. They came in a torrent, for not only was she a big drawing card in her own right, there was the added complication of a July federal election in which she would zealously promote the Liberal cause in speech after speech at election rallies in Ontario, Quebec and New Brunswick. Probably at no other time in her political career would she spend so much time on the hustings as in the late spring and early summer of 1930.

The election that thrust her further into the public spotlight was called against a background of mounting unemployment and economic hardship, notably in the Prairie wheat belt. In the winter of 1929-30, when the Great Depression was really starting to make itself felt, Winnipeg mayor Ralph Webb led a delegation of western mayors to Ottawa to plead for federal assistance. There they were met by an unsympathetic prime minister who refused to accept their arguments for federal aid. He informed the mayors that unemployment assistance was first a municipal, then a provincial responsibility, and dismissed them with the advice to lobby their provincial governments for an unemployment insurance scheme.

King persisted in this stance whenever the unemployment question was raised in the House of Commons, arguing alternately that there was no unemployment problem and that unemployment was a provincial responsibility. His refusal to recognize the calamity was no more graphically illustrated than when, during a debate on the crisis, he told the House that he would not give one cent "for these alleged unemployment purposes." He was prepared to consult with respectful and needy Prairie farmers, but as for those provincial governments that diametrically opposed him, he "would not give them a five-cent piece."

Such a blunt, injudicious statement was quite out of character with the normally evasive prime minister, but he had already determined on a federal election. In preparation for this, his new finance minister, Charles Dunning, brought down a budget which introduced tariff increases on American steel, fruits and vegetables, abolished duties on tea and British china (porcelain, ironstone etc.) and reduced tariffs on other British goods. Although largely cosmetic, this increase in imperial preference provided welcome ammunition for Cairie Wilson who featured it in many a speech leading up to the election. And she gave countless addresses, particularly during the month of July when she made election swings through eastern Canada.

In Ontario, her speaking tour took her to Cobourg, Lindsay, Niagara Falls, St. Catharines, Toronto, and Newmarket, where she addressed a women's rally in a packed Palace Theatre and spoke on behalf of William Mulock, the Liberal candidate for York North. Back in her native province of Quebec she journeyed to the Eastern Townships to stump the hustings in aid of genial Frederic Kay, the MP for Brome-Missisquoi and husband of her cousin Athalie Baptist. Then it was on to New Brunswick, another province to which Cairine Wilson owed special allegiance, because it was here that she had her summer home Clibrig, a 430-acre estate that had been assembled by her father just outside the resort town of St Andrews.

Before going on the election trail the Senator made a June visit to Toronto to attend a reception given in her honour by the Toronto Women's Liberal Association and to address the inaugural banquet of that city's Twentieth Century Liberal Club at the Royal York Hotel. Some four hundred guests thronged the Liberal women's reception at Sherbourne House, including many prominent Conservatives and guests without any political affiliation whatsoever. However, it was not the number of her admirers who turned out that made this reception so memorable as far as Cairine Wilson was concerned; it was the bouquet presented to her midway through the afternoon by two members of the Toronto Caithness Society which had just made her an honorary member. A moving tribute, the bouquet consisted of sprigs of heather that had been gathered in her father's beloved Caithness and tied with a piece of Mackay tartan ribbon.

Fortunately she interrupted her frenetic schedule in Ontario's capital long enough for the *Mail and Empire* staff writer Jessie MacTaggart to catch up with her. The result was a revealing portrait of the new senator in action. Wrote MacTaggart:

> Hon. C.M. Wilson, as she is described officially, arrived in this city yesterday. And she lost no time in proving that a woman senator may be the busiest woman in the world.

> She is also one of the most gracious. Shortly after her arrival at the home of Mrs A. E. Kirpatrick, her hostess, at noon yesterday, although tired from her journey from Ottawa, and with a full program of engagements prepared for her, Senator Wilson found time to talk with charm and interest to the press.

> That is perhaps her most outstanding characteristic, an unusual combination of charm and shrewdness. Her appearance charms. Her voice charms and her conversation charms. But, in her eyes as she smiles, appears a keen appraisal of her hearer, and for all the lightness of her words, the thought they convey has been carefully chosen.

Has Instant Friendliness

It was a very feminine appearing senator who held out her hand yesterday afternoon and with a smile, asked, "You wished to see me?" Surprisingly easy it was to talk to her, for Senator Wilson has that rare gift of conveying instant friendliness. In a moment she was chatting comfortably with her visitor.

She is rather small and slight. Yesterday she wore a soft figured dress. The fact that the colour is forgotten is a tribute to her personality and probably the care with which it was chosen. Her hair is brown and wavy, and although it is short, she wears it brushed straight back from her forehead so that for a moment it seems to be long. Yesterday she wore earrings. One noticed them, for somehow they seemed to epitomize that complete femininity that is so out of keeping with one's idea of a woman senator. ...

Vivacious Talker

Senator Wilson talks vivaciously and smiles often. She moves her hands in a tiny flutter, and often raises them to tuck in a strand of hair. She does it quickly as though it were a mere gesture and quite unconscious...[5]

While the Senator was carrying the Liberal banner in Ontario, Quebec and New Brunswick, enthusiastic members of her brainchild, the Twentieth Century Liberal Association, were doing their best to help get Liberal candidates elected on 28 July. One of these was Odette Lapointe Ouimet, newly elected president of the women's branch of the Twentieth Century Liberal Association and a great admirer of King and his Liberal ideals. In the three months before the election she and nine other officers of the Association, including Cairine Wilson's daughter Olive, fanned out across the country, carrying the message to young Liberals and spearheading the organization of clubs in Canada's larger centres. As a result of their efforts a large volunteer army of young Liberals was recruited to help select candidates, conduct meetings, canvass on behalf of local candidates, and address gatherings of all sizes and descriptions.[6]

Valuable political experience was gained as a result of all this campaigning. But despite the young Liberals' and Cairine Wilson's best efforts the party went down to defeat. On election day the Conservatives under their dynamic new leader R.B. Bennett, the New Brunswick-born corporation lawyer, chalked up a stunning electoral victory: 137 seats for the Conservatives, 88 for the Liberals, 10 for the United Farmers, 2 for the Progressives and 8 for others.[7]

Whatever she may have felt about her party's ignominious defeat, Cairine Wilson did not let it interfere with her friendship with Mackenzie King. In a touching attempt to bolster his sagging spirits, she mailed a gift of Wedgwood plates to Laurier House and extended an invitation to visit Clibrig, where she and the family were then holidaying. Both were duly acknowledged in King's tiny, cramped handwriting in an effusive letter dated 18 August 1930:

Dear Mrs Wilson:

The Wedgwood plates are too beautiful for words. Really in receiving such a gift, I feel much more like a bride on the day of her wedding than as [sic] an ex-P.M. on the morrow of his defeat. I really feel that I am the one who should be mailing presents to you, for if ever a party was under obligation to one of its members, the Liberal party is certainly indebted to you for all that your appointment to the Senate has brought with it of honour and praise to the late administration. You are right in saying that Laurier House has its treasures, but among the most treasured of all will be the beautiful dishes you have sent me, with all that they express of your too kind thought, and far too generous appreciation of any little part I may have had in pleading with you to accept the appointment which has done us all so great honour. Please accept my heartfelt thanks for your lovely gift, which I still hope my grandchildren may even yet inherit! I know of course, that my chances in the way of legacies of the heart are by no means quite so certain as your own. ...

May I avail myself of this note to congratulate you once again for the splendid part you have taken in the party's work and story. We have much to look back upon with pride in the record of the past eight and a half years, but I am certain that history will reserve the beginning of a new chapter in the political history of Canada to your appointment to the Senate, and the truly amazing manner in which you have more than equalled its obligations on all occasions. Let me thank you for the renewed promise

James Layton Ralston, Minister of National Defence 1926-1930 and 1940-1944. Taken in 1936.

of your cooperation in our efforts as a party to press on to even higher and finer achievements both in and out of parliament. This is, I believe, the place of new beginning which the party needs, a place to form and extend a real organization that will be effective alike in propaganda and in the constituencies. Had we had what was needed in these particulars, we would, I believe, have still been in power, notwithstanding New Zealand butter and world depression in industry and trade. I look for great things from the Twentieth Century Liberal Association.

With renewed thanks for your very kind letter and invitation, and for your beautiful gift, and with kindest regards and the best of wishes to Norman, the young people, and yourself, believe me, as always,

Yours very sincerely,

Mackenzie King[8]

The Senator's gift to King was only one of many dispatched over the years to Laurier House. For, in addition to sending a plant on each anniversary of her Senate appointment, she always acknowledged his birthday on 17 December with a present and not infrequently sent him small gifts on other less memorable occasions. Invariably these presents were homey, domestic items — table mats and napkins woven by former pupils of the Mackay School for the Deaf in Montreal, a thermos bottle, a glass bowl, to cite but a few. Only in King's later years did Cairine Wilson alter the birthday routine. Then, instead of sending him a gift for Laurier House, she adopted the practice of mailing cheques to W. L. Mackenzie King III and his sister Catherine, the children of King's nephew Lyon, who was killed in action in 1943 while serving overseas as a ship's surgeon.[9]

Despite Cairine Wilson's unfailing generosity to the party and many acts of thoughtfulness to King, however, the insecure bachelor did not hesitate to snipe at her. He did this in his diary, where with unfailing regularity he heaped praise on individuals one minute and criticism on them the next. One of the more petulant entries involving the Senator was composed on 31 October 1930 when, in one of his periodic attacks against the opulence of the wealthy, King wrote:

At 4 o'clock I went to Senator Carine [sic] Wilson's to tea with Mrs Tweed ? and Miss Belcourt & Hayden.

> Saw over the Wilson home which is one of the most
> beautiful I have ever seen & has a magnificent position.
> It is really lovely within & without. I was disgusted,
> however, in the midst of all this wealth which has been
> made so largely out of the country and the Party to find the
> meeting was to see whether $5,000 could be raised to
> carry on the work of Liberal women. Mrs Wilson ought
> to turn over her sessional indemnity to the Party.[10]

Just why King should attribute a sizeable portion of the family fortune to the Liberal Party is a mystery because all the evidence indicates that it was the reverse that was true: i.e., that it was the Liberal Party that benefited handsomely from the Mackay-Wilson connection. Cairine Wilson, as did her father before her, gave generously to the party. But, in addition to this, she also helped to finance the activities of party-related organizations such as the Twentieth Century Liberal Association and the National Federation of Liberal Women of Canada. Where King personally was concerned, she contributed to a "secretarial fund" established by his good friend Senator Arthur Hardy to offset expenses run up by the party chief as Leader of the Opposition. Indeed, King even confided to his diary on 15 December 1934 that he was "greatly embarrassed in feeling" when he discovered Cairine Wilson's name among a list of subscribers to the fund. There was, in other words, no justification for the Chief's suggestion that the Senator's family owed some of its money to the Liberal Party and that Cairine Wilson herself should donate her sessional indemnity to the party.

The criticism contained in the October 1930 diary entry was mild, however, compared to the broadside that King fired at the unsuspecting Cairine Wilson on Armistice Day that year. In November 1930, he was just a month away from his fifty-seventh birthday and a tired man who could be querulous, suspicious and quick to take offence at imagined slights. He was also an ex-prime minister without the trappings of that office.

> Tonight I waited for Mrs & Norman Wilson to call for
> me to take me to prlt. Hill for the Armistice ceremonies.
> It was their own suggestion (Mrs Wilson's). They never
> came & I was obliged to get on a street-car with the wreath
> I bought this afternoon in addition to the one for Laurier
> House & at the City Hall hailed a man in a car whose name
> I have forgotten. He drove me to the hill, just in time for
> me to place my wreath with the others. I was too late to get
> a rightful place on the platform & did not put the wreath
> on in the right order. When I was coming away I met Mrs

> Wilson who said she was relieved to see me come, as they had not called, they had no word. She was not sure whether the fault was her maid or the secretary's in my office. I phoned Henry later who said he delivered the message to the Wilson's [sic] butler himself this morning — The Wilsons might have phoned to ask if I had received their message — it was the worst neglect I have met with yet, & this the woman I appointed as Senator. She said they were going to the Hockey Match — I felt too incensed for words but said nothing. I however had Henry write.[11]

The wonder, of course, is not that the brooding King was enraged at this perceived slight as that Cairine Wilson found the time to fit in a hockey game that frantic autumn. It seems that she was in perpetual motion after her return from St Andrews, travelling from one speaking engagement to another when not spending time in the Senate or attending meetings of the numerous organizations with which she was closely identified. The list of organizations that she addressed in these months ran the gamut from women teachers' associations and Canadian clubs to doctors' wives' associations and assorted Liberal Clubs. In a sense it foreshadowed what lay ahead of her in the realm of public speaking, for in the years to come she would be in constant demand as a speaker.

Not all of her audiences were adult ones. Sometimes she was called upon to speak to youngsters, as was the case when she addressed a crowded auditorium at the Ottawa Ladies' College shortly after her appointment. Lillian Gertsman, who was then about twelve years of age, was one of the students who heard her that day and to say that she was impressed is an understatement. "I remember that she wore a large picture hat and looked lovely. I was enthralled. She was my ideal," Mrs. Gertsman has recalled.[12]

The progress made by women in the last hundred years, women's influence and women trailblazers, such as Florence Nightingale, were favourite topics, especially in the nineteen thirties when the Senator repeatedly urged members of her sex to inform themselves about the issues of the day and to exercise the ballot. Probably no passage encapsulates her views on this responsibility better than the following, taken from a 1932 issue of the *Canadian Bar Review*. Quoting Franklin Delano Roosevelt, then Governor of New York, Cairine Wilson wrote:

> If every intelligent woman made it a rule to learn something about her local, state or national government every day, more would be accomplished in a year toward governmental reform than by all the books and pamphlets written in a generation.[13]

The Senator believed fervently that much could be accomplished by informed women taking an active role in their communities' affairs. She looked to them to lead the drive for badly needed social legislation, noting that in Ontario it was the women's lobby which finally succeeded, after years of agitation, in having the Mothers' Allowances and the Old Age Pensions' Acts passed. "Woman," she observed in a 1932 address, is by nature a reformer, but the same knowledge which enables her to feed and clothe her family with a due regard for the budget will prevent her from embarking on too sudden improvement schemes."[14]

Even more important in Cairine Wilson's view, though, was the part that women could play in shaping the minds of future generations. Speaking to the annual convention of Zonta International, a professional and business women's service organization, on 21 June 1941, for instance, she observed, "The mother and the teacher mould the characters of the boys and girls during the impressionable years, and if we can inoculate a love of justice, a devotion to ideals, and the wish to serve, we shall have gone a long way to assuring the future of our countries."[15]

She had sounded the same note the year previously when, speaking to the annual meeting of the Women's Teachers Federation at Windsor, Ontario, she had remarked:

> I was much impressed by the opinion of one of our Senators, who said that he would bend every effort in order to ensure the best possible education for his daughters, and would send them to university, for such training would be much more necessary for the mothers than the fathers of the next generation. For my own part, I am not likely to forget some of the principles inculcated in my early youth.[16]

When Cairine Wilson made this observation, in 1940, Canada was at war and the Senator was not so concerned with women's issues as she was with two recently developed preoccupations: refugees and planning for a new world order after the cessation of hostilities. Both themes, but especially refugees and Canada's highly restrictive immigration policy, would figure prominently in her wartime addresses.

A newspaper reporter who heard the Senator speak in the autumn of 1930 was delighted to discover that Cairine Wilson chose her words "delightfully" and spoke without any "trace of that imitation of an English accent that is such a trying addition to the conversation, both in public and private of so many." The journalist then hastened to add that she had nothing against "an educated English accent — it is charming when it comes from someone who has absorbed it on its native heath. But the imitation on Canadian soil is often very painful and we hope the example of the woman senator may be taken to heart by the imitators."[17]

Although the Senator's delivery charmed this particular listener, there is no gainsaying the fact that Cairine Wilson was far from being an impressive speaker in the early years of her Senate career. Even her good friend, Ottawa businesswoman Isabel Percival, has conceded that Cairine Wilson in this period "was one of the worst public speakers" that she had ever heard. Especially distracting to Mrs Percival was her friend's nervous habit of constantly playing with her hands and her gloves. However such was Cairine Wilson's determination to turn in a polished performance that she overcame her handicaps and eventually became an excellent speaker.

The Senator's speeches may not have been distinguished by eloquence, but they were usually well constructed with appropriate vignettes and not infrequently biblical allusions. Sometimes they contained flashes of wit. Never were they pedantic or pompous and only rarely did they excite controversy or fire the imagination.

One noticeable exception was an address that she gave to the New Glasgow Women's Liberal Association during the heat of a provincial election campaign in Nova Scotia. In response to an invitation extended by the women's group, the Senator had journeyed to New Glasgow on 2 August 1933 prepared to give a speech that carefully skirted issues being hotly debated in the local campaign. Beyond expressing the hope that local Liberal candidates would be returned in the forthcoming election, she adhered to her theme, "Women in Politics" and delivered, in the words of her hostess and prominent Liberal organizer, Carrie Carmichael, a "very moderate" address, "her attractive presence & personality carrying possibly the most weight."[18] Shortly thereafter the *Evening News* gave a favourable report on the speech. However this was followed by a "contrary and rather nasty" piece which appeared in a subsequent issue and then, on 11 August, by a venomous letter to the editor that dragged Cairine Wilson's name and that of her father through the political mud. It was penned by a highly partisan Senate colleague of Cairine Wilson, Rufus Henry Pope, onetime president of the Eastern Townships Conservative Association and a farmer and cattle breeder who lived in Cookshire. Writing from that bucolic corner of Quebec, the aging senator reported:

> Dear Editor,
>
> As you know I read your paper with a lot of interest. I like to know about Nova Scotia. I see that you were to have a visit from Senator Cairine Wilson of Ottawa. She went down to tell you folks how to vote. You may not know that she is one of the dwellers in the 'Valley of Humiliation' into which Mackenzie King said the Liberal party was flung for filching about $800,000 out of the

big Beauharnois steal; that was plunder for the 1930 elections. You may not know that Senator Wilson did not see anything wrong about that steal; in fact she stood up in the Senate with the other Liberals, whitewash brush in her hand, to whiten up the sepulchre of disgrace; and she voted to put the whitewash on good and thick so that the public would never know that a gang of her Liberal friends had plundered Beauharnois, lifting the huge sum that I have mentioned for election campaign purposes. Then with Mr King she marched into the 'Valley of Humiliation.'

... She is coming out of the Valley now, and going down to Nova Scotia to give you people lessons in political purity and morality. I suppose she thinks she is purged; and that she is graduated from the Valley, and qualified to stand up as a bright and shining light, and a teacher without guile.

... In one sense I am glad that Senator Wilson is going to help you. She will help your government when people know her and hear her; and remember Beauharnois and the Valley of Humiliation.

I knew her father; and I will tell you a funny story about him. He was Senator MacKay.[sic] He was very rich; so is his daughter. He was Grit of the Grits, and used to give his friends substantial contributions for election purposes. I know that because he told me. He often came out our way on business; and on one occasion after a election in which I was elected for Compton county I happened to meet him. He looked me over, and said; so you were elected; and I said to him I believe I was. That's queer, he said, the Grits out here must be a queer lot. They told me they would beat you. I gave them the money; and here you are elected. I guess I am, I said, and I thank you; you did good work for me, Mr MacKay.

The father helped me; and the daughter will help the Harrington Government. You could not want more. Good luck to you.[19]

Carrie Carmichael was so enraged by the Pope letter that she in turn fired off a missive to Mackenzie King outlining the circumstances of Cairine Wilson's visit to New Glasgow and enclosing a copy of the Pope letter. In his reply the Liberal chief observed, "I do not believe that we have in the public life of the Dominion a more disgusting type of politican than Senator Pope."[20]

Disgusting or not, Pope was certainly unscrupulous in his particular choice of political tactics and in his attempts to make political capital out of the dramatic Beauharnois inquiry, which had enlivened the sessions of 1931. Responding to charges that the recent Liberal government had accepted substantial election campaign contributions from the Beauharnois Light, Heat and Power Company in return for a hydroelectric development permit, the Conservative government had appointed a special Commons committee to investigate the tortuous saga of the so-called Beauharnois project. Their final report, which was adopted by the House on 31 July 1931, implicated three Liberal senators, who were subsequently censured by a special Senate committee appointed to deal with their conduct and actions. A motion by Senator Tanner, the committee's chairman, for concurrence in his committee's report, was debated for several days in the Senate in the spring of 1932. Finally, on 3 May, a vote was taken on the motion and it was passed 34 to 27. The division that Pope alluded to in his letter, was strictly along party lines, Conservative senators voting for and Liberal senators against concurrence in the report. Cairine Wilson, however, was not one of the senators who voted. She and Norman were travelling in Europe, where they had gone to tour Italy with Janet and young Cairine, then attending school in Switzerland. According to the *Senate Debates* it was another Wilson — Senator Joseph M. Wilson (Sorel) — who voted with his Liberal colleagues against accepting the damning report.[21] Senator Pope, in other words, had no grounds for accusing Cairine Wilson of standing up in the Senate "with the other Liberals, whitewash brush in her hand, to whiten up the sepulchre of disgrace."

Away from the hustings, in the Senate itself, Cairine Wilson established herself as a hardworking member noted for her intelligence, her charm and her humanitarianism. Her deep compassion, in fact, earned her a reputation for never turning people away from her office door, be they Canadians down on their luck in the Great Depression or families seeking her help in getting relatives admitted to Canada from Nazi-occupied Europe. Mrs A. H. Askanasy, an Austrian refugee whom she befriended in 1939, expressed it well when she wrote in 1960, "That open door at the Senate building through which any person could come to her office was and is a symbol of her great and open soul, altruistic and generous..."[22] Violet McAlonan Herrington, who was her private secretary in 1947-48, summed up her employer's deep humanitarianism even more succinctly, if less eloquently, "Cairine Wilson never, never turned anybody away from her office."[23]

Not infrequently the Senator wrote to Mackenzie King on behalf of various supplicants seeking employment. In the case of Mrs Henry Cloran, the widow of a Quebec Liberal senator, for example, she reported on 10 March 1936:

> This afternoon we are leaving very unexpectedly on a hurried trip to Europe and I fear that it will be impossible for you to see me before train-time.

> I have, as you know, been very much worried over Mrs Cloran's position, and am particularly sorry to go away without being able to give her any possible assurance for the future. I know that her resources are at the vanishing point and have myself given assistance several times.

> Through all her difficulties I have acquired a great respect for Mrs Cloran and know that she has kept up her spirits remarkably well and that it would be possible for her to give satisfaction in some post.[24]

Helping people was second nature to Cairine Wilson who expressed in deeds what she could not in words and who shared Eleanor Roosevelt's conviction that all useful political activity derived from an interest in human beings and social conditions. For the Senator Liberalism was not so much an ideology as a way of life characterized by earnestness, practical idealism and a deep humanitarianism; it was a quasi-religion that merged with her Presbytrianism to produce a workaholic who strove tirelessly to promote the interests of women and children and to improve the lot of the less fortunate.

In Senate debates the Senator consistently adopted a left of centre position on social issues of the day, thereby placing herself firmly in the progressive ranks of her party. When it came to domestic questions or "soft issues," as they are sometimes called by academics, she demonstrated a particular interest in divorce, health insurance, preventive medicine, infant and maternal mortality, women's working conditions, and education.

By far the most contentious of these was divorce, which was extremely uncommon in Canada until after World War II. In fact, this country had one of the lowest divorce rates in the Western World until the postwar years, adultery being virtually the only recognized ground for divorce during most of Canada's first century. To complicate matters still further for Canadians seeking a divorce, Nova Scotia, New Brunswick and British Columbia were the only provinces that could grant divorces before World War I, although Ontario, Alberta and Saskatchewan acquired this right in the inter-war period. In provinces where there was no access to judicial divorce, parties wishing to obtain one had to appeal to the Canadian parliament for a statutory divorce, an expensive undertaking that limited relief to the well heeled. As alternatives, divorce seekers might have recourse to desertion, legal separation or divorce in an American jurisdiction which, despite having no legal force in Canada, seemed to satisfy public opinion.[25]

Shortly after her appointment to the Senate Cairine Wilson found herself confronted by this explosive issue when the Senate was called upon to debate a bill that would transfer jurisdiction for divorce from Parliament to the province of Ontario. The bill received first reading on 13 May 1930 and two days later third reading after a motion to give it a six months' hoist was defeated 40 to 16. The Senator did not speak to the bill, but she voted for it, eliciting loud applause as she did so. Later she told an interviewer, "Formerly we were distributed reams of material that every member was supposed to read before a divorce was voted upon. It didn't seem to me fair that so many people should have their troubles aired to that extent. And some of them didn't make such excellent reading."[26]

After the final passage of the bill and the transfer of divorce jurisdiction to Ontario residents of that province no longer had to petition Parliament for the passage of a private bill to dissolve their marriage. Instead, they could bring an action in the Supreme Court of Ontario to bring about the same end.

When a measure designed to widen the grounds for divorce in Canada made its debut in the Senate in 1938, the Senator spoke out in favour of more progressive divorce legislation, citing cases of desertion with which she was personally acquainted to bolster her argument that desertion should be one of the new grounds for divorce. Modelled on a recent act of the Parliament of the United Kingdom, the Senate bill provided for three new grounds for divorce in addition to the existing one of adultery: desertion without cause for a period of three years, cruelty, and incurable insanity, which was defined as being under either voluntary or compulsory treatment for a continuous period of five years. Four reasons for decrees of annulment were also outlined in the bill.

As might be expected, Cairine Wilson's support of the bill attracted a lot of attention and with it a flood of letters and callers either condemning or praising her for the position that she had taken.[27] However, the hopes of those who favoured more liberal divorce legislation were soon to be rudely dashed. For although the amended bill had a triumphant passage through the Upper House — and this despite the vigorous opposition of Roman Catholic senators — it met with a resounding defeat in the House of Commons, where debate on it lasted less than half an hour. Not until 1968, six years after Cairine Wilson's death, would Parliament finally enact liberalized divorce legislation.

Although she did not speak to it, Cairine Wilson took a great interest in a bill introduced on 22 February 1935 by Prime Minister Bennett to limit the hours of labour in "industrial undertakings to eight in the day and forty-eight in the week." As was her wont, the Senator studied the bill with the special interests of women in mind and what she found did not altogether please her. The bill's failure to make the eight-hour day mandatory for student nurses was a particular source of concern. As a member of the Victorian Order of Nurses' board, Cairine Wilson was keenly aware of the staggering workloads of student nurses, who provided most of the nursing in acute care hospitals in the nineteen thirties. The hospitals' exploitation of these young women so distressed the Senator that she singled out their plight for special mention in a letter that furnishes a snapshot of a typical day in her life in these years. Writing on 16 April 1935 to Olive and young Cairine, who were then visiting Havana, Cuba, she reported:

> To-day I have embarked upon many undertakings. Just now I am hurrying to the MacMahons for a facial and must attend a Committee meeting from eleven until one. At 2:30 there is a Meeting of the Public Buildings and Grounds Committee, of which I am chairman, and the Senate will sit at three. There is a tea meeting at Bell Street United Church at six, and in a weak moment I agreed to be the speaker on the subject of "World Friendship." The audience will consist of mothers and daughters of the C.G.I.T. group, and I only hope I shall be able to talk intelligently, for at the moment have nothing prepared. I had planned also to comment upon the injustice of legislation which calls for an eight-hour day for certain classes of workers, and which compels nurses to work twelve and study afterwards.[28]

In March 1943, Cairine Wilson rose in the Senate to outline her views on three issues very close to her heart: women's concerns, education and preventive medicine. The occasion was a debate that arose out of the motion of Senator J.H. King, the Government leader in the Senate, to set up a committee to study Canada's postwar requirements (The Committee on Economic Re-establishment and Social Security).

In those early days of 1943, when an Allied victory seemed inevitable, the air was rife with heated debate about what form post-war reconstruction should take. The Canadian government, in fact, had begun studying the question as early as December 1939 when, at the instigation of Cairine Wilson's good friend, Ian Mackenzie, then Minister of Pensions and National Health, it set up a cabinet committee to begin planning for the demobilization and reintegration of Canadian servicemen into Canadian society. When it became apparent that the problems of demobilization could not be studied in isolation, Mackenzie succeeded in having the committee's terms of reference widened to include all phases of reconstruction. To carry out the broadened mandate, he invited distinguished academics, civil servants and agriculture and labour representatives to explore with him ways of planning for post-war Canada in all its many aspects. Thus emerged the pioneering Advisory Committee on Reconstruction whose research team was headed by Dr Leonard March, a noted economist and democratic socialist who had been one of the founding members of the Co-operative Commonwealth Federation. On 16 March 1943, he released what would be the crowning achievement of his social policy career: a blueprint for the Canadian welfare state that proposed, among other things, a comprehensive social security scheme, emphasizing contributory health insurance and a universal program of family allowances and health care ("Report on Social Security for Canada")[29].

When she participated in the Senate debate on post-war Canada, eleven days before the publication of the Marsh Report, Cairine Wilson seized the opportunity to plead for greater recognition of women's issues, remarking, "I have had many communications from women who are concerned that so little attention has been given to their particular problems."[30] She then plumped for increased funding for nursing services and equal educational opportunities for all Canadian children, be they the offspring of rich or poor parents, male or female.

The Senator also made a pitch for a universal program of family allowances, then a hotly debated topic. In doing so, she clashed with Mackenzie King, who was horrified by the costs and the threat to individualism that such a program represented. Equally significant, she opposed the position taken by another leading feminist of her day, prominent Ottawa social worker Charlotte Whitton, who had been waging a determined campaign against a scheme that would pay every Canadian mother an allowance to help offset the cost of child care. Whitton believed that a flexible program of public assistance administered by the provinces and the municipalities sufficed. Universal programs, she contended, threatened massive intervention in family life and should be avoided at all costs.

Cairine Wilson could not accept these views of the outspoken critic and Conservative. As far as the Senator was concerned, family allowances were purely a question of social justice, a means of assuring a basic family income no matter what the earnings or fortunes of the breadwinner. It was her observation that the children of large families were often deprived of necessities and educational advantages. A universal system of family allowances could not help but assist these youngsters, regardless of whether they lived in rural or urban Canada.[31] Her thinking on this subject was much more akin to that of the noted British parliamentarian Eleanor Rathbone, who persistently advocated the adoption of a family allowances' scheme until it became a reality in Britain in 1945. Cairine Wilson had heard the MP speak on this topic during a visit to Westminster in 1934 and had obviously been impressed by her arguments.

Not until the fall of 1943 did the Prime Minister become a reluctant convert to a family allowances program and then only after he had been persuaded that voters in the next election would cast their ballot for the party that they thought would provide maximum employment and a measure of social security. Once convinced of this and of the arguments of his secretary Jack Pickersgill that such benefits do not sap initiative, King zealously pressed the case for family allowances. As a result, the Family Allowances Bill was passed in the summer of 1944 and implemented on Dominion Day 1945. Thanks to this new measure all Canadian mothers, regardless of means, would receive payments on behalf of their children under the age of sixteen.

Before this second major breakthrough was made in the evolving welfare state, Cairine Wilson once again spoke out on the importance of education. She also seized the opportunity presented by the February 1944 debate on the Address in Reply to the Speech to the Throne to champion the adoption of a national health insurance scheme, something that the Liberal government had forecast in its Throne Speech the previous month.

With the speech's reference to a national health insurance scheme or its equivalent very much in mind, the Senator observed on 3 February:

> As no previous speaker in this debate has touched at any length upon health insurance, I should like to deal with some features of this subject. I think that to-day the opinion is very generally held that the national health insurance plan is useful legislation.

> ...We are all aware that Canada is very sparsely populated, with only three and one-third persons per square mile, which is almost the lowest average in the

world. And despite our vast natural resources and empty
spaces, we have become a nation of older people. It would
seem that this defect cannot be cured by immigration,
because the House of Commons Advisory Committee on
health insurance has stated that we can look for no great
influx of healthy youth after the war. These facts make it
all the more important that we should conserve the health
of the people we have. But the very sparseness of our
population increases the difficulty of carrying on such
activities as group medical and health insurance.[32]

Cairine Wilson deplored the rise in mental illness and the lack of
facilities and trained personnel to treat the mentally ill. She drew attention
to the grave problem presented by venereal disease and then focussed on
a perennial concern of hers: maternal mortality. She even touched on the
diseases of middle age, noting "Unfortunately, the diseases of middle age
are on the increase. This may be due in some measure to the greater
longevity of our people, although in this respect I am afraid the Senate has
not such a high record as it once had."[33]

What makes the Senator's lengthy speech so noteworthy, though, is
not so much the stress that it places on the need for a universal health
insurance program as its emphasis on the need for more preventive
medicine. Time and again it returns to this theme because the Senator set
great store by routine medical check-ups, early diagnosis and a healthy
lifestyle. Indeed, her slim figure and youthful appearance in middle age
were testimony to her belief in hard work, "exercise and not eating too
much."

The Senator did not focus exclusively on education and health
questions in her address, however. Before concluding she also urged that
more assistance be given to parents in raising their children.

...I should like to see something done for parents of
young children. It is exceedingly difficult for them to be
welcome anywhere. Although we are asked to become
sentimental over the role of mother, motherhood is not yet
recognized as an essential occupation, nor do we in our
communities give the parents as much assistance as we
might in appreciation of their services to Canada in
bringing up children who, we hope, will be a credit to their
country.[34]

In the Senate Cairine Wilson consistently demonstrated her humanitarianism by advocating the adoption of advanced social legislation. She

also showed that she was a woman of strong convictions who did not hesitate to go against the prevailing tide of opinion when circumstances and her sense of justice dictated that she do so. Such an occasion arose in 1944 with plans to exempt Japanese Canadian soldiers from the provisions of the Soldiers' Vote Bill which provided for the setting up of machinery to enable Canadian servicemen overseas to vote in the approaching general election. No sooner had the controversial bill passed the Commons then it was discovered that one of its clauses disenfranchised "any person whose racial origin [was] that of a country at war with Canada." Since this clause would effectively disenfranchise significant numbers of German and Italian Canadians, the bill began to excite considerable opposition. Claiming that the contentious clause was racist, Senators J.J. Bench and Norman Lambert of Ontario tried to have it removed. They only succeeded, however, in changing the wording so that it applied to Japanese Canadians alone.[35] Taking strong exception to this, Cairine Wilson rose in the Chamber on 28 June and, after referring to the number of representations that she had received protesting the measure, declared, "If we support such a clause as the one to which objection is taken, I do not think we can claim to be opponents of racial discrimination and upholders of democracy."[36]

Unfortunately the bill was returned to the Commons in its amended form. There, the offending clause was further altered amid heated debate to leave disenfranchised those Japanese Canadians who had previously been without the franchise by virtue of their having resided in British Columbia since 1940. Thus was written another chapter in the history of institutionalized racism against this visible minority.

Japanese had attracted hostility almost from the time that they began arriving in British Columbia, a decade after Confederation. Only if they were employed in the mines, the forests and the fishing industry — and if they were not too successful — were they accepted. They were prevented by law from holding certain jobs and were denied the right to vote. Although Japanese Canadians fought with distinction in World War I and voted overseas in the federal election of 1917, they were still denied the franchise after their return to Canada. In the federal election of 1935, the Liberal Party even went so far as to advertise proudly, "A vote for the Liberal candidate in your riding is a vote against the Oriental enfranchisement."[37]

Such was the climate that prevailed when news of the Japanese bombing of Pearl Harbour broke on 7 December 1941. Within hours of that attack Japanese aliens were ordered to register with the RCMP and have their fishing vessels impounded. The coup de grace was delivered in February 1942. Acting on the shabby pretext that they had to be protected from their hostile neighbours, the federal government ordered the expulsion of some 22,000 Japanese Canadians from a 100-mile swath of the Pacific coast. That order signalled the beginning of a process that saw Canada's Japanese minority uprooted from their homes, stripped of their property and dispersed across Canada. By far the largest number, some 12,000, were relocated in British Columbia's interior, often in detention camps in sparsely inhabited areas and isolated ghost towns. The remaining Japanese Canadians were moved to farms in Alberta and Manitoba, to self-supporting projects in British Columbia and to road work and industrial employment in eastern Canada. Paradoxically the relentless campaign to relocate them was led by Cairine Wilson's good friend, Ian Mackenzie, British Columbia's representative in the federal cabinet. The personable bachelor, who frequented dinners at the Manor House, might be a liberal in economics and a champion of veterans' rights and family allowances, but he was also an outright racist, who repeatedly championed anti-Asian proposals throughout his long political career.

Besides speaking out in the Senate against the disenfranchisement of Japanese Canadians, Cairine Wilson lent her support to a pro-Japanese Canadian lobby known as the Co-operative Committee on Japanese Canadians. Other influential supporters included T.C. Douglas, then Premier of Saskatchewan, the Moderator of the United Church, The Reverend J.H. Arnup, and Liberal senator Arthur W. Roebuck.

When the Committee and the Civil Liberties Association of Toronto sponsored a mass rally in Toronto on 10 January 1946 to protest the federal government's intention to deport thousands of Japanese Canadians to Japan, Cairine Wilson was one of the principal speakers. Before a packed house at Jarvis Collegiate Institute, she joined Senator Arthur Roebuck, Rabbi Abraham Feinberg and fellow Candian National Committee on Refugees' executive member B.K. Sandwell, the illustrious editor of *Saturday Night*, in attacking the unprecedented banishment of Canadian citizens for "no crime or reason." In what must have been one of the strongest speeches that she ever gave, the Senator deplored the hyprocrisy and smugness of Canadians who are critical of the intolerance shown towards minorities in Europe but who are themselves intolerant of a minority in their own midst, the Japanese Canadians. Then, after noting that the British North America Act provided for the protection of minorities, she continued:

> I would not like to think that after Canada's endorsation of the Atlantic Charter and signing of the United Nations Charter that we are about to violate those pledges. I wonder what the representatives of the United Nations gathering in London will think of us if we carry out this deportation of Canadian-Japanese.[38]

Cairine Wilson predicted that if Japanese Canadians were shipped to Japan they would become very bitter towards Canada. She also pointed out that deportation would involve serious cases of hardship. "We hear much about the displaced persons in Europe. Why should Canada add to the problems of the world," she asked rhetorically.[39] She might also have asked why one minute she should be lobbying vigorously for the Government to admit European refugees and the next minute pleading with it not to make refugees of Japanese Canadians by expelling them from their own country. The irony of the situation could not have failed to make a deep impression on her.

Cairine Wilson's courage in attacking Mackenzie King's government for its actions against the Japanese Canadians created a lasting impression on courtly Senator Roebuck. For, when paying tribute to his colleague after her death, he referred to that emotional meeting and Cairine Wilson's participation in it. He then observed, "I was filled with admiration and I have always remembered with a certain degree of gratitude to Cairine Wilson, that she had the courage to espouse the cause of the underdog, of the oppressed, of the downtrodden, without any possibility of benefit to herself."[40]

At the insistence of the Co-operative Committee on Japanese Canadians, the Department of Justice referred a deportation test case to the Supreme Court of Canada. The Court heard the case that January and on 20 February 1946 handed down a decision vindicating the Government's stand. However, because it was divided on at least two major points, it did not provide Mackenzie King's government with the unanimous judgment that it sought. This lack of a sweeping decision, combined with the strength of the protest movement, persuaded the Prime Minister to refer the case to the Judicial Committee of the Imperial Privy Council in London for a ruling. After considering only the legal points, it handed down a decision on 2 December 1946 proclaiming the deportation orders valid in all respects.

This was not enough, however, to persuade Cairine Wilson to abandon her campaign to have the deportation orders rescinded. On 30 December 1946, during the Christmas holidays, she wrote to her friend Mackenzie King enclosing a copy of a letter dispatched to the *Montreal Star* by a leading Anglican clergyman who was highly critical of the deportation orders and the Privy Council ruling. In typical fashion, the Senator paved the way gently and referred to personal experience to bolster her case.

You have I know during the past two weeks been endeavouring to cope not only with correspondence of an official nature, but with thousands of messages of personal congratulation and it is possible that for this reason some of the letters to the press may very easily have been overlooked.

> I am particularly impressed by the letter of Canon Davision, which appeared in the *Montreal Star* and of which I now enclose a copy. As you know, I have been very generally concerned, not only about the position in which our Canadian Japanese find themselves, but also about the far-reaching effect deportation may have on Canadian relations with peoples of the Orient. For six months I have had a young Canadian Japanese couple in my own home, and we all, that is, my family and household staff, parted with them with great respect.[41]

The following month, the Senator received the welcome news that the deportation orders had been finally repealed. But this was not before some 3,964 Japanese Canadians had been deported.[42]

Cairine Wilson attended Senate sessions faithfully in these decades and would continue to do so until her death. Dipping into his memories of the years that he served as a Senate page, Richard Greene recalls that the Senator made a practice of arriving early for the afternoon sessions and talking to the young pages about their schoolwork. "A very motherly figure," is how the Assistant Clerk of the Senate remembers her.[43]

Harold King, who became a Senate page in 1940 and went on to become Senate Postmaster, has fond memories of the Senator that span the middle and final years of her Senate career. From his days as a young page, he recalls that Cairine Wilson was always in her seat for Senate sittings unless prevented by illness or travel from being present. And when her friend Senator Dandurand was on the scene, the two senators always left the Senate chamber arm in arm. Later, after going to work for the Senate post office, King used to see the Senator when she came to attend to her mail.

> Unlike most other senators, Cairine Wilson didn't send her secretary to get her mail, but came herself to collect it. At the counter, she would speak to you as if you were one of the family and when she ordered stamps she would always use a roller to moisten them. If one wasn't available, she would instruct you to shove the stamps face-down across the counter. She liked prompt service and always insisted that everything be done properly. But she was always very nice and courteous about it. As a person I admired her.[44]

Above the post office, in the Senate Chamber, Cairine Wilson might speak at length on issues in which she was keenly interested, using notes that had been typed for her by her private secretary. The Senator's most valuable contributions, however, were made not in debates in the imposing, red carpeted Senate Chamber, but in work done quietly behind the scenes, providing assistance to a wide variety of people and in serving as a highly respected member of many Senate committees.

Senator Cairine Wilson in conversation with her friend Mackenzie King. In the background is the Senate entrance.

In Cairine Wilson's day the Senate sat in the Chamber three days a week: Tuesday evening, Wednesday afternoon and Thursday afternoon. The Senator, however, probably spent more than twice as much time in committees that convened on the same days. As a conscientious senator who took her duties seriously, Cairine Wilson found the role that she played in committees, especially the more significant and prestigious ones, far more absorbing and challenging than her attendance at or participation in Senate debates. For committees are where the real work of this much maligned legislative body is done. In the words of Cairine Wilson's colleague and friend, Muriel McQ. Fergusson, they are "the heart and soul of the Senate"[45] because it is in committee that senators study and often rework ill-considered and badly drafted bills that come from the Commons. It is here also that they frequently call witnesses, receive briefs, amass great bodies of research and prepare reports, some of which become landmarks in Canada's political evolution. Cairine Wilson herself would have a hand in drawing up some of these reports, notably the influential report on immigration prepared by the Senate Committee on Immigration and Labour after World War II.

Cairine Wilson belonged to thirteen committees over the years: Joint Committee of the Library; Public Buildings and Grounds; Public Health and Inspection of Foods; Banking and Commerce; Civil Service and Administration; Standing Orders; Immigration and Labour; Internal Economy and Contingent Accounts; Finance; External Relations; Capital and Corporal Punishment and Lotteries; Federal District Commission; and Manpower Requirements and Utilization in Canada. Her stints on some committees were very short. In fact, she sat only one session on the Standing Orders Committee (1935), the Finance Committee (1951), the Federal District Commission Committee (1956) and the Capital and Corporal Punishment and Lotteries Committee (1956). She sat on other committees, though, for virtually the whole duration of her senate career, notably the Library; Public Buildings and Grounds; Public Health and Inspection of Foods; Banking and Commerce; and Civil Service and Administration committees. Most senators are involved with four or five committees in a session and Cairine Wilson was no exception — at least during the 1930s. Glutton for work that she was the Senator sat routinely on as many as seven committees during the nineteen forties and as many as eight towards the end of her career.

In March 1930, just after her appointment to the Senate, Cairine Wilson received a signal honour. Although it was most unusual for a new senator to be thrust into such a role, she was elected chairman of a committee — the Public Buildings and Grounds Committee. It could be that her gift of some small Australian pines to the Government of Canada to plant on both sides of the stone steps in front of the Senate block[46] paved the way for her election. But in all likelihood few people knew about this gift that she made to her country in appreciation of her summons to the Red Chamber. Her nomination to the post was probably a tribute to her recognized leadership abilities and her daily involvement with the running of two large houses, 192 Daly Avenue and Clibrig. But if nothing else, her great interest in gardening would have qualified her for the job. The Senator enjoyed being chairman because she served in this capacity until 1948, when she was replaced by her friend, Senator Norman McL. Paterson. She then took on the demanding chairmanship of the important Immigration and Labour Committee, which in 1947 had thirty-three members.

As a committee chairman, Cairine Wilson called committee meetings, set up steering committees to decide when meetings should be scheduled and who should appear before them, and attempted to get a consensus or agreement on the issues being studied. According to John MacNeill, a lawyer and one-time Clerk of the Senate, the Senator took an active part in asking questions at committee meetings and made a practice of consulting him about legal matters that she did not understand. The noted economist O.J. Firestone, who worked for that celebrated Liberal cabinet minister, C.D. Howe, was another authority consulted by the Senator. To him she posed economic questions that related mainly to current affairs. In Dr Firestone's words:

> She would pursue the subject matter raised in depth, the reasons for the problems faced and what could be done about them. I liked her approach to economic policy matters: Are we doing enough? What are the alternatives?

> Her questions were penetrating, softened by a gentle smile and her great charm. In some respects, she reminded me of my minister. She would drive to the core of an issue and she had little patience with generalities.[47]

When it came to political activity outside the Senate, Cairine Wilson devoted a good deal of time to the National Federation of Liberal Women of Canada, that political nursery which she had so deftly guided into being in 1928. As honorary president, she had expected to play a less prominent part in the organization than she had previously, but with the death of the then president, Mrs W.C. Kennedy of Windsor, in 1934, the Senator found herself thrust into the role of acting president, in which capacity she presided until the 1938 national convention and her election as president. She would remain president until the national convention of 1947, when she was succeeded in that office by Nancy Hodges of British Columbia.

In recognition of her long years of service the Senator was named honorary life president.

In the formative years of the Federation's existence the Senator watched with great interest the indomitable struggle waged by feminists in her native province to obtain the vote for women in provincial and municipal elections. She was not content to watch from the sidelines, though. She returned to her native province to address meetings, agitating for the granting of the provincial franchise to women and calling for a redress of the grievances of Quebec women under the provincial civil code. On 9 March 1934, for example, she gave a radio address on behalf of the League for Women's Rights in which she reminded her listeners, "In the struggle to obtain the franchise it is not the active opposition which is most to be feared, but the indifference which is shown even by the women themselves."[48]

Back home in Ottawa she used the Federation as a forum to promote the cause of her fellow feminists in Quebec. At the Federation's 1932 national convention, for instance, she introduced a resolution urging Quebec members of the House of Commons and the Senate to spare no effort in fighting for the right of Quebec women to vote in provincial and municipal elections.[49]

Certainly the situation in which Quebec women found themselves was paradoxical. When it came to exercising the franchise, they could express their views on national or international issues in federal elections but had no voice in solving problems closer to home such as health and education. To resolve this anomaly, Le Comité provincial pour le Suffrage feminin was established in 1921 as a bilingual association to conduct an "educational campaign to persuade the public and the legislature that women do not wish to have the vote in order to change their sphere in life but rather to raise and improve the level of society in general."[50] In 1927, the committee joined forces with five other Montreal groups to send a delegation to Quebec City to support a private member's bill granting the provincial franchise to women. This would be the first of fourteen such measures to be considered by the Quebec assembly before its iron resistance was finally worn down in 1940 and the women of Quebec obtained the provincial franchise.

This determined struggle had a special meaning for Cairine Wilson because not only did she identify with the dogged persistence and courage of the women spearheading the campaign, she had a personal friend in its leading spokesperson, the able and captivating Thérèse Casgrain. Over the years they often shared the speakers' platform at Liberal functions as Mme Casgrain was, until her defection to the Co-operative Commonwealth Federation, a dedicated Liberal who served as a vice-president of the National Federation of Liberal Women. Moreover, as friends of the

Wilsons, Thérèse Casgrain and her husband, Pierre, a one-time Speaker of the House of Commons and Liberal cabinet minister, attended dinners at the Manor House. In 1934, while the Quebec feminists' fight was still being waged, Cairine Wilson sent a message to them expressing the Federation's great regret that the women of Quebec were being denied the provincial vote. It was a gesture of support much appreciated by Mme Casgrain, who later acknowledged it in her memoirs.[51]

Although Quebec women eventually realized one of their key goals, women elsewhere in Canada were less successful in achieving one of their chief political objectives: increased representation in Parliament and provincial legislatures. Cairine Wilson and those who worked closely with her in setting up the Federation had hoped that it would furnish aspiring female politicians with the necessary political training and leadership skills to move smoothly into successful political careers. With the passage of the years, though, it became all too evident that the Federation was not serving as a stepping stone for ambitious women seeking a political career, that its very existence, in fact, hindered women's entry into the political mainstream, because while it had its own hierarchy of offices comparable to that of its male counterpart, the National Liberal Federation, it had none of the attendant power and therefore little control over the avenues leading to national power.[52] The Federation's failure to groom women for the important political jobs was no doubt a source of disappointment for the Senator, who observed in a 1942 speech that women had not yet "filled a large or prominent place in our parliaments." In that same address she also noted with chagrin that in Canada it had "been exceedingly difficult to secure a party nomination where there [was] a likelihood or even remote possibility of election" and that women were "usually doomed to carry the banner of a forlorn cause."

Still, even if the Federation rarely served as a springboard for entry into a successful political career, Senator Wilson could take consolation in the fact that it did help to further an interest in politics and to educate women about the issues of the day. This function it performed with varying degrees of success from its founding until after the outbreak of World War II, when its head office closed, not to reopen until shortly before the 1945 federal election.

The nineteen thirties were also years when Cairine Wilson figured prominently in the activities of the Twentieth Century Liberal Association. During World War II the Association entered a period of decline and then folded. But in the halcyon years when its members were still young, idealistic, brimming with enthusiasm and not immersed in the war effort, it was a going concern. As an honorary president of the Association's women's branch, Cairine Wilson addressed many of its gatherings, some of which were held in private homes, including her own. From time to time she presided at joint meetings of the women's and men's branches, as was the case in June 1932 when she was one of the judges of a debate conducted at the Chateau Laurier Hotel on Canada's participation in the St. Lawrence Seaway.[53]

Nothing could have gladdened the Senator's political heart more than seeing large numbers of young people enthusiastically involved in the issues of the day and no occasions demonstrated this involvement more forcefully than the Association's three national conventions. At the 1933 meeting, held on 2 and 3 June at the Chateau Laurier, Cairine Wilson addressed a luncheon which her daughter Olive presided over. In her speech on 3 June the Senator touched on such favourite themes of hers as women's place in Canada and the particular appeal that Liberalism has for members of her sex. Then she reviewed the record of the Bennett government, observing in spirited, partisan fashion, "Our house is left in disorder. Mr. Bennett apparently forgets that we associate May with housecleaning." Mackenzie King, a member of her audience, reported that evening on page 154 of his diary:

> The gathering was quite a large one the dining room of the Chateau Laurier being completely filled. Olive Wilson presided. Senator (Carine)[sic] Wilson made a speech, good material, but too obviously prepared by some one for her and committed to memory, a review of the session etc. She had difficulty remembering all the points. I am afraid she is attempting far too much, with the speaking in addition to all else.[54]

In remarking that the Senator was "attempting too much," Mackenzie King was right on target. Only someone with phenomenal energy and an amazing constitution could have maintained the pace that she did without succumbing to health problems. But obviously there were times when she demanded too much of herself and this was one of them. It is to be hoped that her delivery was more effective at the 1936 national convention, by which time the Association could boast 600 clubs nationwide and eight provincial associations. Cairine Wilson could applaud these encouraging statistics and also take pride in the fact that shy, attractive Olive had been elected to succeed Odette Lapointe as president of the women's branch. One wonders, though, what she might have thought of the following incident, recounted by lawyer Sadie Lieff, who was co-chairman of the Association's resolution committee.

It seems that Mrs Lieff was presiding at an afternoon session when a bellhop motioned to her that she was wanted on the phone. She went to the phone where she was informed by Mackenzie King's butler that a table napkin had disappeared from Laurier House. It had obviously been removed by one of the convention's thirty-five delegates who had just attended a luncheon there. On learning this, Sadie Lieff returned to the meeting and announced, "There's a call from Laurier House reporting a missing table napkin." No sooner were the words uttered than a sheepish young man stood up with the AWOL napkin still tucked in his vest.[55]

For most Liberal Party activists who were involved in some way with Cairine Wilson in the 1930s and 1940s, it is her work on behalf of the National Federation of Liberal Women of Canada and the twentieth Century Liberal Association that comes most readily to mind when reminiscing about the Senator. Jack Pickersgill, however, has recollections of a very different sort. His flash-backs centre on the memorial services that Cairine Wilson organized every year to mark the birth of her revered hero Sir Wilfrid Laurier. On her own initiative, she would recruit Liberal senators and members of the House of Commons for a service staged at the foot of Laurier's statue which stands beside the East Block overlooking the Chateau Laurier Hotel. As Laurier's birthday fell on 20 November 1841, the ceremony was always overshadowed by Rememberance Day observances and frequently marred by the weather.

No matter what the occasion, the Senator invariably created an indelible impression with her deep sincerity and her smart, if conservative, attire. Recalling those long bygone days, Kathleen Ryan remarked:

> Most people were impressed by Cairine Wilson's absolute sincerity. Her marvellous hats also created an impression. She was always meticulously and smartly dressed without being high style. She wore a great deal of navy and black and when she was dressed for dinner she was outstanding.[56]

For Marguerite Deslauriers Lamothe it was not only the heady enthusiasm associated with the founding of the Twentieth Century Liberal Association but also Cairine Wilson's example that will long be remembered:

> Mrs Wilson had the will and the competence and she used them. My mother and my aunts used to look somewhat askance at her doings, but thanks to her example I never felt that I couldn't undertake something simply because I was a woman. Because of all the people that we met through her, we became aware of problems in the

community. This is why, for example, I came to sit on the Mother's Allowance Board for Ottawa. Even if she wasn't eloquent, she inspired us to do things. Unconsciously, she was a role model.[57]

Such was Cairine Wilson's prominence in the early 1930s that in late 1934 the Senator was pushed for a cabinet position. One of those who lobbied for her elevation to cabinet rank was Ottawa Liberal powerhouse Olive Skinner, who had considered running in the 1930 federal election, but had abandoned the idea because she lacked the necessary financial resources. Addressing the thirteenth annual meeting of the Ottawa Women's Liberal Club in November 1934, Mrs Skinner, then the club president, asked Mackenzie King outright if he would appoint Cairine Wilson to his cabinet in the event that the Liberals were returned to power in the next federal election. Mrs Skinner based her appeal on the fact that women comprised fifty-two percent of the Canadian electorate and that Liberal women were entitled to a voice in the formation of their party's policies. Observed the speaker, "We have awakened to the fact that what was considered a sheltered and restricted life in caring for the needs of the home is really the centre of influence for the whole life of the nation."[58]

Mrs Skinner's pitch to have Cairine Wilson appointed to the next Liberal cabinet was evidently part of a growing campaign to have the Senator made Canada's first woman cabinet minister because on 7 December *The Detroit News* reported:

...Already a campaign for her elevation to the cabinet is being pushed by the Liberal members of both the House of Commons and the Senate, with strong support by women's Liberal groups throughout the country.

The latter are stressing that, with at least as many women as men voters, they are entitled to at least one cabinet post. It seems unlikely that W.L. Mackenzie King, former prime minister and undoubtedly the successor to R.B. Bennett in this office, can withstand the pressure to name a woman to the ministry.

Mackenzie King did, of course, withstand the pressure, perhaps because he detected signs of ambition in Cairine Wilson. If he did, he shared the views of Arthur Hardy who, when discussing possible cabinet appointments with King that November, remarked that he thought "Cairine Wilson [had] been most ambitious from the start."[59] Cairine Wilson never did become Canada's first woman cabinet minister. That distinction was earned by Ellen Fairclough who was appointed to the Diefenbaker cabinet in 1957. Whether the Senator regretted not becoming Canada's first woman cabinet minister is not known. But we may be sure that she was thrilled to receive recognition of quite a different sort some years later. On 28 May 1941, amid an idyllic spring-time setting of budding orchards and green dykeland, she received her first honorary degree: a DCL from Acadia University, her son Ralph's alma mater.[60] The following year she was invited to receive an honorary degree at Queen's University's autumn convocation, but had to decline that invitation; she was scheduled to attend a women's conference in New Jersey on 14 October and speak at a large meeting in New York on 17 October. The degree was finally conferred on her on 12 May 1943.

The honorary degrees may have been small consolation for a cabinet appointment. We shall never know. We do know, however, that freedom from the onerous responsibilities associated with a cabinet portfolio allowed the Senator to dedicate herself to the League of Nations Society in Canada and the cause for which she should be chiefly remembered: refugees.

6

CHATELAINE OF THE MANOR HOUSE AND CLIBRIG

On most questions Cairine Wilson was down to earth and realistic. One noticeable exception was her view of herself. As so often happens when we attempt to define ourselves, she conjured up a self-image that contradicted the facts in at least one important respect. Despite all the time that she devoted to outside interests and commitments after her appointment to the Senate, Cairine Wilson still regarded herself as first and foremost a wife and mother whose deepest loyalty was to her husband and her family. When being interviewed for personality profiles she made a point of stating that she assigned top priority to her husband and her children. However, even if this observation flew in the face of reality, the fact remains that home was still the centre of her emotional universe. It was the place where she raised eight children, relaxed with jovial, easy-going Norman, and entertained countless visitors from all walks of life. It was the place where she reaffirmed the traditional values that had played such an important part in her upbringing and that predominated in the social circles in which she moved.

When queried about her eight children who formed such an important part of this lively household, Mrs Wilson invariably referred to her "two families," the first composed of the four oldest offspring: Olive, Janet, Cairine and Ralph; the second made up of the four youngest: Anna (often called Peggy), Angus, Robert and Norma. Norma was only four when her

The garden at the rear of the Manor House showing the Felix de Weldon fountain with sculptures of Michael and Joan Burns, grand-children of Cairine and Norman Wilson. Seated is Alice Wilson, wife of Angus Wilson, and standing nearby are James Gill, another grandchild, and gardener Louis Hansen.

mother was elevated to the Senate, Olive twenty. With the exception of
Janet, who was a student in Paris, all the children were living at home,
which was then the large red-brick house at 192 Daly, but which was soon
to be the palatial Manor House in suburban Rockcliffe. It was a time in
Cairine Wilson's life when you would have expected her to be preoccupied with child-raising and to have pronounced views on the subject. And
such was the case, as one journalist discovered when she interviewed the
newly appointed senator for an article in the June 1930 issue of *Canadian
Home Journal*. Seated in her homey office with its family photos, Senator
Wilson dwelt at some length on her philosophy of child-rearing. She
applauded the idea of parents' establishing a close relationship with their
children, but then observed:

> This business of companionship with children can go
> too far, as it does in some homes in the United States
> where the children call their parents by their first names,
> criticize them openly, refuse to keep any reserve at all
> themselves or permit their parents to do so. But, with
> saneness and common sense dictating, parents and child-
> ren should be able to establish a bond of closest friendship
> which also recognizes the authority and direction due to
> parenthood and superior age and knowledge.[1]

The front of the Manor House in 1949. Seated is Cairine and
Norman Wilson's grandson, James Gill. Standing are daughter-in-
law, Alice Wilson, and gardener Louis Hansen.

When giving her views on child-rearing, she was probably recalling her stern, forbidding father and the strained relations that existed between him and his sons Angus and George. These and her somewhat bitter memories of the formality that reigned in the sombre household at Kildonan probably made her wish that she had been raised in a sunny, more relaxed atmosphere. But Cairine Wilson found it difficult to become close to most of her children when they were growing up. Both her natural reserve and her deep distrust of lavish displays of affection, to say nothing of the long hours that she spent away from home, militated against it. In a letter to her friend Mackenzie King, on 17 December 1932, she hinted at her longing for a warm relationship with her offspring. Alluding to King's birthday on that very day and to the death of his beloved mother on 18 December 1917, she wrote:

> I understand all that December 17 means to you and shall always remember the very sad days of 1917.
>
> My children will, I fear, scarcely be as faithful as you have been and I only regret that I never knew your mother. Perhaps she might have taught me how to train my sons.[2]

North aspect of the Manor House c 1930.

The front entrance of the Manor House framed by a graceful archway which was incorporated in the gatehouse that had been cut through the original stables and coach-house block.

Because of the Senate appointment, Anna, Angus, Robert and Norma, Cairine Wilson's second family, saw very little of their mother in their formative years. Somewhat to their chagrin, they were left often in the care of old family retainers, such as Betts, the butler, Clifford, the chauffeur, and Eva, the nanny, who raised Norma almost singlehandedly. Like the children of other wealthy establishment families in that day and age, the three youngest Wilsons ate in their own dining room, which, at the Manor House, was located off the kitchen, alongside the main dining room. When they did visit with their parents, it was usually in the late afternoon following their return from school, the girls having come from Elmwood, a private girls' school, and the boys from Ashbury, its male counterpart. At this hour of the day the elder Wilsons could usually be found comfortably ensconced in the dark walnut-panelled library, browsing through the daily papers and partaking of that most civilized of British rituals, afternoon tea. Norma has recalled that after she had returned from Elmwood, she might "dance" into the library to talk to her parents, but then again she might not, for this hour was not reserved for the youngest Wilsons.[3] Sunday evening, on the other hand, was always set aside for the youngest children because this was when the Senator made a practice of reading to them at bedtime. For this magical hour, she chose biblical stories or chapters from some of the children's favourite books: the Dr. Doolittle series by Hugh Lofting and works by Thornton Burgess.

Although she spent little time with her children after her elevation to the Senate, there is no doubt that Cairine Wilson loved them dearly, especially Angus, who perhaps reminded her of her revered older brother of the same name. In the one extensive file of personal correspondence that survives — letters that she wrote to her namesake when young Cairine was away from home — there are copious references to the children's activities, some of which contain hints of the Senator's dry sense of humour, as for example, the epistle that she wrote on 28 September 1937:

> Yesterday Anna and I visited Dr Hooper who removed the stitches, and as far as we are able to see, there is likely to be no scar, for there is only a slit to mark the spot, although Anna says that the cyst was exceedingly difficult to remove. Dr Hooper is certainly not of the garrulous nature and I find that he prefers to be questioned more regarding his horse than about his patients.[4]

Many large families have at least one child who is a source of untold worry and concern, from childhood right through adulthood. The Wilson family was no exception. In this case, the child was Anna (also known as Peggy), a sensitive youngster who had the misfortune to be born after the four oldest children and before Angus, Robert and Norma. Hers was the characteristic plight of the middle child, surrounded by more aggressive and/or accomplished siblings. Intimidated by bright, vivacious Janet and teased unmercifully by all three older sisters, Anna became insecure and lazy. Today she would probably be called a "slow learner," although outside the academic classroom she demonstrated a real talent for such disparate pursuits as crossword puzzles and art. Her mother was advised to provide her with special tutoring but, in another of those rare refusals to grasp the obvious, rejected the idea. Apparently Cairine Wilson just could not face the fact that a child of hers had special needs and that Anna's lack of motivation and laziness could have an emotional basis. When the Senator did realize this, Anna was well on her way to becoming an alcoholic. Her addiction to the bottle would remain with her for life and pose many a trial for her mother and the family.

Olive, too, was a source of heartache for her mother but for very different reasons. Perhaps it was because she nursed a secret longing to be an only child or maybe it was because she resented having to compete with Janet who outshone her when the two sisters ended up in the same class at Elmwood. Whatever the explanation, this shy, retiring daughter rejected her mother when growing up and went out of her way to seek affection from her Aunt Anna, who was only too happy to provide it. Relations between mother and daughter became more strained when Olive became very interested in the son of a leading Roman Catholic family in Ottawa. The relationship ultimately broke up and Olive married Alan Gill, a promising young scientist, on 22 January 1938 in a ceremony in the Manor House drawing room. Unfortunately for Olive and her mother's peace of mind the marriage brought its fair share of problems because Alan, although brilliant, was difficult, changing jobs frequently after the Second World War, and, once yanking his young family off to Peder Bay, near Victoria, to live under extremely primitive conditions. Further difficulties arose when he developed diabetes and later had to have a leg amputated. Olive's marriage, in other words, was tailor-made to arouse her mother's ever-present sympathies for the underdog, and in characteristic fashion Mrs Wilson provided whatever she could in the way of moral and financial support.

Only with her grandchildren did Cairine Wilson begin to mellow and become really discerning about the needs of the different personalities in her expanding family. As so often happens with mothers, she was more at ease with her grandchildren than with her own children. To her own offspring she often appeared cool and distant, but this was not the case with her grandchildren. With them she did not hesitate to reveal her great warmth in small, subtle ways, such as recognizing grandson Donald Davies's love of liquorice. Whenever he came to visit she made sure that there was a bowl of his favourite candy on her bedside table.[5]

Cairine Wilson, daughter of Angus Wilson and his wife Alice, cherishes warm memories of her grandmother as does her younger sister Joanna. "There was a distance there," observed Cairine, "but we always felt that she cared about us and loved us." This care and love expressed themselves in the Senator's efforts to broaden her granddaughters' intellectual horizons. After her husband's death, and when Cairine and Joanna were still very young, Senator Wilson often drove to Cumberland on a Saturday to visit her son's family and spend a couple of hours with the girls helping them with their stamp collections. She herself collected stamps and from the correspondence that poured into her Senate office she selected duplicate stamps to give to her granddaughters. Through her

Senator Cairine Wilson and daughter-in-law, Alice Wilson, shown in the Manor House garden in 1949.

long-standing friendship with Mother St Thomas, Senator Wilson also arranged for the girls to have private French lessons at Jeanne d'Arc Institute, a non-denominational hostel for single girls started by Mother St Thomas in 1917. On Fridays after school the girls would be collected by Clifford, the chauffeur, and driven to the Institute on Sussex Drive, where the much loved, roly poly mother superior would have them memorize *Aesop's Fables* in French. Following the lessons, Cairine and Joanna would be picked up by Clifford and chauffeured to the Manor House for dinner.

For Cairine there is also the tender memory of her grandmother's promise to take her on a cruise of the Saguenay River. Unfortunately the Senator died before she could carry it out.[6]

Until his incapacitating illnesses of later years, Norman Wilson provided constant support and encouragement to his wife. He clearly loved and admired Cairine, who loved and needed him. Essentially a serious, modest woman, with a sustaining passion for good works, she benefited from his leavening influence and ego-bolstering approval. It is true that their separate paths frequently took them in different directions, but it is also evident that they shared many interests. The obvious ones were family and politics. But travel and entertaining also ranked high on the list.

Norman and Cairine Wilson made many trips to Europe in an age when affluent Canadians did not fly thirty to forty thousand feet above the Atlantic in a silver jet but instead crossed the ocean on a well appointed passenger liner which resembled a luxurious floating hotel. Janet Burns has especially fond memories of a trip that her parents took in 1932 when she and her sister, Cairine, were attending school at Marmand, just east of Lausanne, Switzerland. The senior Wilsons came over for the Easter holidays, collected the girls, and then took them on a whirlwind tour of Italy and France. Janet reported, "Neither of us ever had more fun or a more relaxed time with our parents. We both still talk about that holiday and remember it with pleasure."[7] It was when she and Norman were returning from that memorable holiday that Cairine Wilson discovered just how alert members of the fourth estate can sometimes be. When the Canadian Pacific liner, the *Empress of Australia*, docked at Father Point, in the Gaspé, the Senator found herself surrounded by members of the press; they had spotted the name Mrs Norman Wilson on the passenger list and immediately associated it with Canada's first senator. Her cover broken, Senator Wilson was forced to confess, somewhat sheepishly, "I thought the use of my own name would be a perfect alias."[8] So closely did she identify with the traditional view of marriage that she considered her husband's name to be hers.

Less exotic travelling took them regularly to Toronto, where Janet settled after her marriage and where they often attended the Royal Winter Fair, a showplace for Canadian livestock and thoroughbred horse jumping, which attracts working farmers, riders from elegant hobby farms on the city's fringe and city dwellers alike. Before his death in 1931, they usually shared a box at the fair with Jack Cameron, husband by his first marriage of Norman's sister, Ida. Cairine and Norman Wilson's interest in this Toronto institution and Establishment mecca continued for as long as they were able to make the trip.

Norman Wilson on the golf links. Photo taken in the early 1930s.

At home in Ottawa they entertained frequently, first in their large homes on Daly Avenue, and then at the Manor House. When the family lived at 192 Daly, Cairine Wilson combined the traditional role of wife and mother with that of gracious hostess and tireless worker for assorted charities and church committees. To these more conventional roles she added that of political organizer, in which capacity she welcomed the leading Liberals of the day into her home. She would probably have laughed at the suggestion that she held a political salon at 192 Daly, but that was what it was, because in this large red-brick house with the Queen Anne details she provided an attractive meeting place for people to swap political ideas and reconcile divergent views on the issues of the day. Her enthusiasm and energy were such that in the 1925 federal campaign she would return to Daly Avenue between committee meetings and speeches to see that the children were put to bed, go from a ward meeting to a church function and still play an active part in all the committees on which she served.[9]

Family photo taken in front of Clibrig in 1943. Back row left to right: Norma Wilson (now Mrs James Davies), the Senator, Cairine Wilson, Norman Wilson. Front row left to right: Joan Burns (now Mrs John Addison), Din (Janet) Burns, Michael Burns and mother Janet Burns (née Wilson).

At the French-styled Chateau, which they called the Manor House, the Wilsons entertained men and women from all walks of life, from governors-general and prime ministers to recently arrived refugees from Europe. Sometimes the event was a function in aid of a local organization closely associated with Cairine Wilson: The Zonta Club of Ottawa, a professional and business women's service club to which the Senator belonged; the Ottawa branch of the Canadian Save the Children Fund, which she helped to launch in the 1940s; The Young Women's Christian Association of Ottawa, on whose board she served; the Bronson Home for elderly women, which she served as a board member; and Elmwood School. (She played a prominent role in its early history, providing generous practical and financial assistance along with Mrs H.S. Southam and Mrs Edward Fauquier.) For organizations such as these, a well organized tea, served with sterling silver tea service in the Manor House gardens, was a big attraction and a large money-raiser. Dr Bliss Pugsley, a longstanding Zonta member, has recalled that people came from far and wide to the annual Zonta tea held at the Manor House the first Saturday in June:

> For twenty-six years the sun shone on it; only once did we have to move indoors. Both the gardens and the greenhouse were open to the public. There were flowers galore and people just loved to wander and look. They could also tour the main house and many did. It was certainly a very popular annual event.[10]

A particularly colourful fund-raising event was staged on 3 June 1950 at the Manor House. According to the *Ottawa Journal*:

> Brilliant sunshine, after a wet morning, favoured the garden party of the Union Nationale Française d'Ottawa, which took place on Saturday afternoon from four until seven o'clock at the Manor House, which Mr Norman Wilson and the Hon Cairine Wilson put at the disposal of the organization. The garden party was in aid of flood and fire victims of Canada, under the patronage of the French Ambassador and Mrs Hubert Guerin, the Rt Hon the Chief Justice and Mrs Thibaudeau Rinfret and Mr Norman Wilson and Senator Wilson.

> More than 400 members of the French colony and their friends, the diplomatic corps, and prominent Ottawa men and women, chatted among the lilacs and tulips to the sound of the band of the RCMP, whose brilliant red

coats framed in the grey stone half-circle of the drive, lent
a picturesque background to the party.[11]

Alixe Carter, a writer and Zonta member, has deeply etched memories
of a very different type of function held at the Manor House. This one
involved fifteen to twenty debutantes who received instructions from
Cairine Wilson on how to curtsy to their Excellencies, the Bessboroughs,
at their annual drawing room. Left to her own inclinations, Alixe Carter
would not have become a debutante. But she was eager to please her
favourite aunt, Gertrude Bennett, the first director of the Ottawa Civic
Hospital's school of nursing. So one day, shortly before the drawing room
was to take place, Alixe and Marmo Cross, another Westerner, went to the
Manor House to practise curtsying under Cairine Wilson's supervision.
Since their fathers were both good friends of the Conservative prime
minister of the day, R.B. Bennett, the young women drove to the Wilson
residence in R.B.'s chauffeured limousine. Not surprisingly, this invited
all kinds of comment, especially on the part of a shocked Janet Wilson
who, when she saw them alight, immediately asked "What in the name of
heaven are you doing riding in the Prime Minister's car?"

Having advertised their families' Conservative sympathies, Alixe and
Marmo entered the Manor House. After they had lunch they and the other
debutantes withdrew to the living room to practise curtsying. As everyone
wore a long dress with a train, this was not the easiest maneuver to execute:

> We had to go so far down that many people toppled
> over, and there was a great deal of giggling. But Cairine
> Wilson was very friendly and not the least bit intimidat-
> ing. There was none of the school marm about her.[12]

The Wilsons often entertained personal friends and acquaintances,
many of whom were prominent in their respective fields. For Cairine
Wilson was a woman who felt a need not only for friendship and
intellectual stimulation but for something larger: for a community of
friends and acquaintances who could share her enthusiasms and broaden
her horizons. Norman helped her to fulfill this need by accompanying her
on visits to "important people" and by playing the role of genial host,
which he did with great frequency until illness intervened in his later years.
Sometimes they entertained at the exclusive Country Club in nearby
Aylmer, Quebec, but as a rule they hosted luncheons and dinners at the
Manor House, where guests were entertained in a large formal dining
room with silver-toned oak panelling and soft antique red hangings. On
such occasions the indispensable Betts was much in evidence: a towering
figure whom one guest, the British art critic, Eric Newton, once recalled

as "modelled on Kensitas [the tall, lank, dark-suited gentleman that formed part of a cigarette motif] in appearance and on Jeeves in behaviour."[13]

When her daughter, Cairine, was away from home, her mother kept up a steady stream of correspondence with her. Nearly every letter contained at least one mention of a recently staged dinner or luncheon. Thus, on 4 November 1935, the Senator reported in typical fashion:

> On Thursday we had a successful dinner party, at which the American Minister and Mrs Armour were guests of honour. The others were: Colonel and Mrs Crerar and the former's sister, Mrs Gallagher, Colonel and Mrs Sherwood and Mrs Stevenson, the Charlie MacLarens, Mr and Mrs Frank Ahearn, Mr Norman Archer and the Honourable Ian Mackenzie. We had two pumpkins on the table and the urn filled with fruit, so Betts said it looked like a harvest festival.[14]

Nearly every Wednesday evening when the House and the Senate were not sitting, Cairine Wilson invited senators and members of the House, many of them Chateau Laurier residents, to dinner. Two Westerners were among the regulars: James MacKinnon from Edmonton who, before being elevated to the Senate in 1949, served as a cabinet minister under Mackenzie King and Louis St. Laurent, and gregarious Ian Mackenzie who, as Minister of National Defence between 1935 and 1939, oversaw the rearmament of Canada's armed forces. He subsequently became Minister of Pensions and National Health, in which portfolio he pushed for the extension of social benfits. It was while serving as Minister of Pensions and National Health that the Scottish-born politician played a key role in the events leading to the evacuation of Japanese Canadians from British Columbia's coast in 1942. In 1948, he joined Cairine Wilson in the Senate

The Nova Scotia-born lawyer and Liberal cabinet minister, James Layton Ralston, who was always known as Layton, was another regular at these dinners. Colonel Ralston was a selfless and devoted patriot who drove himself unmercifully when Minister of National Defence in the Second World War. Like his good friend, Cairine Wilson, he seldom spared himself in his work, being conscientious to a fault. Like her, he was also a public figure who could take an unpopular stand on a controversial issue. One such occasion arose in October 1944 when, after visiting Canadian troops overseas, he recommended to Cabinet that well-trained soldiers who had been conscripted under the National Resources Mobilization Act for home defence be dispatched overseas. He made his recommendation secure in the knowledge that Mackenzie King would oppose it, but fully convinced that there was no viable alternative given the unexpectedly high casualties in Italy and northwest Europe.

King did oppose his minister's plan. Prophesying that conscription would destroy national unity and bring about the downfall of the Liberal Party, he began an unrelenting and devious campaign to force Ralston out of the Cabinet and replace him with a minister who would continue the voluntary system of recruitment for overseas service. Matters finally came to a head on 13 November when King informed his cabinet that Ralston had never withdrawn a letter of resignation that he had submitted two years earlier and that General A.G.L. McNaughton, who disliked Ralston intensely, must be brought into the Cabinet without delay. Upon hearing this, the Minister of National Defence confirmed his resignation letter, and then rose, said good-bye to his colleagues, and left the room — alone.[15]

King's despicable treatment of Ralston and his departure from the Cabinet upset Cairine Wilson greatly. But true to form she continued to maintain unswerving loyalty and faith in her leader. Still, she must have found it difficult to forgive King for his actions, especially as they were directed against a friend of such outstanding patriotism and courage.

Often Mackenzie, MacKinnon and Ralston were joined at these dinners by Fred Kay, the husband of Cairine Wilson's cousin, Athalie Baptist, and by witty Jack Elliott (J.C.), a Liberal cabinet minister from southwestern Ontario, who was Postmaster General in the closing years of the 1930s. Kay, a man of considerable charm who had earned a law degree at McGill University, resembled Norman Wilson in that both were born in 1876 and both were by inclination farmers and politicians. First elected to the House of Commons as a Liberal in 1911, Kay was reelected four times before his defeat in 1930, when he returned to farming fulltime at Philipsburg, Quebec.

Cairine Wilson's longtime political colleague, Ernest Lapointe, was another frequent guest as he was at other Wilson social functions, such as Janet's wedding, where he toasted the bride, and Olive's nuptials, when he toasted the bride's parents. Large of frame and big of heart, with a commanding voice and great charm, Lapointe made a lasting impression on the Senator. There is no doubt that her quiet sense of humour appealed to him because as his daughter, Odette, has remarked, "Father enjoyed Mrs Wilson. She must have had a sense of humour."[16] In 1949, eight years after Lapointe's death, when writing to King, Cairine Wilson noted rather wistfully, "We are pleased and flattered that you will be present at the wedding [Norma's marriage to Jim Davies in May 1949], although we shall miss our dear Ernest."[17]

Besides entertaining frequently at dinner, Cairine and Norman Wilson made a practice of inviting large numbers of guests to Sunday lunch. These luncheons became one of Ottawa's most celebrated institutions, known far and wide for their heterogeneous guest list and stimulating conversation. On these occasions members of the family mixed with relatives, parliamentarians, civil service mandarins, old friends, and sometimes guests from outside these circles. In the years immediately preceding World War Two and during the war itself, this company often included highly educated, cultured refugees, many of them Germans who had fled Nazism.

One such refugee was William Heckscher, a man of grace, style and wit, who eventually became an internationally-known art historian and a member of Princeton University's Institute for Advanced Study. To escape Nazism, Heckscher went to Britain where, in 1940, he was interned as an enemy alien. From there he was transported to Canada and imprisoned along with other German and Austrian refugees in one of several internment camps located in Ontario, Quebec and New Brunswick. Released early in the war, he took up an academic teaching position — his first ever — at newly established Carleton College (now Carleton University) in Ottawa. It was here, in the nation's capital, that he first met Cairine Wilson, who frequently invited him to lunch at the Manor House. Some forty years later this former internee would observe:

> She was exceedingly kind and my feelings for her were of limitless admiration. She was as a human being someone very special. Judicious and witty (and by 'witty' I mean that she had a kind of eighteenth century Voltarian esprit), she saw human beings and she also had the ability to see through human beings. She had people in her entourage who, politically, seemed somewhat too radical and absolute and I am sure that she knew this but her way of dealing with such problems was utterly different from what I had learned and seen in Europe. The sharpest remark about someone who thwarted her plans in a brutal and stupid manner was "not very helpful."[18]

Kurt Swinton, who became a Toronto businessman after the war, was another former internee who attended Sunday lunches at the Manor House. Like his friend, Bill Heckscher, he played a leading role in the school that was established in the internment camp at Farnham, Quebec, where, as a qualified radio engineer, he lectured on popular science, including atomic theory. Because he was fortunate enough to have a first degree relative in Canada — his mother — Kurt Swinton was one of the first internees to be released. Immediately after obtaining his freedom on 18 February 1941 the energetic engineer went to Montreal, determined to obtain a job that would put his expertise to work on behalf of the war effort.

His attempts to obtain employment in Canada's largest city, and in Ottawa which he visited after leaving Montreal, were to no avail. However, while he was in the nation's capital, he became a protégé of Cairine Wilson, who may have lobbied successfully on his behalf because one morning he awoke to find that he was a commissioned officer in the Canadian army.[19]

Two of Cairine Wilson's closest friends regularly attended these Sunday lunches. They were Beatrice Belcourt and Elizabeth Smellie, both spinsters and both trailblazers. Beatrice Belcourt was a tall, stately woman with dark hair and eyes and impeccable taste in dress. The daughter of a Liberal senator, Napoleon Antoine Belcourt, she worked as a public relations officer for Radio Canada in Ottawa at a time when it was most unusual for a woman to occupy this type of position. Outside the office this energetic, charming woman employed her journalistic skills on behalf of the Free French, helping to raise funds for that organization and arranging for the short wave radio station WRUL in Boston to transmit messages from French Canada to Occupied France.[20] She also sat on the board of the Victorian Order of Nurses and the executive committee of the Canadian National Committee on Refugees, which was headed by Senator Wilson.

Elizabeth Smellie, a tall, somewhat plain-looking woman, was noted for her organizing genius and quick sense of humour that delighted in small, everyday incidents. Warm and outgoing, she had distinguished herself as a pioneer in public health nursing where she earned the affection of all those who worked for her. In World War I she had risen from the position of nursing sister to that of assistant to the Matron-in-Chief, Royal Canadian Army Medical Corps Nursing Service. After the war she became Superintendent of the Victorian Order of Nurses, in which capacity she came to know Cairine Wilson, who sat on the organization's board. Their friendship continued during the war years, when the nursing trailblazer organized the Canadian Women's Army Corps, and into peacetime with her return to the VON and then retirement in Ottawa.

There was also a small coterie of friends who came regularly for Sunday afternoon tea, which was invariably served in the large formal drawing room that ran the width of the Manor House. One such friend was Captain Brian Simpson, an ex-Montrealer who worked for the Department of Veterans Affairs. Another was Sir Lyman Duff, who has been described as probably the least-known important Canadian and conversely as the greatest jurist and chief justice this country has produced.

Like his good friend Cairine Wilson, Sir Lyman was a staunch Liberal, a political affiliation that he maintained rather indiscreetly through all his years on the bench. He was reserved both in his public and in his private life. Flamboyancy was as foreign to his nature as it was to the Senator's. But there the similarities end because, although he was sober of mind, Sir Lyman was an alcoholic whose abuse of the bottle and near catastrophic binges almost prevented him from being appointed Chief Justice of the Supreme Court of Canada in 1933. To add to his problems, he was hopeless at handling money, frequently allowing his personal finances to get completely out of control.

Cairine Wilson first came to know the jurist in the 1920s, probably after the death of his wife, Elizabeth ("Lizzie"), in 1926. From correspondence that survives in the Duff papers, it is evident that she knew Sir Lyman as early as 1927, when they both lived on Daly Avenue and she solicited a donation from him for the Ottawa Welfare Bureau.[21] By the 1930s she was writing to him as a concerned friend, offering suggestions and assistance. In June 1934, forinstance, she reported:

> After I returned home yesterday I opened the New York Times and discovered at once the advertisement of the Mid-night Sun Cruise on the Steamship, Rotterdam. It seemed exactly what would be most suitable, and I am, therefore, sending the paper in case you would like to make enquiries,

> Many years ago I travelled on the Holland-American Line and I know that the boats are most comfortable, scrupulously clean and the food excellent. The ocean trip will, I feel sure, be just what you require, and I sincerely hope that Miss Duff's back is better today.[22]

The reference to Miss Duff was to Annie, one of a pair of teetotal, spinster sisters, both teachers. Annie, who was eight years younger than her brother, had retired from Toronto's Parkdale School in 1930 after teaching there for over thirty years. A shy, rather homely person, she was absolutely devoted to her brother as was her older sister, Emma, who had earned an international reputation for herself as a Toronto kindergarten teacher and writer of children's stories. When it became all too evident that alcohol and personal finances were getting the better of their brother, the two sisters resolved to take him in hand. Emma, who could not afford to stop teaching, remained in Toronto, but in 1932 Annie moved to Ottawa to be with Lyman. She found the jurist in deplorable physical and financial condition but, undeterred, she immediately set about reforming him. As a first step, Annie barred liquor from the house. Lyman occasionally smuggled some into his library or bedroom, but from the time of his sister's edict, he never again offered guests an alcoholic drink in his home. Annie hired a cook and housemaid, saw that her brother ate properly, and supervised his household and personal expenditures. She kept such a tight rein on his disbursements that the one-time spendthrift soon found himself constantly short of ready cash. But so successful was the salvage campaign that by early 1933, if he had not conquered his afflictions, Duff at least had them under control. His recovery was so successful that by March of that year Prime Minister Bennett felt that he could ask the jurist if he would succeed F.A. Anglin as chief justice of the Supreme Court of Canada.[23]

To Annie and Emma Duff goes most of the credit for Duff's improved health, indeed his survival. But others also lent a helping hand, one being Cairine Wilson. It is difficult to establish just what role the Senator played in his rehabilitation, but we can be reasonably sure that she told him a few home truths and provided valuable moral support in the form of little kindnesses and words of encouragement. Whatever she did, the Duffs were very grateful. Hints of their gratitude and of the real loss that Cairine Wilson felt on the death of Emma, with whom she corresponded over the years, are contained in a letter that the Senator wrote to Annie Duff in April 1935.

> My dear Miss Duff,
>
> We have passed through some very difficult times together and I am particularly sorry that I cannot be with you and your brother to-day. Please tell the Chief Justice that I appreciate his thoughtfulness in telephoning himself to let me know the very sad news.
>
> It is quite unnecessary to state that I have always loved dear Emma Lorne Duff from the first letter that I received and that Norma is proud of her book, as well as the letters.
>
> I never liked to think that one so valuable to the children of Canada should be laid aside and be forced to suffer. It is a great satisfaction to have known such a woman and I shall certainly cherish the memory of our hours together.
>
> My heart is full of sympathy for you and Sir Lyman and with a great deal of love...[24]

Cairine Wilson's little acts of thoughtfulness — arranging for Duff and his sister to have the use of Clifford and the car for a day, sending him information about cruises — were completely in character. For the Senator was invariably thoughtful of others. No matter how crowded her timetable, she never seemed too busy to send flowers, books and notes of personal cheer to ailing friends and sympathy and understanding to those who had lost a loved one. Many a time her black Mercedes sedan rolled up to the entrance of the Senate block, loaded with fresh flowers and produce destined for distribution to retired politicians and church ministers and old friends. On such occasions the Senator's private secretary was assigned the task of dividing everything up and arranging for delivery to the intended recipients. If the secretary had her own car, as in the case of Violet McAloran Herrington, she might distribute the flowers and produce herself.[25]

Mrs Wilson sent engagement and wedding gifts to countless friends, acquaintances and relatives, and kept in touch by mail with friends who lived outside Ottawa. One of these friends was Myra Macdonald Punnett, who served as Senator Wilson's private secretary from the mid-thirties to November 1941, when she left to be married and live in Rochester, New York. To this day Mrs Punnett treasures Cairine Wilson's friendly and newsy letters, some of which were written by hand when she must have had many other demands on her time.[26]

Cairine Wilson's deep sense of social responsibility and compassion were very much a part of her everyday life. When she lived in the small town of Rockland, Ontario she performed little kindnesses for workmen and their families. In Ottawa she routinely called on retired family servants and elderly friends and relatives, and arranged for Clifford to take residents of the Elizabeth Residence (a home for elderly women) for drives. And every Sunday afternoon, as religiously as she attended Sunday morning worship at St. Andrew's Presbyterian Church, she visited shut-ins at St. Vincent Hospital, a chronic care institution.

Cairine Wilson was fortunate in having incredible energy and stamina. Otherwise she would never have been able to accomplish all that she did. She was equally fortunate in having excellent staff at home (At the Manor House the indoor and outdoor staff totalled ten) and a daughter, Cairine, who was prepared to expedite innumerable errands and oversee the running of the Manor House and Clibrig. No sooner had the Senator returned to Ottawa from St Andrews, for example, than she started writing letters to her daughter instructing her regarding work that she wanted carried out at Clibrig. So dependent was she on young Cairine for this type of assistance that she might hint strongly that her daughter cut short a holiday and return home to the Manor House as soon as possible. On 4 November 1935, for instance, the Senator, who was then in Ottawa, wrote to St Louis, Missouri, advising her vacationing daughter that it was quite all right for her to be popular with their old St Andrews, New Brunswick friends, the McK. Jones, "but naturally, we want you home just as soon as you can be spared."[27]

Another indispensable member of the household was Betts, the butler. Cairine Wilson recognized just how valuable he was to her when she told the following story. She had planned (with Betts's assistance, of course,) a large dinner party to which the newly arrived Japanese ambassador had been invited. The latter, it was believed, was a widower who would be arriving unaccompanied. Great was the Senator's consternation, therefore, when Betts announced the arrival of the ambassador *and* his daughter. At the same time that he reported their arrival the butler gave Mrs Wilson a sign that she was not to worry. Knowing that the young aides de camp at Government House welcomed outside dinner invitations, he immediately phoned the Governor General's residence to request an extra male guest. No sooner was this done than a breathless aide arrived at the Manor House to take his seat at one of the two additional places that had been hurriedly set on Betts's order. The butler had reorganized all the seating arrangements without missing a single announcement.[28]

When Cairine Wilson was away from Ottawa, there was no place that she would rather be than Clibrig, the sprawling family estate located on the outskirts of the resort town of St Andrews, New Brunswick in Atlantic Canada. From her early twenties until the last year of her life, when two broken hips prevented her from leaving Ottawa, she spent most of every summer there, surrounded by members of her family and later by increasing numbers of grandchildren. Husband and wife both contributed to the upkeep of the Manor House, Norman using funds from his astutely managed investments for this purpose. Cairine, however, assumed full responsibility for Clibrig. It was considered her property.

As its name suggests, Clibrig (named after the highest mountain in Sutherlandshire, Ben Klibreck or Beinchlibrig, as it was sometimes written) has strong Scottish associations; in this case it was Cairine Wilson's Scottish-born father, Robert Mackay. The Montreal businessman and Canadian Pacific Railway Company director was persuaded to buy the property by the CPR's president, his good friend Sir William Van Horne. Sir William, who owned "Covenhoven" and the 500-acre island on which it stands, Minister's Island, not only sang the praises of St Andrews to his fellow CPR director, he also helped to arrange the purchase of the main parcel of land that makes up the Clibrig estate. This done, the railway magnate gave instructions as to where certain trees should be planted and, as a further token of his friendship for the Mackays, painted a landscape mural that was placed above the dining room fireplace in the main house.

The property on which the Mackay summer house was built comprised several parcels of land, the principal one being a 320-acre farm that the previous owner, Nathan Bleakney, had acquired in 1885 from his uncle, Sir Charles Tupper, a Father of Confederation and, for two months in 1896, Conservative prime minister of Canada. When the ailing and somewhat difficult Bleakney sold the estate to Cairine Mackay's father in 1905 it comprised an assortment of farm buildings and a picturesque stone house that had been erected in the late eighteenth century by Captain James of St Andrews. Having acquired this property and shore lots fronting on Chamcook Harbour, Robert Mackay proceeded to build his summer home atop a gentle hill that sloped in majestic style from its highest point down through woods and open fields to the harbour. From the rear of the house, which overlooked historic Passamaquoddy Bay, one could see nearby Minister's island and part of the huge Van Horne estate. Indeed, when the tide was out, the Mackay and Van Horne families could visit each other by driving across the floor of the bay. Only a few miles away, on rugged Campobello Island, were the summer homes of Franklin D. Roosevelt and his mother, Sara D. Roosevelt.

Robert Mackay's summer home was impressive with its spacious back verandah, half-timbered exterior and abundance of rich rubbed wood in the interior finishing. It was certainly large, having two bedrooms on the ground floor and nine on the second storey, four of which were servants' quarters. In the thirties, when it was owned by Cairine Wilson, it employed an indoor staff of seven, a chauffeur and three full-time gardeners. However, although it was large, it was probably no larger or more pretentious than other notable houses in the area, many of which were built by wealthy Canadians and Americans in that golden age between 1890 and 1914 when the upper classes spent fortunes fulfilling their wishes. Dubbed "Newport of the North," in the pre-World War Two years, St Andrews attracted wealthy visitors in search of bracing sea air and a congenial ambience. They found both in this quaint seaside town which had been settled originally by United Empire Loyalists from the nearby state of Maine. From a dour Scots-covenanting village it had grown into a shipbuilding town and then, when the building of schooners was abandoned, into the most exclusive summer resort in the Maritimes, with the Canadian Pacific Railway's famous Algonquin Hotel as its chief drawing card.

Senator Robert Mackay and his family became prominent members of the summer community and each year returned to relax and renew old friendships. Following her mother's death at St Andrews in 1912, Cairine Wilson packed up her children and journeyed every summer to Clibrig to supervise the running of the household for her widowed father. However, after his death, in 1916, it was her older sister, Anna Loring, who acquired the 420-acre estate. In 1918, when she was living in England, she purchased it from the Mackay estate for $60,000[29] and then rented the property to Cairine Wilson for one year. The following year, 1920, Anna Loring sold the north section of Clibrig to her sister, who then commissioned an architect to draw up plans for a large severe-looking house that looked as if it belonged on an estate in southern England. The grand design never materialized. In 1922, Anna's husband, Rob Loring, died suddenly and shortly thereafter his widow sold her 96-acre share of Clibrig to her sister for $100,000. As Anna explained in a letter to Cairine, "I estimate the cost of Clibrig has been to me approximately $114,884.84 plus various items not mentioned & so after deducting the $112,000.00 already paid by you to me, I think the price of $100,000.00 (one hundred thousand dollars) is a fair one."[30]

Now that the entire estate belonged to her, Cairine Wilson was free to introduce sweeping changes to Clibrig, but because of her abiding love of tradition she chose not to. Like her father before her, she retained the farm and the charming late eighteenth century stone house, which was then occupied by the farm manager. Major improvements were delayed until the mid-thirties when she built a colonial style white clapboard house for her daughter Janet's use and added some rooms to the top storey of the main residence.

The front entrance of Clibrig, the Wilson summer home at St. Andrews, New Brunswick. It was razed in 1972 to make way for a smaller, more functional house built for Cairine Wilson's daughter Cairine.

Cairine Wilson's love of Clibrig was born of many things, not least of which was a life-long devotion to the traditions of her family. In this respect she closely resembled her father. She also inherited a love of nature from the gruff, undemonstrative senator. Like the true Highland Scot that he was, Robert Mackay felt a kinship for the world of growing things, regarding the old elms of Kildonan, his Montreal home, as his friends; and his long walks on the top of Mount Royal as treasured opportunities to commune with nature. It was this fondess for nature that took him summer after summer to St. Andrews, where the sea air and the varied and rugged landscape reminded him of his native Caithness.[31] It was this same love that drew his daughter to St Andrews and Clibrig.

Cairine Wilson's love of nature expressed itself most visibly in her attachment to the farm at Clibrig and in a deep interest in flowers and gardening. The farm was a working farm run by a manager and three assistants. Its large vegetable and fruit gardens supplied most of the fresh produce used by the family and the staff while its hens furnished fresh eggs and its ten head of Jerseys abundant cream for the making of butter and hand-cranked ice cream.[32] When vacationing at St Andrews, the Senator left many decisions regarding the farm's day-to-day operations to Norman, who, of course, was a farmer by upbringing and training. During their summer sojourns there he habitually tramped out of the house at seven o'clock in the morning to consult with the farm manager. So, when her husband became incapacitated by illness, it was only natural that Cairine would try to find another member of the family to assume overall responsibility for this part of Clibrig. Her choice was her eldest son, Ralph, to whom she conveyed the farm in 1953 in the hope that he would maintain it as a viable operation. This he managed to do for almost three decades. Then economics caught up with the farm and in the 1980s, under his administration, it virtually ceased to operate.

Fortunately some of the beautiful flower beds survived, lovingly maintained by young Cairine, who inherited her mother's interest in gardening. One of the Senator's favourite pursuits at Clibrig was tending the flowers in the large beds that adorned the lawn on the east side of the main house, which was demolished in 1972. When Angus Wilson conjures up memories of his mother, one that comes most frequently to mind is that of her gardening very early in the morning in rubber boots at Clibrig, where the cool nights and heavy dews encourage plants to grow profusely and produce bright blossoms. Often she was teased about the quart-size oil cans that kept large bunches of flowers fresh while they were being transported to local churches, hospitals and friends' homes.

Cairine Wilson not only loved gardening, she was by all accounts knowledgeable about flowers and their cultivation. Early in the year it was her habit to prepare an order for flower and vegetable seeds, which she then gave to her secretary to type up and send on to the supplier. As soon as the order had been filled, the Senator dispatched a collection of seeds to Burt Gowan, Clibrig's head gardener for planting in the estate's greenhouse.

She invariably arranged most of the flowers for display in the house, much to the delight and edification of Margaret Doran, who used to visit the Wilson family at St Andrews as a friend of Olive.

> We used to start the day with family breakfast in the breakfast room off the main dining room. Then afterwards we would all go to the flower room to choose from an assortment of old rubbers. After we had donned them, we trouped out to the garden with scissors and baskets to cut flowers. The Senator always arranged some iris in a lovely clear glass bowl and decided where the other vases of flowers would be arranged in the living room. She knew every plant by its botanical name. I really enjoyed learning about flowers from her.[33]

When planning her garden at Clibrig the Senator would inundate young Cairine with instructions:

> I ordered from Ormiston Roy in Montreal, four peony roots for ourselves and two for Sara Childs [a close friend from Pittsburgh, Pennsylvania], who asked about them. I said at the time that I thought Ormiston Roy was the best and cheapest. Those for Sara Childs have been included with my order but Burt may pick them out from the numbers - 5 and 98. I selected these for the reason that they flower later. Burt will be able to plant them in her garden but, as you know, the ground will require fertilizing. Tell Burt I hope to send some good dahlia tubers from here as well as the Siberian Iris and two other varieties — as well as additional lythrum, some of which we could make good use around the pond.[34]

The Senator's fastidious attention to detail expressed itself not only in the hard slogging work that she did on behalf of refugees, but also, it seems, in the routine management of her homes in St. Andrews and Ottawa.

In 1984, over twenty years after Cairine Wilson's death, F. Earle Martin, president of Toronto's Cedarvale Tree and Landscape Services, recounted an anecdote that illustrates vividly both the Senator's love of her garden at Clibrig and the magic so often wrought by her quiet air of authority. Reported Mr Martin:

> Some of our men were working for one of our most cherished clients, Senator Cairine Wilson, at her residence in the charming setting of Rockcliffe when one day the Senator telephoned to our Toronto office and asked us not to bother mailing our men's weekly pay cheques to Ottawa because she had sent the whole crew off to attend to the trees at her summer home at St Andrews-by-the-Sea!

> Well now, you can imagine the flap around our office. There were several other clients in Ottawa waiting to have their trees looked after and now our fellows were a thousand miles away in New Brunswick! We had to send another crew to carry on and it was just as well that we did because we acquired other clients in St Andrews-by-the-Sea.[35]

Cairine Wilson also enjoyed sailing with Ralph, Angus and Robert on Ralph's boat, and games of golf. Norman adored the sport and seized every opportunity that he could to head off to the links at St Andrews. Rarely was he accompanied by his wife, for apparently she usually golfed with George Babbit, the manager of the local Bank of Nova Scotia. When the weather was obliging, Cairine Wilson also enjoyed nothing more than relaxing and sipping afternoon tea with a few friends on the verandah at Clibrig. Although she did not favour ladies' afternoon Bridge parties (especially in Ottawa), she did play the game in the evening after dinner. Indeed, at Clibrig, it was not unknown for the Senator to arrange evening Bridge parties of eight to ten tables. In her later years Bridge yielded to Scrabble. She became an avid fan of this word game, despite losing repeatedly to members of the family. "We could always beat her because she insisted on trying for big words," observed Janet Burns.[36]

Uninterrupted peace and quiet were rare commodities at Clibrig because when the Wilson children were growing up and later when grandchildren and their parents came to visit the house bulged with people and resounded with activity. When Margaret Doran made her first visit in the early thirties, the family booked an entire sleeping car for the trip and then packed it with family members, their friends and staff. While they were en route, other staff members, who had preceded them, feverishly readied the rambling Tudor-style house for the family's arrival. Later in the decade, Cairine and Norman Wilson, instead of shipping their touring car ahead, began driving down, taking two days to make the journey.

Nearly every summer that Margaret Doran visited St Andrews the entire Wilson household and their friends participated in a giant picnic held on a picturesque island in the Bay of Fundy. To reach their destination everybody crowded into a chartered fishing boat which could accommodate about sixty people. By general agreement the highlight of the St Andrews's social season was the mammoth garden party that the Wilsons staged each August for up to three hundred people, some of whom came from great distances to attend this special event. Unlike other functions held by the summer residents, this one included both summer visitors and townspeople: the grocer, the butcher, the bank manager, any local entrepreneur or businessman who came within the Wilson family orbit during the summer. It also included children, some of whom, like the Magee sisters from Montreal, sported outfits that had been made or purchased especially for this occasion.[37] While the youngsters cavorted on acres of lawn, their parents stood on the back terrace, exchanging gossip and savouring homemade ice cream and cakes to the background music of a three-piece orchestra hired from the Algonquin Hotel. Many of these same guests were among those invited earlier in the season to Sunday lunch at Clibrig, where adults ate in the main dining room and swarms of children lunched in their own dining room.

A regular feature of life at Clibrig when the children were growing up was private French lessons given by different school teachers. One such instructor was Swiss-born Madame Heime, a thick-set, frumpy woman with highly rouged cheeks. For one or two summers she loomed up almost daily, accompanied by her tall, lanky husband. She began the day by giving a French lesson to the Senator, then breakfasted with the children and their visiting friends. Those who made it to the morning meal early enough could escape her company and French instruction. But lunch was another matter. At this repast everybody had to speak French.

Then there was the Sunday visit to historic Greenock Presbyterian Church, whose graceful spire and white clapboard exterior remind one of so many old New England churches. Every Sunday morning at Clibrig the Wilsons and the children, plus assorted house guests, would drive in a convoy of cars down the long hill to St Andrews and then across town to the glistening white church with the carved bright green oak tree on its steeple. Installed in the family's mahogany box pew, located seven rows back from the pulpit, they would spend an hour or more sitting bolt upright on hard seats.

Cairine Wilson's association with Greenock Presbyterian Church was not limited to Sunday worship and financial support. She also purchased new window shutters, provided flowers from Clibrig's gardens for its services, and furnished items for its annual bazaar. She made some good friends among the church's congregation. One was Margaret Best, the daughter of a onetime minister of the church, Alexander Mahon, and wife of Charles (Charley) Best, the co-discoverer of insulin. The Bests were frequent visitors to Clibrig, where in 1937 they celebrated their thirteenth wedding anniversary. So close was the friendship, Cairine Wilson became the godmother of their son Charles, who later became a Conservative Member of Parliament. She also took an active interest in the senior Best's work, attending a luncheon arranged by him to spearhead the establishment of the Canadian Diabetic Association and contributing substantial funds to the Charles H. Best Institute of the University of Toronto.

From left to right: Dr. Charles H. Best (Charley), his wife Margaret, daughter-in-law Eileen Best holding grandson, and son Charles Best, Senator Wilson's godson.

Horne Russell, the portrait painter, was another visitor to Clibrig. After arriving in Canada from his native Scotland, Russell had gone to work for the Canadian Pacific Railway as a commercial artist. He then turned to painting fashionable Montreal society, which he even followed during the summer months to St Andrews and nearby St Stephen on the Bay of Fundy. Cairine Wilson's parents were among his patrons as was Cairine herself, who commissioned portraits of Janet, Olive, young Cairine, Ralph and Anna. When the one-time president of the Royal Canadian Academy was building his own summer home at St Andrews, he stayed at Clibrig. It was from here that a saddened Cairine Wilson wrote to Mackenzie King on 9 July 1933 reporting the death of her friend and then adding,..."I have spent every spare moment with Mrs Russell, who is wonderfully courageous and most unselfish."[38]

The Bests and the Horne Russells were among many well-known visitors who received hospitality at Clibrig. Among the instantly recognizable names in a guest book that still survives are those of Franklin Delano Roosevelt, who visited the Wilsons in August 1936, Alexander of Tunis, a visitor in August 1949, and the Bessboroughs. The Earl of Bessborough, who was the Governor General of Canada from 1931 to 1935, and his beautiful and charming wife, Roberte, were good friends of Cairine Wilson. The Senator attended the christening of their Canadian-born infant son in September 1931 and took great pride in seeing her beloved Angus serve as a page at the viceregal drawing room in February 1933. When the Bessboroughs visited St Andrews, as they did on several occasions, they invariably enjoyed Wilson hospitality. In July 1934, the viceregal couple and their eldest son, Lord Duncannon, paid an informal visit to the summer resort. While the Earl of Bessborough and his wife made the Governor General's private railway car their home, Lord Duncannon stayed with the Wilsons who also gave a dinner for his parents.

Other names from the guest book, if not quite so illustrious, nevertheless represent the cream of the Canadian establishment in pre-World War Two days: people like Lucile Pillow from the wealthy Montreal Pillow family; Senator Charles T. Ballantyne, a prosperous Montreal businessman who served in Sir Robert Borden's wartime cabinet; Elizabeth Maxwell, wife of the well-known Montreal architect, Edward Maxwell; Elwood Hosmer, the only son of Montreal multimillionaire Charles Rudolph Hosmer; Sidney C. Oland, from the Halifax brewing family; Marguerite Shaughnessy of the Montreal CPR family and a friend from Cairine Wilson's childhood; and Kate Reed who had the distinction of being one of the Square Mile's first career women by virtue of her job as interior decorator for the CPR hotels, managed by her husband Hayter Reed. Then there is Cairine Wilson's friend, handsome, American-born Henriette Davis, the divorced wife of Sir Mortimer Davis, the Jewish tobacco tycoon from Montreal; and, from the United States, such close friends as Sara Childs from Pittsburgh, Pennsylvania; Jura Hall, a widow from Berkeley, California; and the McKittrick Jones of St Louis, Missouri.

One name that does not appear in the guest book is that of Mackenzie King, who was the recipient of many invitations to visit Clibrig. He made at least one visit, in August 1932, during the depths of the Great Depression. After his return to Ottawa, the lonely bachelor wrote in his fine delicate hand:

> The egg cup will be a symbol of the cup of happiness flowing over, for it will ever recall one of the most delightful visits I have ever had anywhere anytime. I continue to think of the great charm of your home and its surroundings, of the dinner parties and receptions, of the delightful and distinguished people we met, and of the other incidents too numerous to mention, but each with some special feature of its own. Particularly will I recall with delight at all times the walks with Norman and yourself, and the glimpses of the young people. Home life and home scenes to a bachelor, have a charm it is impossible to express in words.[39]

Like so many other busy executives, Senator Wilson was not content to leave all her work at the office. It followed her to St Andrews, where mail was forwarded daily from the office and where she dictated replies to her private secretary, who usually stayed with the family in the main house. While at St Andrews, the Senator also seized the opportunity to visit other centres in the Maritimes to address groups of Liberal women and Women's Institutes meetings. Although born and bred a city woman, she had enormous respect for the women of rural Canada, particularly those enrolled in programs of the Women's Institutes, one of her favourite causes. On one speaking engagement, for example, she revealed her admiration in no uncertain terms when she observed:

> The women of rural Canada are perfectly wonderful. I want to know them better. Travelling through the various provinces, I have been particularly impressed by the interest they displayed in the programs of their Women's Institutes, which have done so much to educate them in politics and economics. They seemed to me more alert, more eager to learn, more vitally interested in the country's affairs than most of the women in our cities.[40]

Besides addressing women's groups, Cairine Wilson toured county fairs and, in St Andrews itself, attended graduation exercises at the Charlotte County Grammar School. She also made a practice of dispatching books from Ottawa to St Andrews for use by local schools, which owed many prizes and scholarships to her generosity. As well, she faithfully supplied fresh flowers and produce to all of the churches at St Andrews for their summer bazaars. Her generosity aside, it was invariably Greenock Presbyterian Church which emerged the winner in terms of gross sales, much to Norman Wilson's delight.

The Senator never spared herself, participating in local endeavours at St Andrews and other New Brunswick towns as earnestly as she involved herself in national or international projects. She became widely known throughout the province and when she died she was remembered with affection, gratitude and pride. Clibrig was more than just a place for her to enjoy nature and entertain large numbers of establishment figures. It provided a reason for this conscientious humanitarian to identify strongly with another Canadian province and a have-not province at that. And in as much as she could relax anywhere, Clibrig was the place where she could experience the greatest relief from outside pressures.

and superior age and knowledge. As far as groaning over the modern generation is concerned I am afraid I cannot subscribe to it. They have taken the law very much into their own hands in many matters, but they are also awakening to a sense of national responsibility which youth has never recognized before. There is always a period of instability following any war, and this one, due perhaps to the unusual prosperity which so quickly followed the post-war depression, has lasted longer than usual. But the pendulum is swinging back again, and I feel that it will swing farther than before. The girls of today who have not been too prudent in the desire to express their freedom from conventional bonds, will not, as the mothers of tomorrow, allow their daughters —or sons—the same liberty they demanded for themselves. I do not think of course that they should have had all the liberty they have demanded. Girls who are out late at night, especially if they must come home some distance by motor, should, I think, be chaperoned. Not that the girl and her companion cannot be trusted . . . but because the chaperone provides protection from any whisper against the young people which unchaperoned opportunity might start."

"Have you studied child psychology?" Mrs. Wilson was asked.

"No, I haven't," she replied smiling. "I've no doubt there is much that is valuable in it, but I have never had time to study modern psychology as applied to the child. I have been busy bringing up a large family on a sane psychology of my own, which is after all merely common sense. I would not myself wish to send very young children to what almost seems to be, in practice if not in intention, experimental schools. I would feel that both my child and myself were missing something very precious by being separated during those impressionable, years when affectionate, understanding and maternal guidance

are fundamentals in preparing the child for its direct contacts with life."

"Of course I do think that routine is very important, and that one cannot over-estimate the value of correct feeding. But those are matters of common sense and simple instruction, whereas intensive psychological study might seem, on first analysis to be rather like impaling baby re-actions on an experimental pin and tagging the resultant wriggles."

"As far as the physical condition of my children is concerned it has always been a matter of grave consideration, but I must confess that I haven't fussed about them. I never acquired the habit of taking any of them to a doctor —a child specialist—every month to be examined. When they have been ill with the usual maladies of childhood I have nursed them myself, with of course the help of the regular nurse-maid. The family doctor who brought several of them into the world, attended them in these illnesses, for I felt that he would understand them better perhaps than another doctor. If, of course, anything serious developed I would never hesitate to call in the best of expert help, but as for fussing about them, following rigidly laid down rules which penalised all the rest of the family . . . as for weighing them

before and after feedings and all that modern efficiency . . . I simply never have had time for it. I believe in making as few rules as possible, but in following those which are made."

"The cultural development of children is most interesting to watch, for no two will re-act similarly to the same environment. There is no doubt that surrounding a child with beauty will make some impression on the mind . . . but where one child will develop a keen and critical appreciation, another may merely assume that beauty is inevitable, and so accept it much as three meals a day are accepted."

Mrs. Wilson has entered the Senate of Canada as its first woman member without any idea of cutting a wide swathe and making sweeping revolutions in that august body.

"I'm not thoroughly convinced yet that I should have accepted the appointment," she said smiling, "I'm not sure that by being a Senator I can do as much or more than I could by being just Cairine MacKay Wilson and working, as I have now for nearly twenty years, without the obligations, the dignity . . . and of course the undoubted thrill, of my appointment to the Senate."

And this young woman who two years ago organized a gathering in Ottawa of Liberal women from all of Canada, and by her inspiration and sincerity and enthusiasm welded them together into the National Federation of Liberal Women; who for years headed the Ottawa Liberal Women's Club, was active in the Eastern Ontario Liberal Women's Association and who still finds time to act on numerous church and welfare committees, sighed softly . . . and then thrust out her chin a little . . . not belligerently at all, but as though she were facing, four - square with head up the new responsibility and honour which has been given her.

"You have asked me," she *(Continued on page 96)*

(Continued on page 96)

Hon. Cairine Reay Wilson

Angus MacKay Wilson

Robert Loring Wilson

¶ Here we see Canada's first woman senator with all but one of her eight children. To have been permitted to converse intimately with Senator Cairine MacKay Wilson in her office in the Parliament Buildings, Ottawa, was a privilege. To take tea with her in her home, meeting her husband and all of her children but Janet who is studying in Paris, was to be specially privileged in meeting Cairine Wilson, woman, wife, and mother in the setting which permits of no camouflage or artificiality—a real home. There is a delightful speech and camaraderie between the children and their parents and no one who has met them in their home and seen the happiness and love which is so evident there could possibly doubt the sincerity of Senator Wilson's belief that normalcy is the right of every child.

Janet Wilson

Norma Wilson

Anna Wilson

Olive Wilson

Corinne Wilson

The Senator with portraits of seven of her eight children.

7

GO IN PEACE TO LOVE
AND SERVE THE LORD

One of the dismissals given at the conclusion of the Anglican communion service in *The Book of Alternative Services* reads "Go in peace to love
and serve the Lord." It is not an injunction that guides very many of us in
this day and age, but it was certainly one that governed the life of Cairine
Wilson, who was above all else a devout Christian for whom Christian
doctrine and social action were utterly inseparable. Reared as she had been
in Scottish Presbyterianism, she believed deeply in personal responsibility
and the concept of stewardship, the conviction that individuals should use
their talents and money to benefit others. As an adult she worried
constantly about the conscientious sharing of her wealth and gifts, always
asking herself if she were truly doing enough to serve the needs of others.

Unlike a lot of children raised in homes where church attendance and
bible readings loom large in the life of the family, Cairine Wilson never
turned her back on formal Christianity. All her life she remained committed to her church and its works. By her own admission, hers was a simple
faith, but a steadfast one. When queried on this subject by the journalist
Norma Phillips Muir, the Senator replied, "I feel that there is no more
stabilizing influence in life, nothing that gives it a deeper and sweeter
significance than religion. I'm afraid my faith is very simple, but it is very
sure. It has always been a part of me." [1]

Simple as Cairine Wilson's faith was, however, it served the Senator
well throughout a crowded life that brought her into contact with a wide

variety of people and required her to brook a great deal of frustration in the pursuit of some of her objectives, especially those relating to the admission of refugees to Canada. In short, it was a faith that enabled her to look beyond the foibles and sins of men and institutions and develop an inner peace that was invaluable in times of vicissitude and struggle.

Cairine Wilson gave generously of her time and money to the Presbyterian church. As a senator she laid numerous cornerstones and addressed countless women's missionary society meetings, occasionally delivering some blunt reminders that her audiences did not want to hear. She did this on at least one occasion, 20 June 1948, when she pleaded for adequate salaries and pensions for Presbyterian ministers. The Senator made her pitch after confessing how horrified she had been to discover that the maximum stipend for members of the clergy was only $1,800 a year.[2] As an indication of how strongly she felt on this question, she willed $5,000.00 — no mean sum in 1959, when she made her will — to the Pension Fund of the Presbyterian Church in Canada.

In addition to addressing innumerable meetings and participating in church dedication services, the Senator wrote articles for the *Presbyterian Record* and took part in fund-raising campaigns, such as the April 1948 campaign on behalf of the Presbyterian Advance for Christ in the Toronto area. She also contributed to the upkeep of individual churches, one being St Andrew's, Cumberland, to which she donated a new organ.[3]

Not surprisingly, Cairine Wilson made the Presbyterian Church in Canada one of the chief beneficiaries of her will. Besides remembering its pension fund, she gave $5,000.00 to the Church to assist in the education of young women wanting to serve it in a fulltime capacity. She also left cash legacies to: St Andrew's Presbyterian Homes Incorporated; the Presbyterian College in Montreal, which her great-uncle Joseph Mackay had helped to establish; Greenock Presbyterian Church in St Andrews, New Brunswick; the Women's Missionary Society of the Presbyterian Church in Canada; and the Women's Guild of St Andrew's Church, Ottawa.[4]

It is no small irony that the Senator found herself towards the end of her life supporting one of the parties responsible for an ugly controversy that had decidedly unchristian overtones. It is equally ironic that this crisis embroiled the church where she and her family worshipped when in Ottawa, St Andrew's.

St Andrew's, at the corner of Kent and Wellington Streets, has the distinction of being the oldest Presbyterian church in the nation's capital. In the 1930s and 1940s, it was also closely identified with Ottawa's wealthy and powerful families. On its communion rolls could be found such illustrious names as Booth, Bronson, Toller, Fleck and Chrysler. At one time or another the rolls had also contained the names of prominent political figures, such as Sir Sanford Fleming and the Hon. Frank Oliver.[5] Before he died in 1940, in Ottawa, Lord Tweedsmuir, the Governor General, worshipped there. Mackenzie King was a faithful member until his death in 1950. In fact, King played a key role in engaging The Rev. Dr Ian Burnett, the minister who was at the root of the controversy that split St Andrew's' congregation and opened wounds that have yet to be staunched.[6]

Andrew Ian Burnett, who became a good friend of Cairine Wilson, emigrated from Scotland to Canada in 1943 because of a shortage of ministers in this country. The son of the manse, he had graduated from the University of Edinburgh and had been ordained in 1931. When he was inducted into St Andrew's, in June 1943, he came highly recommended by two eminent Scottish clergymen who had lauded his "preaching and organizing ability and his successful work with boys and young people."[7] Before long the new incumbent was impressing members of the congregation with his writing talents and his sermons, which, in the words of one partisan "lifted you right out of your seat." Among his many devoted admirers was Cairine Wilson, who in a letter to her friend, Mackenzie King, in 1950, reported, "Norman and I attended the service for Mrs Leathem [the widow of a former minister of St Andrew's and a friend of Cairine Wilson] this afternoon and once more I was impressed by the simplicity and beauty of Mr Burnett's prayers."[8]

Despite his many gifts, however, Dr Burnett succeeded in antagonizing powerful members of the congregation. When Mrs Burnett left her husband in 1958, these dissidents used the marriage breakdown as an excuse to mount an all-out attack against him, citing the church teaching that a man who cannot keep order in his own house cannot be expected to keep order in his church. The ferocious struggle that ensued split the congregation into two factions: the Ianites (so called because they supported their minister) and the Agnesites, who rallied to the side of Mrs Burnett. In an effort to resolve the crisis, Dr Burnett tendered his resignation in 1959. However, the Ottawa presbytery refused to accept it. And so the dissension continued into 1960 until finally the inevitable happened: In the fall of 1960, the presbytery ordered the dissolution of Ian Burnett's pastoral tie with St Andrew's, effective 1 October 1960.

His dismissal was a bitter blow to Cairine Wilson, but unlike many other supporters of Ian Burnett, she did not leave St Andrew's. It was her church and despite all that had happened she could not sever her ties with it. She also continued her friendship with Dr Burnett and made a substantial contribution to the annuity that St Andrew's established for him. Ironically Dr Burnett would die almost ten years to the day after Cairine Wilson's death.

Fortunately high drama of this sort did not characterize other organizations with which the Senator was closely associated. Which is just as well, because she was involved with a plethora of institutions and committees during her lifetime. A militant Christian, Cairine Wilson dedicated much of her life to causes that benefited mankind. Not for her a faith that focussed almost exclusively on the believer's relationship with God and personal salvation. In her view Christianity should be not only an integral part of one's day to day existence but a powerful force in the fight for social justice and a better world.

The Senator's dedication to perceived duty, her compassion and her earnestness meant that her involvement in community and national organizations rarely took the form of tokenism. Usually she was an active participant who gave freely of her time and her money.

Senator T.A. Crerar, when paying tribute in the Senate to Cairine Wilson after her death observed:

> Senator Wilson was not a great intellectual, and I think that she was the better for that. People with strong intellects often lack imagination and sympathy. Her qualities were the qualities of the heart and I would remind honourable senators that in the Book of Proverbs, where great wisdom is distilled, there appear these words: "Keep thy heart with all diligence, for out of it are the issues of life."

> And that was essentially true of Cairine Wilson: gentle, honourable, courageous and sympathetic. Her heart went out to every good cause: it throbbed for everyone in trouble or distress, and she gave not only of her time but of her substance to try to remedy as far as lay within her power the injustice and the wrongs of a long-suffering world.[9]

The onetime cabinet minister certainly did not err in describing Cairine Wilson as a great humanitarian. As the member of King's cabinet most directly concerned with immigration and refugees, he had seen first hand how indefatigably the Senator had worked on behalf of the cause closest to her heart, refugees. He was also quite correct in saying that she was not a great intellectual. However, Senator Crerar ignored the fact that his late colleague had a good intellect and political acumen of a high order. These assets, coupled with her amazing organizing abilities and her tremendous energy, might have propelled her into a career if she had been reared in a different age and in different circumstances. Indeed, she probably would have carved out a brilliant career for herself as a business-woman given her outstanding aptitude for finance and organization, skills that were conspicuously evident in the keen interest that she took in her own investments and in her astute handling of money generally. Born as she was into a wealthy Montreal family in the late nineteenth century, however, Cairine Wilson could never quite shake off the conventions that governed her exclusive social circle. So as an adult she channelled her energies and talents into a multitude of "good works," goaded by a deep compassion, the social gospel and a need to prove herself.

These causes were so numerous that it would be next to impossible to name them all. Still, there are some that merit special mention because they absorbed a lot of her time or because they help to illustrate the wide range of her interests. One of these was the Mackay Institute, which figured prominently in the lives of several Montreal Mackays over the years. A life governor, Cairine Wilson followed the affairs of the privately-run institution in great detail, especially after she was appointed to the board of managers in the 1930s. Despite all the demands competing for her attention she would correspond regularly with the principal, advising on improvements required to the aging buildings and, where necessary, authorizing expenditures.[10]

The Senator's involvement in the family-dominated institution was not only an advisory one. In addition to advice and time, she gave generously of her money. She and her sister Anna Loring, for instance, purchased the residence occupied by the principal and then, in 1951, deeded it to the school. Cairine Wilson also contributed to the school's running expenses and made the Institute one of the principal beneficiaries of her will. Even with the tight rein that she attempted to keep on school renovations, though, she must have had many an occasion for misgiving, for sister Anna, who was president of the institution from 1935 until 1950, had extravagant ideas about how things should be done. This led her into conflict with her brother Edward Mackay, who was also on the board, and helped to embitter relations between them and make things difficult for her sister Cairine. Fortunately the school was rescued from its precarious financial situation by a merger with the School for Crippled Children in 1960. The resulting institution, the Mackay Centre for Deaf and Crippled Children, preserved the Mackay name, but the merger never received Anna Loring's blessing. Cairine Wilson, on the other hand, welcomed it.

Mrs Wilson's association with the Mackay Institute led to her involvement with the Ontario Association of the Deaf. She provided valuable assistance to this organization by serving as honorary campaign chairman of its scholarship appeal in the late 1940s and spearheading the drive itself with a donation of $1,000.00.[11]

Cairine Wilson's affiliation with The Victorian Order of Nurses and the Ottawa Young Women's Christian Association stemmed naturally from her great interest in the well-being of women and children and in health matters generally. She was introduced to the work of the VON by her genial friend Senator George P. Graham, who was president of the organization from 1927-1938. While a member of the VON's national board in the 1930s Cairine Wilson chaired a development and expansion committee that vigorously publicized the work and aims of the order. When its functions were taken over by the Education And Publicity Committee, she chaired that committee. To assist the VON's publicity campaign, she financed the production of a 35-mm film, "The Little Black Bag," which was shown in commercial cinemas across Canada in 1937 and 1938.[12] No doubt because of her significant contributions, she was elected a vice-president of the VON in 1944.

A life member and honorary president of the Ottawa Young Women's Christian Association, the Senator participated in the 1955 drive to raise funds for improvements to the local YWCA building. Five years later she wrote to various Ottawans regarding the proposed amalgamation of the local YWCA and YMCA and the option secured on the Auditorium property, which later became the location of a new Y building. As she so often did to assist worthwhile causes, she provided the grounds of the Manor House for YWCA functions. One of these was a large garden party staged in June 1948 in aid of the World Reconstruction Fund of the YWCA.

Although not one of the founders of the Ottawa Neighbourhood Services in 1932, Cairine Wilson took a keen interest in the work of this private welfare agency, which was established in the depths of the Depression to meet the emergency clothing and footwear needs of Ottawa families on relief at that time. She faithfully attended its annual meetings and often supplied good ideas. At the time of her death she was its honorary president.

Much greater demands were made on her time by Ottawa's Shernfold School, located on Bronson Avenue in the old Erskine Bronson home and run by the Sisters of St John the Divine, an Anglican order. The first of its kind in Canada, the residential school was established in 1927 under the auspices of the Canadian Welfare Council to provide training and care for mentally retarded girls. Cairine Wilson, who became an honorary president, was on the original board of directors, which also included those Liberal powerhouses, Mrs Charles Thorburn and Senator Andrew Haydon. Another board member was the Wilsons' friend Ken Greene.[13] The Senator continued her involvement with the School right up until its closure in 1947.

Mrs Wilson was also associated with the Canadian Welfare Council which she served from 1930 onwards. She sat on the board of Canada's major national child welfare agency from 1943 until 1947, when she became an honorary vice-president. In May 1961, in appreciation of her faithful support of the Council's aims and work, the President conferred a Council life membership on the Senator.[14]

Senator Wilson's participation in national and community organizations even extended to membership on a committee that selected and presented gifts to the wives of departing governors-general. The Senator mentioned such a presentation in a letter to Mary Craig McGeachy, who was then working for the league of Nation's secretariat in Geneva. In her missive, dated 23 March 1940, Cairine Wilson reports that the previous day she, Mme Lapointe, Mrs Gardiner, Miss Duff (Sir Lyman Duff's sister), and Mrs Lawrence Freiman had gathered at Government House to present a mink coat from the women of Canada to Lady Tweedsmuir, the widow of the recently deceased governor general.[15]

Committees and organizations with an international orientation also made claims on the Senator's time. The most conspicuous of these was the Canadian-American Women's Committee, which had its genesis in a New York conference staged by the American Federation of Women's Clubs and other women's organizations in November 1941. Cairine Wilson attended that conference as one of a handful of prominent Canadians invited to participate. Like her Canadian colleagues, she had been asked to inform the conference about the role that Canadian women were playing in the war effort. For their American sisters were convinced that their country would soon be entering the conflict and they were eager to establish what contributions they could make to the Allied cause.

Once back in Ottawa the Senator spearheaded the establishment of a committee that would develop closer links between Canadian and American women. The springboard was a conference of delegates from American and Canadian women's organizations held in the nation's capital in May 1942. Cairine Wilson assumed the chairmanship of the resulting Ottawa-based committee, known initially as the Canadian-American Women's Committee on International Relations. That October the American section was formed in New York under the chairmanship of dynamic May Hall James, an academic whose career included the chairmanship of the Division of Liberal Arts, Quinnipiac College, Hamden, Connecticut.

Although autonomous, the two sections worked closely to further mutual appreciation and cooperation between Canadians and Americans by increasing the information flow between Canada and the United States. In pursuit of their objectives, they arranged educational conferences, field study trips for women college students and teachers, exchanges of children's art, lecture tours, Canadian film showings in the United States and student exchanges between Smith College, the prestigious American women's college, and the University of Toronto. Cairine Wilson's pride in her Scottish ancestry is no more evident than in her reference in a letter to some of these fortunate exchange students. Writing to her daughter Cairine in 1945, for example, she said: "Yesterday I entertained the two girls who are to go to Smith at lunch and have just now had a call from the candidate who is going from Brampton and I think three at least have good Scotch names."[16]

As chairman of the Ottawa committee, Cairine Wilson recruited local women who figured prominently in women's organizations, held conference dinners at the Manor House, contacted senior Canadian officials to give talks and kept up a steady stream of correspondence with the forceful Dr James. Because she was large in stature and dominant in personality, the American chairman may have caused Cairine Wilson to feel "pushed" at times, as Dorothy Bishop, the secretary of the Canadian section, has expressed it. However, the Senator never let this interfere with her determination to improve channels of communication between Americans and Canadians. In any event, the two women appear to have been good friends during the course of their twenty-year partnership.[17].

Cairine Wilson's association with the Unitarian Service Committee of Canada began with its founding in 1945. The Senator's involvement with this relief agency was almost foreordained given her friendship with its Czechoslovakian-born executive director Dr Lotta Hitschmanova. (This is the legendary figure whom Charlotte Whitton, the onetime pugnacious mayor of Ottawa, once informed, "You are the one woman I know with more energy than I myself burn!") When asked by her friend Lotta Hitschmanova to become honorary chairman of the USC Ottawa committee in June 1945, the Senator accepted immediately.[18] That August the Executive Director received a certificate of registration for "the Unitarian Service Committee of Canada Fund," which permitted it to operate for one year. According to the terms of the certificate, however, fund-raising activities were limited to members and supporters. By using her influence and submitting details of the Committee's foster parent scheme and the thousands of dollars worth of medical supplies that it had shipped to Europe, Cairine Wilson managed to get the restrictions lifted in February 1946. Henceforth the Committee was able to raise funds from the general public as well as from its Unitarian supporters.[19] As this achievement demonstrates, Cairine Wilson could play an invaluable role in smoothing the passage of various applications through the government buraucracy. It was a task that she often assumed but she did not always produce the desired results.

The prodigious amount of work that Mrs Wilson performed for these voluntary organizations and the large sums of money that she gave to worthwhile causes alone entitle her to the label "great humanitarian." But her humanitarianism also found expression in the positions that she adopted as a senator on social questions and in the work that she did for two very special organizations: the League of Nations Society in Canada and the Canadian National Committee on Refugees.

8

CITIZEN OF THE WORLD

It was almost inevitable, given her strong streak of idealism and humanitarian interests, that Cairine Wilson would take up the cause of the League of Nations. And so she did. In the early 1930s she joined the League of Nations Society in Canada. She mounted the public platform on behalf of the world body and by 1933 had become so involved in the Society's work that she was appointed to its national council and executive committee.[1] Four years later her leadership qualities, celebrity status and tireless promotion of the League propelled her into the presidency. In an organization whose executive ranks were packed with men (Two notable exceptions were Agnes Macphail, the first woman to become a Canadian MP, and Isabel Armstrong, the journalist, who were members of the executive committee in 1934) she became the Society's first and only woman president.

Cairine Wilson became an apostle for the League because she believed fervently that the world body represented the best hope for peace and order in a troubled world. Indeed, like other Canadian internationalists, she felt that its machinery offered the only hope for preventing another world conflagration such as World War I, which had seen the world's leading nations almost exhaust their resources in the work of slaughter and destruction.

In 1914, when Mrs Wilson was raising a young family in the Ontario mill town of Rockland, Canadian soldiers had gone off to the war with a light heart and an easy step. In the long line-ups outside recruiting stations some of these men had even worried that hostilities might be over before they could see action. The shelling, the gas, and the indescribable mud and squalor of trench warfare on the blood-soaked Western front soon drove reality home. Before it was all over, some 60,000 Canadians would be killed and 138,000 wounded, proportionately far more casualties than this country incurred in World War II[2]. Included in this toll were many of Canada's finest and most talented young men, some of whom Cairine Wilson probably knew personally.

When the world was still reeling from this greatest of human tragedies, the League of Nations came into being. It was founded in 1920, to promote international co-operation and to prevent future wars by establishing open, just and honourable relations between nations. Although its Assembly attracted most of the public's attention, much of the world body's day- to-day work was conducted by the permanent Secretariat or commissions. These were nominated under the League to investigate and control international evils such as the traffic in narcotics, to promote intellectual co-operation, to abolish slavery, to protect minorities and to curb the spread of malaria, typhoid, and tropical diseases. Because of her humanitarian outlook and longtime involvement with women's and chidren's issues, Cairine Wilson would take a special interest in the work of the Health Organization and those bodies that dealt with more strictly humanitarian affairs — the control of the drug traffic, the protection of women, child welfare, the refugee problem and the abolition of slavery.

The Canadian society was a national volunteer organization with headquarters in Ottawa. Among the public figures instrumental in launching it in 1921 were noted Liberal Newton Wesley Rowell and Sir Robert Borden, both of whom were committed to organizing Canadian public opinion in favour of the League and the "new diplomacy." The Society's aims, therefore, became primarily educational as it strove to make Canadians aware of the horrors of war and the dangers inherent in the old system of diplomacy.

Many of the Society's major figures were friends of the Senator such as Ernest Lapointe, who was elected president of the organization in 1933 and who may have played a key role in interesting Cairine Wilson in the Society; Raoul Dandurand, who was the first Dominion delegate to be president of the League Assembly and later Liberal leader in the Senate when Cairine Wilson was elevated to the Red Chamber; and Agnes Macphail. She had first-hand experience with the League, having been the first Canadian woman to attend a League of Nations conference as a delegate.

To carry out its mission, the Society established branches in cities across Canada and obtained corporate memberships from many national organizations, including the Imperial Order Daughters of the Empire, service clubs, the National Council of Women and the Canadian Legion. It became the agent for the League's publications in Canada, published an impressive quarterly, *Interdependence*, and organized lecture tours for experts on the League as well as national radio broadcasts and conferences on League issues. But as Senator Wilson and her colleagues in the Society were to discover, persuading Canadians and their government to support the kind of world body that could enforce world peace was asking the impossible. Because of their geographical isolation from Europe and Asia, Canadians could not see how the League could protect them from military aggression. As for the Canadian government, it viewed the League as a European instrument controlled by Europeans and used (if used at all) to serve a European need for collective security.

What Canada favoured was a league that promoted co-operation in economic, social and health questions, and arbitration and conciliation in the peaceful settlement of disputes. Cairine Wilson lauded these aims too, but, unlike King and most other Canadians, she also subscibed whole-heartedly to the concept of collective security. Only if the League's members united to oppose aggression, she believed, could peace become a reality. It was a conviction that she would defend stoutly in the years to come, so vigorously, in fact, that, in 1938, she would risk her reputation by publicly denouncing the Liberal government's approval of the Munich Agreement. Before taking that brave stand, though, she would devote a good deal of time and energy to a much less controversial undertaking: pleading for a study of the League's work and accomplishments.

Typical of the addresses that she gave on this theme was one that she delivered on 25 November 1931 to the Women's Canadian Club in London, Ontario. She began with a survey of the life of Florence Nightingale and followed this with a description of the League's Health Organization. Next came a review of the world body's attempts to crush the international opium traffic and its efforts to rescue women and children who had been forcibly deported to the interior of Asia Minor during the hostilities that accompanied the break-up of the Ottoman Empire. In closing, she urged her listeners and women across Canada to study the League's work and achievements. Then she observed:

> ... we cannot change the customs and habits which have endured for thousands of years in a moment. The league represents a step towards the ideal, and with our encouragement should accomplish much in the future.

> I well remember the words of a medical friend of mine as he looked at our first baby. With the usual maternal pride, I thought such a child had never been born, but gazing pityingly down he murmured, "The higher the species the slower the development."[3]

This homespun vignette with its snippet of dry humour was entirely in character with Cairine Wilson. Life might be serious and speeches might be weighted with significance, but this did not mean that there was no time for gentle self-mockery and Aristotelian wit.

The Senator lost no opportunity to lobby for the League cause, which needed all the support that it could get during the cash-starved Depression years when governments were cutting down on their international commitments. Whether her audience was a rally of Liberal women, a women's service organization or members of a social workers' club, she tried, if at all possible, to interject a word about the world body and its achievements, especially those in the health and humanitarian fields. Probably her most distinguished audience was to be found in the Red Chamber itself, where, on 17 November 1932, she moved the following resolution:

> Resolved, that in the opinion of the Senate there should be no curtailment or interruption in the continuity of the work of the League of Nations dealing with social and humanitarian questions and particularly with that section which relates to the opium traffic, the traffic in women and children, and child welfare.[4]

Cairine Wilson informed her male colleagues that she had made the resolution in response to a request that she had received from the head office secretary of a large international women's organization based in Geneva. Just who this person was she did not say, but we can be sure that it was someone who was familiar with the Senator's longstanding involvement with women's and children's issues and did not wish to see Canada curtail its contributions to this valuable League work at a time when many other member states were in arrears in theirs.

After moving her resolution, Cairine Wilson went to considerable pains to enlighten her fellow senators about the League's attempts to combat a scourge that still defies concerted attempts to crush it: the international drug trade. When she spoke on this theme, it was with the alarming knowledge that in 1919, on a per capita basis, Canada actually led the world in illicit drug trafficking[5]. Fortunately, the Senator could report that this country, in an effort to curtail the trade, had strengthened its Narcotics Act and assigned its administration to a newly created department of health. Still later, Canada had attended League-sponsored conferences in Geneva and signed conventions limiting and controlling the manufacture of narcotics.

No sooner had she finished speaking to her resolution than the debate was adjourned. When it resumed less than a week later, J.H. King, a senator from East Kootenay, B.C., made a vigorous defence of the

League's efforts to curb the illegal drug traffic. He was soon followed, however, by an Edmonton senator, who was less than enthusiastic about Cairine Wilson's resolution: W.A. Griesbach, the one-time "Boy Mayor of Edmonton." Senator Griesbach observed:

> If this resolution had been drawn in such a way as to show the activities of the League of Nations in the order of the importance that we attribute to them, thus giving social and humanitarian questions, the opium traffic and the traffic in women and children a relative place in the list, I should have been glad to support it. But we are asked to deal with one subject to the exclusion of all others, and to assert that there should be no curtailment or interruption in this work. The League of Nations has many important tasks before it at the present time, and, for the reason that I have already mentioned, it has a limited income; consequently, I gravely question the wisdom of the Senate solemnly asserting that in its opinion this matter is paramount in importance to all the other activities of the League of Nations. I think that at this distance we should be well advised to let the League of Nations decide for itself what are the important questions to be dealt with, and what place this particular question should occupy on its agenda.[6]

He was followed by Senator Wilson's friend, Raoul Dandurand, who hastened to remind his listeners that "The women of nearly all countries have been very much interested in social and humanitarian problems, and I commend the action of the honourable member from Rockcliffe in drawing our attention to the importance of the work carried on in this field.[7] Finally, in summing up, he opined, "While I recognize that dealing with humanitarian problems is but a part of the important work carried on by the League, I do not think there is any harm in expressing the opinion that the activities of the League in that direction should not be curtailed."[8]

To Cairine Wilson's great relief, the resolution was adopted the next day, 24 November. She had not spoken in vain. Canada would maintain her existing level of support for the League's humanitarian work. Nor did the Senator speak in vain on 16 May 1934 when she rose once again in the red and gold Senate chamber to make a passionate defense of the League of Nations and to castigate war. She did so against a background of mounting world tension brought on by the Great Depression and the repeated failure of the dwindling free world and the League of Nations to respond adequately to threats to world peace. Fresh in everybody's mind was the failure of a League-sponsored disarmament conference to adopt any broad or constructive measures and Germany's withdrawal from the conference and the League itself in 1933. Even more ominous had been the Manchurian crisis, which had erupted in 1931 with the establishment of a Japanese puppet state in the Chinese province. The League of Nations sent a commission to investigate and then recommended that Manchuria be returned to Chinese control and that Japan enjoy economic privileges. Japan, however, did not regard this as a satisfactory solution and in March 1933 formally withdrew from the League.

It was now patently obvious that a great power might defy the League with impunity. With the world situation deteriorating rapidly, Cairine Wilson began to fear that many Canadians, who had begun to take an interest in foreign policy and disarmament, would rejoin the apathetic majority or, worse still, would swell the ranks of the League's critics. One of these was the noted isolationist, Senator A.D. McRae, who had been a brigadier-general in the First World War. On 1 February 1934, he informed his Senate colleagues:

> We are a small nation — ten and a half million people — to be taking part in this European embroglio. We are far from the continent of Europe. With the certainty of war before us, I want to call the attention of this honourable House and of the country to the opportunity that we have at this time to withdraw with honour from the League of Nations — an opportunity which subsequent developments many not afford.[9]

Some six weeks later, after giving due warning, he moved that the Senate express the opinion that Canada should withdraw from the League of Nations and cut off further funds to the world body. Debate on this motion raged intermittently in the Senate for over a month. When her turn came to refute the isolationists' arguments — on 16 May 1934 — Cairine Wilson prefaced her remarks with the two-edged observation that "were it not for the interpretation given by Germany to the motion of the honourable senator from Vancouver concerning the withdrawal of Canada from the League of Nations, the members of the Senate would have every reason to be grateful to the honourable gentleman for he has given us the opportunity of listening to many able opinions on the subject."[10] She then proceeded to demolish Senator Griesbach's assertion that the League of Nations Society in Canada had fallen largely into the hands of pacifists and to attack Senator Black's contention that war was now carried on in a more humane manner. Drawing on her experience as a woman, the Senator said:

> For the wife or mother who loses a son or husband, it makes little difference that 99 percent are saved if the one in whom she is vitally interested loses his life or returns home a helpless cripple. That war is carried on in a more humane fashion, however, was effectively disproved yesterday by the honourable senator from Montarville, for he gave a most vivid description of the slaughter and devastation in the late world conflict. It is not necessary for me to enlarge upon this.

> ...We have to learn different habits as individuals. Can we not as nations be reasonable?[11]

The Senator also dwelt on the international arms trade and pronounced herself firmly on the side of those who advocated a world-wide ban on the manufacture and sale of armaments. Then she returned to a theme close to her heart: the League's achievements in the health and humanitarian fields.

On 31 May, Senator McRae's motion was defeated, or, as the *Senate Debates* so quaintly phrase it, "negatived." Cairine Wilson could take comfort in the fact that her passionate attack on war and her stout defense of the League had probably played a role in this defeat.

Promoting the League of Nations from the public platform demanded far less of Cairine Wilson's time, energy and political acumen than helping to guide the affairs of its Canadian lobby, the League of Nations Society in Canada. Like so many national volunteer organizations, it was plagued by difficulties in recruiting new members and beset by financial problems, all of which were exacerbated by the Great Depression and the League of Nations's diminishing stature. It was also handicapped by disaffection in the regions with the way things were done at headquarters in Ottawa and by strong differences among the membership with regard to policy. To further complicate matters when Cairine Wilson was at the helm, some of its objectives were covertly torpedoed by her friend Mackenzie King, himself an honorary president of the organization.

The Senator's work with the Society would take her often to its national office, which, after several moves, finally found a permanent home at 124 Wellington Street. The grey-stone building, in which the Society rented a suite of dark rooms on the second floor, was just a short distance away from the Senator's office: almost directly opposite the West Block and close to the celebrated Rideau Club, for close to three-quarters of a century the elysium of Ottawa's top professional men, civil servants and businessmen and a favourite luncheon haunt of Norman Wilson. At one time it had housed a bank, but when Cairine Wilson frequented it, it had been turned over to offices and to at least one apartment, that of the journalist Charlie Clay, an active member of the Society whom the Senator befriended and assisted in small ways.[12]

In these dingy quarters, the Senator met frequently with key players in the organization, chief of whom were Dr Henry Marshall Tory, the noted educator and scientist, who had been with the Society since its inception, and Robert Inch, a one-time journalist. When Cairine Wilson became president of the Society, the three would form a de facto triumverate, with Dr Tory the "elder statesman." One astute observer who often had occasion to watch the three in action was Dr John Robbins, who worked for the Society's International Literature Service in the 1930s. According to this distinguished educator and humanitarian Dr Tory thought very highly of Senator Wilson, and she in turn often deferred to him. However, even if she frequently submitted to his views, Cairine Wilson still had decided opinions of her own. Robbins has also recalled that the Senator never spoke in a forceful way and that even after she became president of the Society she never tried to dominate proceedings. Some fifty years later John Robbins also had nostalgic memories of the time that Cairine Wilson invited him to lunch with her in the Parliamentary Restaurant in order to discuss some items of Society business. The young father was babysitting a two-year-old son at the time, but the Senator, not the least bit apprehensive, said, "Bring him along." The child gave her a lively time, but in characteristic fashion she maintained her composure and did not become ruffled.[13]

The other member of the triumverate, Robert Inch, also had great respect for the Senator. He had been Dr Tory's secretary at the National Research Council when Tory was president of the federal agency. Introduced to the League of Nations Society in Canada by Tory, he soon became the hardworking editor of the organization's magazine *Interdependence*. From there he went on, in 1935, to become the Society's paid national secretary, a position that he filled until his resignation in 1942. To those who knew him well, Bob Inch had two outstanding characteristics. The first, which was surprising in so mild-mannered a man, was his courage. This, allied with his deep conviction, often led him to urge his strong views about the role of the organization on those who disagreed with him, be they a reluctant government or members of the Society itself.

Equally important was Inch's dedication. When he believed in something, such as a peaceful world order, Bob Inch translated this belief into an almost fanatical commitment. As a member of the League of Nations Society in Canada he poured his life into the cause and often, in the process, adopted an aggressive and combative course that alienated other Society members and made things very difficult for himself and his colleagues.

This was the Bob Inch that Cairine Wilson came to know well after he left the volunteer ranks to become the paid national secretary: an utterly selfless worker for the League, but one who courted mounting criticism because of his freewheeling tactics. Fortunately she and Inch shared similar views on most issues. First and foremost was the belief that the Society should adopt a strong stance vis-a-vis the principle of collective security. It was a position fraught with danger for the Society as both discovered in 1935 just after Inch had been appointed to his new post and when Senator Wilson was an honorary vice-president of the organization and a member of its national council.

National Research Council Archives

Dr Henry Marshall Tory, 1933.

Collective security and the Society's position on it were burning issues in the summer of 1935 when it became all too evident that Italy was bent on aggression in Ethiopia. Debate became even more heated when Italian troops invaded the African kingdom on 3 October and the Canadian government was forced to take a stand on economic and military sanctions against the aggressor. At first it appeared that the Conservative government of the day might be prepared to endorse a wide-ranging list of sanctions. R. B. Bennett, the Prime Minister, had earlier authorized the Canadian delegate in Geneva, Howard Ferguson, to promise that "Canada would join with other members of the League in considering how, by unanimous action, peace can be maintained."[14] In doing so, Bennett had overridden the strong objections of the Under-Secretary of External Affairs, O.D. Skelton, who was vehemently opposed to the imposition of sanctions, claiming that they had little public support and might lead to a general war or at least conflict with the United States which, as a non-member of the League, would continue trading with Italy anyway. While Bennett was at the helm, Skelton's advice on sanctions was ignored and Howard Ferguson was unleashed to act at his own discretion. This resulted in Canada's accepting membership on the Committee of Eighteen, where it was determined what sanctions should be levied against Italy and where Canada proposed an immediate embargo on munitions' shipments. Shortly thereafter, however, the Bennett government went down to defeat in the October 1935 federal election and Mackenzie King and the Liberals were returned to power. With King once more prime minister, Skelton reasserted himself with renewed vigor.

Before Skelton could make his influence felt, though, Howard Ferguson resigned, to be replaced by another Canadian representative who shared Ferguson's thinking on sanctions, Dr W.A. Riddell. Riddell was deeply committed to the principle of collective security and he exploited the hiatus between the old and new governments to press, with French concurrence, for additions to the list of embargoed exports to Italy. In the absence of fresh instructions from Ottawa, he moved in the Committee of Eighteen to add oil to the proposed list of embargoed products and thereby make economic sanctions a truly effective weapon. This bold proposal was quickly endorsed by the Committee and then submitted to the Assembly for its approval, but not before triggering a violent reaction in Rome, which declared that oil sanctions meant war. In Canada, news of these developments set off a vigorous controversy and King became alarmed. A month later, on 2 December, the Government sternly rebuked Riddell with the statement that he "represented only his own personal opinion ... and not the views of the Canadian government."[15] When questioned later by journalists, King replied that his policy was essentially that of sanctions if necessary but not necessarily sanctions. This specious argument was not lost on Europe, however, which saw it for what it really was: an abandonment of the policy of collective security. In November the League did institute economic sanctions against Italy, but they were far from comprehensive and Mussolini's troops continued to advance in Ethiopia. The following May the King of Italy was proclaimed Emperor of Ethiopia.

The confrontation between Italy and Ethiopia had assumed crisis proportions by the time that Inch took up his new position as national secretary in June 1935 and in characteristic fashion he acted quickly to move the Society further into the arena of public debate by forcing the Government's hand on the sanctions issue. That August, acting on behalf of the Society, he fired off a forceful letter to Winnifred Kydd, a member of both the Canadian delegation to the League Assembly and the Society's national council. In this missive he advocated, among other things, that Canada press for a full debate on the Ethiopian question and, then, if circumstances warranted it, call for the levying of collective sanctions against Italy. When the letter was brought to Bennett's attention, he castigated it as "interference" in government business and wrote to Inch suggesting that his efforts vis-a-vis the Ethiopian question indicated a greater interest in politics than in world security.[16] Shortly thereafter, on 31 August, the Society sent Inch to Geneva as a Temporary Collaborator, thereby preventing him from pursuing a political action campaign in Canada.

After the formation of the new Liberal government, the Society called for a meeting of the national council to discuss the position that Canada should take with regard to the application of economic and military sanctions. It hoped that such a forum would provide for an expression of public opinion for the Government's guidance, but little did it realize that the meeting would quickly dissolve into two warring camps, one representing the advocates of economic and military sanctions, the other the anti-sanctions faction. Cairine Wilson attended that fateful November 8th meeting at the Chateau Laurier Hotel as did John W. Dafoe of *the Winnipeg Free Press*, the acknowledged king of Canadian editors and the most influential spokesman for those Canadian internationalists who advocated a policy of collective security through the League.[17]

When resolutions put forward by each of the two factions were defeated, a compromise was finally achieved with the presentation and carrying of two other motions. The first, which was moved by a vote of 14 for and 4 against, endorsed the action of the Canadian government "in agreeing to co-operate in the imposition of economic and financial sanctions in order to restore peace in the present crisis." The second, which was carried unanimously, urged the Canadian government "to make it clear that it is prepared to co-operate in a determined and collective effort to solve by peaceful means the territorial, economic, population and other problems of the world as part of a settlement which will include the strengthening of the sanctions obligations of the League and the conclusion of a treaty providing for a substantial reduction of national armaments."[18] Those who felt strongly that the League should function as a conciliator and as an enforcer of economic as opposed to military sanctions had managed to carry the day. The complete abandonment of a militant sanctions policy, however, would destroy much of the Society's vigor in the next few years.

Since no record was kept of the individual votes cast, we can only speculate on how Cairine Wilson voted on the various resolutions. We may be sure that she voted for military and economic sanctions, given her unrelenting championship of collective security. Her unflinching belief in this doctrine is illustrated forcefully in an address that she gave to the 1942 annual meeting of the national council when she said in part:

> Perhaps we have not yet realized that this nationhood imposes on us much greater responsibilities, and that, as a country of sparse population and rich in natural resources, we must share with others less fortunately placed. We must have cohesion of the international community of the future, consideration for the prevention of war, insistence upon legal procedure for change, and a sharing of economic advantages; and we must support this international order by economic and, as we now realize, by military action. We have been too prone to think of peace as merely a static matter, and that we could shelter ourselves behind an imaginary Maginot line of pacts and alliances. To attain security and to maintain peace we must be prepared to sacrifice and even to take up arms if necessary.[19]

One of the most striking features of this address is the extent to which it echoes Cairine Wilson's constant preoccupation with sharing. Just as she believed that she, a pillar of Canadian society, should use her wealth and talents to benefit mankind so did she believe that well endowed countries like Canada should share their resources with the unfortunate peoples of the world. Equally notable, of course, is the speech's emphasis on the principle of collective security. In espousing this doctrine and rejecting pacificism, the Senator differed markedly from such leading Canadian feminists of her day as Laura Jamieson and Alice Chown. Both these women were pacifists, but whereas Jamieson rejected outright the idea that peace could be achieved through the League of Nations, arbitration or disarmament, Chown worked hard for the world body and a new international order based on universal disarmament, compulsory arbitration and a league of democratic nations. She joined the Toronto branch of the League of Nations Society in Canada and became a spirited worker for the cause. As time wore on, however, the labour and social services organizer became more and more disillusioned with the Society's "academic" viewpoint and its refusal to pitch its message to the masses. Consequently, in 1930, she led a group of determined supporters out of the Toronto branch and spearheaded the formation of a separate entity, the Women's League of Nations Association dedicated to developing programs for "ordinary people." Not until 1933 did the Society try to resolve the situation and not until two years later was a compromise solution reached.[20]

Alice Chown's radical ideas and direct approach contrasted sharply with those of Cairine Wilson. Still, the Senator was not averse to picking up some pointers from the forceful Miss Chown. After seeing a sample of her propaganda, for example, Cairine Wilson wrote somewhat apologetically to Robert Inch:

> Thank you so much for allowing me to see one of Miss Chown's real efforts. I understand now why you considered mine lacking in style.
>
> According to your advice, I have agreed to speak for Miss Chown in Toronto, and only hope I shall be able to further the cause of the League of Nations.[21]

It is evident from this excerpt that Cairine Wilson was entrusted with the task of trying to persuade Alice Chown and those of her supporters who had defected from the Society to return to its fold. Since many of the women did eventually rejoin, the Senator probably succeeded in her mission, once again demonstrating how persuasive she could be in her own quiet way.

Senator Wilson took on the chairmanship of the national executive committee in June 1936 at a time when the membership was still deeply divided by the sanctions controversy and the Society's energies were being sapped by bitter controversy. The new responsibilities were thrust on her at the Society's annual meeting when those present named her temporary chairman in the absence of the national executive committee chairman, C.G. Cowan. Brokenhearted by the Society's complete abandonment of a comprehensive sanctions policy, he had stayed away from the meeting. Although it placed her in an extremely difficult position, Cairine Wilson substituted for him and then when Sir Robert Falconer was incapacitated by illness, she assumed the dual position of acting president of the Society and acting chairman of the national executive committee. In June 1937, at the annual meeting, she was elected president, a position that she combined with that of national executive committee chairman (except for a short interval when Dr T.H. Leggett held office) until Warwick Chipman, K.C. was appointed chairman of the national executive committee in 1939.[22]

She had the distinction of being elected president by the largest number of registered delegates yet to attend an annual meeting: 139. They came from across Canada, from Vancouver in the West to Sydney, Nova Scotia in the East. Even more significant, 83 of the delegates, i.e., 60 percent, were women[23], women who were proud of Senator Wilson and looked to her for leadership. At this milestone convention, held in the steel-making city of Hamilton, Ontario, their votes would make it possible for her to become the first and only woman president in the Society's history. Just over a year later, in September 1938, the Senator would climax this first with still another achievement: election to one of the vice-presidencies of the International Federation of the League of Nations Societies.

When Robert Inch looked back on this conference five years later, he recalled that it was "not altogether a milk and water occasion."[24] This suggests that the meeting gave rise to quite a lot of sparring and much heated debate. Notwithstanding the acrimonious divisions over collective security, the conference finally resolved — no doubt urged on by Cairine Wilson and Inch — to take a strong stand on this concept. Accordingly, it took the bold step of sending the following cable to Mackenzie King, then attending an Imperial Conference in London:

> The fifteenth convention of the League of Nations Society in Canada feels bound to call the Prime Minister's attention to the insistent demand of many of its branches and of the convention itself that Canada should accord wholehearted support to the League and pursue no policy in London or Geneva impairing collective security or reducing the League to a consultative body.[25]

The tone of the meeting and the content of the telegram would serve as important indicators of what lay ahead in Cairine Wilson's presidency.

As president of the Society, the Senator would need all the political acumen, tact and stamina that she could muster, for to say that she inherited a difficult situation is an understatement. She would not always succeed in smoothing ruffled feathers and in reconciling divergent views. That would have been next to impossible given the make-up of the executive and the strong convictions of many of its members, to say nothing of Bob Inch's combative nature. But along with the determined national secretary, she would force the Society to take a stong stand in support of the League and a general collective peace system.

In pursuit of this objective the Senator and Inch had to brook both overt and covert opposition. One of the key players in the game of covert opposition was Mackenzie King who did not want to see the Society succeed in popularizing the concept of collective security. His particular target was a campaign that Cairine Wilson and her colleagues launched in May 1937 to recruit new members and obtain additional funding from the private sector. To reach its goal of $15,000 in new subscriptions, the Society set up a national finance committee under the direction of the indefatigable and energetic Dr Tory. Clifford Sifton of Toronto offered to solicit business support and to this end met with eleven of Canada's leading insurance executives in October 1937. As a result of the hearing that he received, Sifton went on to interview the Superintendent of Insurance in Ottawa and Mackenzie King, an honorary president of the Society. Shortly afterwards, however, the interest that the insurance companies had expressed mysteriously evaporated and Sifton's campaign collapsed. Determined to retain complete control of foreign policy, the Prime Minister had intervened to prevent the Society from realizing its aim of leading public opinion and influencing the making of foreign policy in favour of collective security.[26] Notwithstanding the failure of Sifton's campaign, the Society did succeed in getting its finances in order during Cairine Wilson's presidency. However, if it had not been for sizable contributions made by the Senator and Tory, the Society, according to the educator-scientist, would have ceased operations altogther in the late 1930s. To keep it afloat, Cairine Wilson donated $1,000 and Dr Tory $500. Anna Cooke, a prominent member of the Ottawa branch, guaranteed $200.[27]

Cairine Wilson intervened most effectively and dramatically in favour of collective security on 2 October 1938 when she issued a bold statement condemning the Munich Agreement, which had just delivered the German-speaking part of Czechoslovakia, the Sudetenland, to Hitler in return for his promise that this would be the last of his territorial demands in Europe. This abject surrender of Czechoslovakian territory had been precipitated by a ranting speech that the Chancellor made on 12 September insisting on self-determination for Czechoslovakia's Sudeten Germans. Hard on the heels of this came a demand for the immediate annexation of the Sudetenland to Germany. In response, the Czechs mobilized and the British and French leaders discussed the possibility of concerted action. Throughout jittery Europe people scanned the skies, watching for the approach of bombers which would announce the outbreak of hostilities, but they looked in vain. Determined to prevent war, for which Britain was unprepared, Prime Minister Neville Chamberlain arranged a meeting for 29 September at Munich. Here, he, Mussolini and Premier Edouard Daladier of France met with Hitler and arrived at a "compromise" which turned over the Sudeten-rim lands to Germany and effectively crippled the whole Czech economy and transportation system. Czechoslovakia was lost to Germany, but Europe was yanked back from the brink of war.

Chamberlain returned to England, beaming and confident. To the ecstatic crowds, who welcomed him in London, he announced that the agreement promised peace to Europe, and the people, believing him, cheered the 69-year-old prime minister. On the other side of the Atlantic, Mackenzie King greeted the news of the pact with jubilation. All summer long he had watched the simmering Czech crisis with growing apprehension, fearing that if the Czechs resisted Hitler's demands, Germany would invade the beleaguered republic. If this happened, Great Britain would be drawn into the conflict and Canada would have to come to her aid. It was a prospect that Mackenzie King could not stomach, for he knew that although the majority of Canadians would probably accept this decision, there were others who would not. If war came, the country would be divided and the Liberal Party shattered. Such a horrendous possibility was enough to crush King's spirit and help bring on a debilitating attack of sciatica that confined him to bed for two weeks. So it is not surprising that when the news of the Munich Pact was announced the Prime Minister was overcome with relief. "I came to my library, knelt down and thanked God for the peace that had been preserved to the world," he confided to his diary.[28]

Later the Prime Minister called O.D. Skelton, the Under-Secretary for External Affairs, to say that he wanted him to arrange for a cable to be sent immediately to the British prime minister, declaring, "The heart of Canada is rejoicing tonight and my colleagues in the Government join me in unbounded admiration at the service you have rendered mankind."[29]

Not all Liberals shared their party leader's enthusiasm for the Munich Pact. Among the small number of detractors was a group of young Liberals who huddled around a restaurant table shortly after Chamberlain's "Peace in Our Time" speech. It was their custom to meet frequently in this nondescript Sparks Street establishment and on this particular evening they engaged in long and earnest discussion about the agreement and the British prime minister's promise of peace. Among those present was the National Federation of Liberal Women of Canada's legal adviser, George McIlraith, who would later assist Cairine Wilson in her work on behalf of refugees. As he remembers it, everyone who met around the table that

September evening opposed Chamberlain's actions. They all thought that the compromise would ultimately lead to war. The next day McIlraith met the Senator and learned that she too felt the same way. Despite her position in the Liberal Party, however, she would speak out fearlessly against the agreement.[30]

Cairine Wilson found absolutely nothing to rejoice about in the Munich settlement. Unlike millions around the world, who believed or hoped that the acquisition of the Sudeten Germans would satisfy Hitler and forestall further aggression, she foresaw only a perilous descent into war. Canadians, she concluded, must be warned of this; they had to see the Munich Agreement for what it truly was: a craven measure which spelled disaster for Czechoslovakia and invited further German expansion. Never a person to shirk her duty as she saw it, she invited Robert Inch and Dr. Tory to her Senate office to discuss the situation and decide how the Society should respond to it. They met on Saturday 1 October at noon, just hours before King, the representatives of Germany, Italy, Great Britain and France, and other dignitaries celebrated the Munich Pact in a hurriedly convened ceremony in Confederation Square. The proceedings, which would have appealed to the Senator's highly developed sense of irony, were King's idea. Still overcome with joy and relief at the news of the Munich Agreement, the Prime Minister had telephoned the deputy minister of the department of Public Works to ask if the winged figures of "Peace" and "Liberty" could be raised to the top of Canada's almost completed National War Memorial in a special celebration to mark the signing of the accord. The result of this call was the ceremony which unfolded in the fading light of a magnificent autumn sunset on 1 October and which featured the portly Prime Minister pulling the controlling rope that set the statues in place.

It was against this backdrop that the three Society officers agreed that a statement on the agreement should be issued and that each should prepare a draft. Dr Leggett, who was chairman of the National Executive Committee and who could not attend this portentous meeting, was consulted by Inch. Then, the following evening, the Senator and her colleagues drew up a final draft at the Manor House and sent a copy to the Canadian Press wire service. They had acted with an admirable sense of good public relations, because by drawing up a critical statement and then releasing it before Chamberlain reported to the British House of Commons, the Senator and her fellow officers ensured good press coverage of the Society's position. But it was not a step that Cairine Wilson took lightly. For daring to issue a statement in her own name, correctly setting the Munich Agreement in its disastrous context, she risked alienating many people in high places, chief among them Mackenzie King. This she realized full well. In fact, the

Senator's private secretary at that time, Myra Macdonald Punnett, has recalled Cairine Wilson telling her that she thought that she might be asked for her resignation from the Senate because of her independence.[31]

Mrs Punnett's recollections of the Senator's resolve and courage are also supported by those of Robert Inch, who, four years after the drafting of the statement, informed a meeting of the Society's National Executive Committee, "Senator Wilson was most determined and aroused, declaring, if I might repeat it, that she would make a declaration even if it cost her her Senatorship."[32] Just as she was loyal to her friends so was Cairine Wilson loyal to the Liberal Party. But never did she allow this loyalty to override a question of principle. Whenever she felt strongly about something, she spoke out, no matter how unpopular and harsh the views that she held. Rarely, if ever, though, did she excite animosity, perhaps because she was adept at projecting a harmony that reflected her own inner self.

Just what pressure was brought to bear on the Senator to renounce her position on the Munich Agreement is open to question. The onetime university president, James Gibson, who was on secondment from the department of External Affairs to Mackenzie King's staff in 1938, has reported that the Prime Minister went to great lengths to persuade Cairine Wilson to back down from her statement. Although he had not been aware of it at the time, claims Gibson, "insistent pressure was brought upon Senator Wilson by the Prime Minister to disavow the public stand of some officers and members of the League of Nations Society following the Munich proceedings in 1938."[33]

Whether or not King did exert direct pressure, the fact remains that his right-hand man in Quebec, Ernest Lapointe, did. The Minister of Justice had left to attend the League Assembly in Geneva just before the Prime Minister was forced to bed by sciatica, but when the turbulent developments in Czechoslovakia threatened to plunge Europe into war, Lapointe shortened his stay at King's request and returned to Canada. On 4 October, the day after Cairine Wilson's statement had hit the press, he strode into the Prime Minister's East Block office. There, after a discussion of cabinet business, Lapointe "expressed cordial disapproval of Cairine Wilson's attitude and that of the League people."[34] He then went on to say that he would accept the Society's invitation to dinner and there he would drive home to them how completely misguided they were.

On 4 October the *Evening Citizen* published excerpts from the statement listing four truths that the Senator claimed should be recalled during the mistaken rejoicing over peace:

> Our leaders continue to subscribe to a concept of
> anarchy which actually permitted the World War of 1914

and which might well have permitted its repetition in the last few hours.

A surrender which is almost complete [under] the threat of naked force.

The dismemberment of Czechoslovakia is presented as a fait accompli.

The new barbarism represented by Germany may now be free to extend to the Black Sea and other continents.

In support of this stand, J. Napier of Montreal wrote to the Senator:

It is so easy to follow the "mob hysteria" of adulation, sponsored and encouraged by a servile press, that when, as in your case, we find a personality, high in affairs of state, with the *moral courage* to differ from small minds in high places, it is a privilege to offer whatever support we can, even if such support be, as in the writer's case, of a very non-influential character.[35]

Napier also noted that *The Gazette* [Montreal] had refused to publish a letter of his critical of the agreement, prompting the Senator to reply:

With you, I regret exceedingly that the press in Great Britain and also in our own country has given the public little opportunity to express opinions critical of Prime Minister Chamberlain. I have also been puzzled over the various statements, more or less inspired, which are given for our consumption and the crisis through which we have passed has left us with many misgivings. It is discouraging, particularly when our clergymen take the attitude adopted by Canon Gower-Rees on Sunday last, but I value the pronouncement of Reverend Leslie Weatherhead before almost 3,000 in the City Temple at London on October 2nd.[36]

To her good friend, Sir Lyman Duff, the Chief Justice, she wrote:

It is a great satisfaction to know that you approved of the pronouncement which was issued in my name and which the Secretary of the League of Nations Society and I prepared with great care. We did not wish to give unnecessary offence and yet realized that the time was most critical and some statement should be made.[37]

Napier's and Duff's reactions to the Munich settlement and the Society's response to it were, of course, decidedly atypical. Much more representative of Canadian opinion as a whole was that of the well-known Liberal politician, Paul Martin, who became a national officer of the Society in 1933 and served as president of the Windsor branch in 1931 and 1932. He welcomed the pact, believing that it removed the threat of war and provided Britain with badly needed time to strengthen her defences.[38] Dour Edward Mackay did not mince words when condemning his sister's stance on the Agreement. "There is Cairine condemning Chamberlain. What does she want — all our boys going off to war?[39] Events would prove Cairine Wilson and Robert Inch correct in their assessment of the situation, as the noted Canadian foreign policy expert, F.H. Soward, realized when he observed, "One of the sanest comments on the Munich settlement, made almost immediately after its publication, came from the national president of the League of Nations Society in Canada, Senator Cairine Wilson."[40]

Having refused to back down from the Society's Munich statement, Cairine Wilson set out, at Robert Inch's urging, to ensure that a firm believer in collective security was elected chairman of the Society's national executive committee. Summoning up all her powers of persuasion, she appealed to members of the committee in December 1938 to elect Warwick Chipman, K.C. to this position in a mail ballot. Observed the Senator:

> Among those who came forward in active defense of the Society at the time of the Munich Settlement and who urged us to press forward Warwick Chipman, K.C. of Montreal was one of the most outspoken. On several occasions he expressed himself as being in favour of an intensive immediate effort on behalf of our objectives and it was obvious that here was a man to whom we should look for leadership and assistance.[41]

Her efforts obviously paid off because Chipman was elected to this influential post. In 1942, however, Mackenzie King would appoint the Montreal lawyer minister to Chile, thereby removing him from the Society.

Cairine Wilson's early years as president of the Society were indisputably the most dynamic and exciting in its history. There was the organization's response to the Munich Agreement. It not only thrust the Society into the limelight, it also sowed more discord among the members and triggered a spate of resignations. One of these was tendered by Dr Leggett who resigned from the chairmanship of the national executive committee, claiming that the organization would have attracted thousands of new members had it adopted a pro-Munich stand.[42] But there were also other developments that, if not as dramatic as the Senator's Munich statement and its aftermath, are nevertheless noteworthy.

In addition to its fund-raising campaign in 1937, there was the successful Peace Action Week that the Society mounted in November 1938, employing radio broadcasts, public rallies and a dinner to take its message to the general public and persuade it to support a policy of collective security. As part of her contribution to the organization's accelerated publicity campaign, Senator Wilson spoke to various groups in Montreal, Kingston and Toronto in the closing months of the year. When not charging from one speaking engagement to another on behalf of the Society, she worked hard to launch a new Society-sponsored committee, the Canadian National Committee on Refugees and Victims of Political Persecution. Soon it would become a refuge for those Society members like herself who wanted to work towards more practical and rewarding ends.

As the war clouds darkened in the summer of 1939, the Senator began to ask herself seriously if the Society had outlived its usefulness. There had been times in the past when she had become discouraged by reverses suffered by the League of Nations, but never had she lost the faith. Even in its darkest hours, the world body had never been for her the "League of Notions," as Clifford, the chauffeur, referred to it, but a practical force for preserving peace in the world. Now, however, developments were making it all too apparent that the world body could not prevent the outbreak of another world war. And, if the League failed in its most important mission would not the Society become useless? These were questions that kept nagging away during that eventful summer of 1939, especially during the portrait sittings at Clibrig when the Senator discussed the ominous situation in Europe with sculptor Felix de Weldon.

After her return to Ottawa in September, Cairine Wilson and other leading officers of the Society thrashed out the whole question of the organization's future. Warwick Chipman and Robert Inch were convinced that the lobby could make a valuable contribution to the war effort, but this view was not shared by all the members of the national executive committee. Among the dissenters was Cairine Wilson. Like Dr Tory, she had come to the reluctant conclusion that the outbreak of hostilities had robbed the Society of most of its relevance. As far as she was concerned, the Literature Service and the refugee work should be continued, but everything not related directly to "immediate needs" should be allowed to wait until the war's end.[43]

Evidently her and Tory's views were shared by many other Society members because it was eventually decided that the organization should maintain a low profile until the conclusion of hostilities. This policy of "winding down" was anathema to Bob Inch, whose fervent enthusiasm for the cause and penchant for undertaking projects without the authority of the executive, led him into frequent combat with Cairine Wilson and members of the national executive committee throughout the period 1939-1942. Finally, in October 1942, the Committee asked for and received the national secretary's resignation. By then, however, Cairine Wilson had resigned as president (She had done this earlier in the year) to devote more of her time to an interest that would absorb most of her energies for the next six years: refugees. She had served the cause of the League of Nations well, but she would make a still more valuable contribution to the cause of refugees. Indeed, the work that she did on their behalf would represent the pinnacle of her public career. Nevertheless, she never abandoned her belief in a world body dedicated to peace and international co-operation. And, after the official establishment of the United Nations in 1945, she joined six other interested parties in signing an application for a federal charter for the United Nations Association in Canada, the successor to the League of Nations Society in Canada.[44]

9

MOTHER OF THE REFUGEES

Cairine Wilson had been president of the League of Nations Society in Canada for a year when she embarked on what would become the most important campaign of her life: the fight to open Canada's doors to the hordes of desperate refugees who had escaped the engulfing Nazi tide and who were seeking a new life in Canada. To help pry open these doors, she would spearhead the establishment of the Canadian National Committee on Refugees (CNCR) and through it wage a tireless struggle against isolationism and shortsightedness, carrying the battle into the halls of Parliament and the offices of government bureaucrats.

When the Senator first took up the refugees' cause — in 1938 — Canadians were stubbornly opposed to large-scale immigration. With unemployment rampant, they took the view that immigration threatened scarce jobs in an economy where, in 1933, almost one-quarter of the labour force was unemployed. Coupled with this was a widespread reluctance to become involved in Europe's quarrels and problems for Canadians, like their neighbours across the border, had no wish to act as custodians of the world's conscience. Although refugees could bring badly needed skills and talents, they were definitely not welcome — at least not by the Canadian government and a large part of the population. In 1930, when Canadians were becoming preoccupied with the economy, the Canadian government passed an order-in-council which admitted only those immigrants who had enough capital to establish and maintain themselves on farms. This was followed, the next year, by an order-in-council effectively banning all non-agricultural immigrants unless they were American or

British. As a result, immigration plummeted from 1,166,000 in the decade 1921-31 to 140,000 between 1931 and 1941.[1] How many of these immigrants were refugees is impossible to say because the label "refugee" has varying definitions. Also, statistical compilations drawn up by immigration officials, then employed by the Immigration Branch of the Department of Mines and Resources, do not identify "refugees." Nevertheless, if an estimate made in May 1938 is any guide, Canada admitted only 10,000 refugees between the end of World War I and 1938.[2]

The year 1938 threw into sharp relief the whole refugee question, because by then world opinion could no longer feign ignorance of the ruthless warfare that the Nazis had been conducting against Jews and other minorities, such as gypsies, pacifists, Freemasons and Communists. Persecution of the Jews was especially severe and more particularly after the German invasion of Austria in March of that year. Following the collapse of Chancellor Kurt von Schuschnigg's government, Austria's 200,000 Jews were subjected to such savage treatment that the persecution in Germany seemed moderate. Rabbi William Margolis, spiritual leader of Ottawa's United Jewish community, alluded to this when he said in an address in New York shortly after the invasion:

> Five years ago and for some time thereafter, when the Jewish people warned the world that Hitlerism means havoc, the cry was ignored and dismissed as a Jewish false alarm. It was lightly thought that the Jew was lamenting his own lot of affliction. Today the world realizes that once again the treatment of Israel is the barometer of civilization, even as the status of all minorities reflects the tide and progress of human liberty.
>
> What now? Will the democratic nations still sit back and practise the lamentable laissez faire of 'watchful waiting'? Will they permit Hitler to make the next move — probably the fateful one for humanity?[3]

The year that marked the fifth anniversary of the National Socialist regime in Germany was also the year in which the Evian conference was held. Named after the French health resort on Lake Geneva where it was staged, the Evian conference was the outcome of President Roosevelt's bold initiative to bring together thirty-two nations to discuss the worsening refugee situation brought on by Hitler's invasion of Austria. The author of the plan was Roosevelt's Undersecretary of State, Sumner Welles, who hoped that the United States, by making this move, could deflect pressure from critics of the Administration's immigration policy and forestall attempts to lower immigration barriers.

Had the Canadian government appreciated the true motives behind the American initiative, it might have reacted differently when it received a formal invitation to attend. As it was, the Government felt extremely uncomfortable for it knew only too well that attendance at the conference implied an interest in helping to alleviate the refugee problem by liberalizing immigration laws and admitting sizable numbers of Jews. This was a prospect that the shrewd temporizer, Mackenzie King, could not face. The Prime Minister might have wanted to act on humanitarian grounds (In November 1938, for example, he had written in his diary, "The sorrows which the Jews have to bear at this time are almost beyond comprehension. Something will have to be done by our country.") But he was loath to ignore political realities. And one of these was Quebec's attitude toward refugees in general and Jews in particular. Anti-Semitism existed throughout Canada, but in Quebec it found its most overt and ugly expression, thanks to the impact of the Great Depression and the revival of French Canadian nationalism. French-language newspapers, from moderate organs such as *Le Devoir*, to ultranationalist papers such as *La Nation, L' Action Nationale* and *L' Action Catholique*, spoke out against opening the doors to Jewish refugees. Equally vociferous were French Canadian members of Parliament and such Quebec organizations as the St Jean Baptiste Society and the provincial Knights of Columbus. Lowering the barriers to immigration, particularly Jewish immigration, was therefore a step that the King government was not prepared to take. National unity had to be preserved at all costs.

As a result, the Canadian government stalled for several weeks. At last it agreed to attend the conference but principally because it did not want to be associated with Fascist Italy, the only country to turn down Roosevelt's invitation.[4] Canada need not have worried that the conference would force a liberalization of immigration laws on the participants. Despite many lofty statements of principle, the proceedings' only real achievement was the establishment of a permanent organization to coordinate refugee resettlement programs, the Intergovernmental Committee on Refugees, and even this body was largely ineffectual.

It was against this background that Cairine Wilson first took up the cause of refugee immigration. There were, of course, vocal proponents of a more liberal immigration policy: leading spokesmen for the Jewish community, which was then making a last ditch, dramatic attempt to help save Jewish refugees; newspaper editors and commentators in English-speaking Canada; prominent members of the Protestant churches; the Co-operative Commonwealth Federation Party, particularly its leader, M.J.

Coldwell; and various pro-refugee organizations. The Canadian government and the population as a whole, though, were resolutely opposed to a liberal immigration policy.

It is difficult to establish exactly when the Senator first took up the cudgels on behalf of the refugees, but it was probably in the autumn of 1938, shortly after her friend Constance Hayward returned from a visit to Europe. A lecturer and organizer for the League of Nations Society in Canada, Constance had gone to Geneva to attend the League Assembly as a Temporary Collaborator. It so happened that her stint at the Assembly coincided in part with the proceedings of the Evian Conference, with the result that she became well informed about developments there as well as elsewhere in Europe. What she learned upset her greatly, but what perhaps moved her most deeply was the hyprocrisy and posturing of many Conference delegates, who pretended to be concerned about the refugees' plight yet were reluctant to open their countries' doors to the victims. So this compassionate woman with the long, oval face and patrician features returned to Canada determined to heighten public awareness of the refugee problem and soften the Canadian government's stand on immigration. If Senator Wilson had been concerned about the refugee question before her friend's landmark visit to Europe, she became more so after hearing Constance's reports of conditions on the Continent. From then on the refugee problem would absorb more and more of her time and energy. There would be no turning back.

We know by the Senator's own account that she became deeply involved with the cause after the Munich Pact and the subsequent arrival of the first group of Czechoslovakian refugees in Canada.[5] There is no doubt that she was deeply affected by the predicament of these newcomers, because two years after their arrival in this country she observed, in an address to the Halifax branch of the Canadian National Committee on Refugees, "Their lives have been very difficult and lonely, but they have been very courageous."[6] When commenting on the plight of these Czech refugees, she was probably recalling some of the pitiful tales that had been brought to the attention of the CNCR in the past year. One in particular illustrated the kinds of hardships faced by many of the newcomers who settled in northern Saskatchewan and on the Alberta-British Columbia border. This case involved a desperate farmer, living near St Walburg, Saskatchewan, who wrote to a Czech friend in Toronto requesting a loan of eight dollars and the use of an old parambulator. The loan, reported the farmer, would offset the travel expenses of his young daughter who was eager to return home from a Saskatchewan town where she had just finished the school year while the baby carriage would make life easier for his wife, who wanted to have her infant beside her when she toiled in the fields. The couple were putting in a sixteen to eighteen-hour working day, but were still unable to accumulate enough money to pay for their daughter's travel expenses or to purchase enough fodder for their livestock.[7]

Constance Hayward. Photo believed to have been taken in the 1960s.

When we consider the conditions under which many of these Czech settlers were living, Senator Wilson's remarks were certainly not misplaced. Nor were the sentiments expressed in the text that she and Dr T.H. Leggett, chairman of the National Executive Committee of the League of Nations Society in Canada, wrote to accompany a public appeal for contributions to the Society's National Aid to Czechoslovakia Fund. On 15 October 1938, when the fund was established, the two spokesmen wrote:

> No one can follow the heartrending course of events in Czechoslovakia without desiring to help. We hope that Canadians will respond appropriately. One million, two hundred thousand Czechs have now had their land, homes and even their household furnishings incorporated into the Third Reich. Thousands of anti- Nazi Germans have also been included and what remains of the Czechoslovak state hesitates to welcome them for fear that the Reich will once again extend its territorial claims to encompass them. With winter rapidly approaching, thousands of persons are without shelter, food and clothing. Even at this great distance we cannot escape feeling some of the torments of this proud people as it bows before a totalitarian regime. The fact that as a nation we're obligated, morally and otherwise as well, to aid in protecting Czechoslovakia from external aggression adds to our present responsibilities. We invite contributions large and small.[8]

Although the appeal was issued jointly by Cairine Wilson and Dr Leggett, the text suggests that it was written, if not entirely by the Senator, then at least largely by her.

When the Senate began her uphill battle to secure the admission of refugees, she was one of a rare breed. Given her family background, she might have been expected to condone Canada's highly selective, self-serving immigration policy. After all, Canada's establishment was then characterized by a certain provincialism and a deeply ingrained belief that anybody who spoke a language other than theirs was inferior. It was also pervaded by anti-Semitism which, although usually unvoiced, was nevertheless an insidious part of everyday life. Cairine Wilson, however, was one establishment figure who could transcend these attitudes and become an indefatigable fighter for the refugee cause. Her abundance of compassion and her long-standing interest in assisting the more deserving of society's unfortunates certainly had something to do with it. So did colourful tales of the time her ancestors were chased off their crofts in

Sutherland by the sheep clearances. Unquestonably her recognition of the valuable contributions that educated and talented refugees could make to Canadian society played a role. Whatever the significance of each of these reasons Cairine Wilson became an unflagging champion of refugee immigration and promoter of refugees' interests.

The homey office down the hall from the Senate entrance became the headquarters for the Senator's personal campaign. Here, she would spend untold hours writing letters, making phone calls, interviewing supplicants, and meeting with colleagues who waged the battle with her. One of these was George McIlraith, the young, bespectacled lawyer who served as solicitor for the National Federation of Liberal Women of Canada and who was then on the threshold of a long parliamentary career. In his own Senate office, over forty years later, he recalled these meetings, noting that they invariably started around 8:20 in the morning so that people like himself could get to their own desks by nine. No mean organizer himself, he marvelled at Cairine Wilson's quiet resolve and capacity for hard work.

> I have often thought that the various refugees who have succeeded so well in Canada and have contributed so much to this country have never sufficiently acknowledged or appreciated her work because she was a terribly shy person and very modest. For a woman of her position and wealth, her modesty was almost unbelievable.[9]

One of the first cases to be brought to her attention was that of a Viennese pediatrician who had a brother in McGill University's faculty of medicine. Catherine MacKenzie, then principal of Montreal's High School for Girls and a member of the League of Nations Society in Canada, sounded the alarm when she wrote to the Senator on 24 November 1938 informing her that the McGill hematologist, Dr Rudolf Gottlieb, wished to arrange for his brother and sister-in-law to come to Canada as soon as possible.

> There will be all necessary guarantees that he and his wife would not become a public charge. The case is very urgent as persecution has already begun. Would you kindly speak to Mr Crerar [Minister of Mines and Resources] to ask him what can be done?

> ...I know that you feel as I do about the persecution of intellectual workers and the more eminent the greater the distress and the more urgent it becomes to act for their relief.[10]

The persecution had indeed begun. The plundering and murdering had broken out in earnest some two weeks earlier on 10 November 1938 when, on the orders of Reinhard Heydrich, head of the SS Security Service, the worst pogrom to date was launched. "Kristallnacht" ("Crystal Night") — so called because of the broken glass from Jewish businesses, homes and synagogues that littered Austrian and German streets — was the opening salvo in another Nazi-organized campaign to terrorize the Jews. Before the orgy was over, hundreds of Jewish homes and stores would be plundered and razed; and countless Jewish men, women and children would be yanked from their homes, shot, beaten, or hauled off to concentration camps.

Cairine Wilson wasted no time in pulling the necessary strings and using her influence on behalf of the Gottlieb family. Indeed, she acted so quickly that Catherine MacKenzie was moved to write:

> I am very grateful to you for your interest and prompt action in the case of Dr Karl Gottlieb. It was kind of you to call at school and I am very sorry I missed the pleasure and honour of seeing you.

> I am certainly with you in your courageous stand in the present world situation and in your defence of the downtrodden and unfortunate. Like other women I know who are interested in public events, I feel it a comfort that we have a senator of our own who feels as you do and acts at once.[11]

Fortunately the Senator's efforts were not in vain, because on 18 December 1938, a jubilant Catherine MacKenzie wrote:

> My very sincere thanks and Dr Gottlieb's for your help and influence in obtaining permission for his brother Dr Karl Gottlieb to enter Canada. I admire your stand on the refugee question and deplore Dr Manion's [leader of the Conservative party 1938 - 1940] even if it appears a popular vote-getter in the province of Quebec. It is easy to resent Germany's treatment of the Jews when we do not open our doors to them, very cheap sympathy that![12]

Catherine MacKenzie's denunciation of Robert Manion was triggered, no doubt, by an address to a Quebec audience that the national Conservative leader had given a few days earlier. Manion, who was married to a French Canadian, had attempted to woo Quebec's sympathies by stating that he was opposed to any immigration as long as a single Canadian was out of work.[13] Predictably, his remarks were lauded by the French Canadian press. But they were also praised by most Liberals.

In her role as a lobbyist for the refugee cause, Senator Wilson pitted herself against cabinet ministers and officials from the two government departments most closely involved with immigration: the Department of Mines and Resources, which had jurisdiction over immigration, and the Department of External Affairs. Before these opposing forces, she would plead the cases of individual refugees in an attempt to obtain special permits for them. In the process she would make such a nuisance of herself that a cabinet minister would refer to her as "the home of all lost causes."[14]

After the Liberal Party's return to power in 1935, the cabinet minister ostensibly in charge of immigration was Thomas Crerar, the Minister of Mines and Resources. But Crerar was not particularly interested in immigration. Even if he had been he had little time to devote to the question, because the Immigration Branch was only one of four separate and distinct branches into which his department was divided. The one-time Prairie radical and founder of the Progressive Party therefore left nearly all decisions relating to immigration to the Immigration Branch's director, Frederick Charles Blair.

National Archives of Canada PA 114604

Frederick Charles Blair (left) and E.A. Collins following investiture at Government House, Ottawa, November 1943.

A native of Carlisle, Ontario, where he was born of Scottish parents in 1874, Blair was a dedicated civil servant who had joined the Department of Agriculture in 1903 and two years later become an immigration officer. From this position he had risen to become director of Mines and Resources' Immigration Branch in 1936. Here he reigned supreme for seven years, assiduously overseeing every aspect of his department's activities and enforcing rules and regulations to the letter.

Unfortunately for those refugees clamouring to get into Canada, Blair was the perfect instrument of the government's anti- immigration policy. Notwithstanding the highly restrictive immigration law, he could recommend the issuance of special permits. However, Blair rarely chose to do so, because he believed strongly that immigration should be discouraged. To complicate matters still further for prospective immigrants, the director of Mines and Resources' immigration branch disliked Jews. This meant that he was particularly opposed to refugee immigration, equating the label "refugee" with Jew. In short, he became the force to be reckoned with.

Anne Sedgewick Carver, whose parents were great friends and admirers of Cairine Wilson, recalled a meeting that she had with the bureaucrat in 1938. It had been inspired by a letter that she had received from a young Jewish friend, who had written to her from Austria requesting information about emigrating to Canada. After she related the Austrian's story, Blair replied, "You must realize, Miss Sedgewick, that there is a rising tide of anti-Jewish feeling in Canada. There is no way we can assist this man to come to Canada. However, the situation might be different if he had private means." Mrs Carver, then a young idealistic student, was so appalled by this attitude that she left the meeting feeling deeply ashamed of Canada for having such a policy and for employing an individual like Blair who was apparently comfortable with it.[15]

Ironically, it was this upright, devout Baptist of Scottish descent that Senator Wilson would frequently lock horns with over the years. When his obduracy proved too much, she would sometimes protest to the Prime Minister. After one such complaint, Blair responded, "All the cases that Senator Wilson has brought to my attention in the past four years have been Jewish."[16]

Besides spending every hour she could snatch from her Senate and other duties to lobby for the admission of individual refugees and their families, Cairine Wilson also spoke out on behalf of Europe's homeless. Not content with badgering government officials and appealing to organizations, she took to the airwaves and other public platforms to advertise the plight of this group and to urge a liberalization of Canada's immigration policy. Time and time again she propounded themes, which, even today, are still relevant: Immigration barriers must be lowered to allow skilled and cultured immigrants to settle in Canada; this country needs talented artisans, scientists, industrialists and creative artists to introduce new capital, to exploit undeveloped opportunities, and to create new industries and employment.

Senator Wilson also enlisted the aid of refugees themselves in her efforts to promote their cause. Notable among these was Mrs. A.H. Askanasy, a Jewish refugee from Vienna, who settled in British Columbia and later established citizenship courts for women in western Canada. In the winter of 1938-39, while she was in Ottawa, Mrs. Askanasy addressed several groups, including a large meeting staged in the Manor House's billiard room and luncheons that the Senator held in her honour at the Parliamentary Restaurant and the Chateau Laurier. It was this last occasion that Cairine Wilson's good friend, Isabel Percival, remembered so vividly almost forty-five years later. According to the doughty president of Ketchum Manufacturing Company, the newly arrived refugee tried to impress upon her hand-picked audience the gravity of the situation in Austria, but failed miserably. It seems that the six or so ladies assembled at the luncheon table that day just could not believe her tales of Nazi-organized terrorization of the Jews. Finally the guest of honour blurted out, "It's obvious there's no way I can convey to you the seriousness of the situation in Austria."[17]

* * * *

All these efforts on behalf of the refugee cause take second place, however, to the role Cairine Wilson played in helping to found Canada's foremost non-sectarian refugee pressure group, the Canadian National Committee on Refugees and Victims of Political Persecution (CNCR). She spearheaded its founding in the fall of 1938, shortly after she had been elected a vice-president of the International Federation of the League of Nations Societies and at a time when the League itself was beginning to seem almost irrelevant. Spurred on by the new pogroms in the fall of 1938, the Canadian lobby, under Senator Wilson's leadership, began to mobilize to fight for a liberalization of Canada's immigration policy. To this end, the Executive Committee passed a resolution on 15 October authorizing the establishment of a new body, the Canadian National Committee on Refugees and Victims of Political Persecution, later shortened to the Canadian National Committee on Refugees. To provide a springboard for the organization's formal launching, the committee also began making arrangements for a national conference on refugees to be held that December under the joint chairmanship of Senator Wilson and Dr T.H. Leggett.

When it convened at the Chateau Laurier in Ottawa on 6 December, the conference brought together about a hundred and forty delegates from some twenty-five English-speaking organizations, including such disparate groups as the Anglican Church of Canada, the National Council of Women, the National Council of Canadian YMCAs, the Royal Architectural Institute of Canada, the Canadian Jewish Congress, and two organizations that Cairine Wilson herself had been instrumental in launching: the Twentieth Century Liberal Association and the National Federation of Liberal Women of Canada. Among those who participated in the prolonged, and sometimes heated, discussions was voluble Charlotte Whitton, with whom the Senator often had many a heated argument. At the opening session, the social worker made an impassioned plea for care and restraint, insisting that the Committee not allow itself to be carried away by impetuosity, no matter how humane its motives. There were other refugees besides those who had been driven out of Germany — refugees in Spain, Poland, Italy, parts of Russia, the Baltic states and China — and the Committee, Whitton said, should confine itself to statements of principle and not attempt to deal with questions it was not competent to handle.

She then warned against concentrating large numbers of immigrants in Canada's principal centres of population, observing that even among such professions as doctors, lawyers and teachers there was bitter opposition to certain forms of immigration. Finally, she suggested that the federal government provide money to establish refugees "elsewhere" or, as she later explained, "in areas and countries now but semi-settled and set apart for such purposes."[18]

Cairine Wilson did not share Whitton's views. Refuting one of the social worker's later observations, she pointed out that many of those present had given a great deal of thought to the problem and that the Committee was therefore entirely competent to formulate detailed proposals. There had been enough stalling and prevarication. Canada had a duty to help these people and should act now.

Another speaker, the Reverend Dr Claris Silcox of the United Church of Canada, also took issue with Whitton. Like Wilson a pro-refugee advocate, he lamented the fact that the Government had not heeded a warning issued by the Social Service Council of Canada in 1936 to draw up long-range plans for admitting and resettling thousands of refugees. Now, he stressed, there was no time for long-range planning. The Government must act at once to help resolve an urgent problem.

Silcox painted a moving picture of what it was like to be a pro-refugee lobbyist, besieged day after day by heart-rending appeals from concentration camp inmates and other unfortunates. Some of these refugees, he insisted, should be admitted to Canada. In fact, if the Canadian government acted more humanely and idealistically, the economic problems facing the country might well be solved.[19]

Listening to Dr Silcox, Cairine Wilson must have reflected on the numerous letters from refugees that she too had received in recent months, many from highly qualified professionals, but a large number from people in less exalted walks of life. As she pondered Silcox's stirring exhortation to the Canadian government, she must have wondered what it would take to prod the cabinet into a more humane refugee policy.

Some inkling of just what the Committee and its supporters were up against was provided by an informal meeting which had convened earlier that day in the sandstone Langevin block on the corner of Confederation Square. There, in T.H. Crerar's office, some twenty-five members of the Committee, led by Cairine Wilson, had listened to the well-intentioned, but somewhat misguided minister outline the perceived difficulties faced by his government in lowering immigration barriers. Several familiar arguments had been resurrected: money assigned to the resettlement of refugees might be better spent assisting Canada's unemployed; all sorts of subterfuges were resorted to in an effort to get people into Canada and if visitors' permits were issued indiscriminately, there would not be enough ships to bring to Canada all the people who wanted to come; certain countries would infiltrate refugee ranks with fifth column elements; and the Government could only act when public opinion was behind it.

Another stumbling block was Crerar's conviction that the Nazis' actions against the Jews had a strictly economic motive. As the minutes of that meeting dryly record it: "Mr Crerar thought that action against the Jews in Germany was purely economic, that is, the wealth of the Jews was being seized to assist German finances, and fear was expressed of what might happen if Germany got away with it. Other countries might be tempted to take similar action."[20]

The following morning, in a whirlwind session, the Committee passed a series of resolutions calling for the appointment of an executive committee and the mounting of an ambitious education program to combat anti-Semitism and to fight for a liberalization of Canada's immigration policy. With the adoption of these resolutions, Canada's leading refugee organization began to take shape.

More groundwork was laid that afternoon when the Senator led an eleven-member delegation to the Prime Minister's office in the East Block on Parliament Hill. They informed King and nine members of his cabinet that "the growing intensity of the persecutions and sufferings of thousands of these unhappy people constitutes a great challenge to the reality of our humanitarianism; and that our loyalty to our democratic principles and traditions, and our hope for them, make it imperative that we render what help we can in this urgent situation."[21]

Unfortunately this plea failed to goad the Prime Minister into action. Those looking for a positive response received only a suggestion that an approach be made to the provincial governments. King might accede to Cairine Wilson's personal request for an interview, but he was not prepared to promise anything, even to representatives of a fledgling pressure group headed by a long-time friend and dedicated supporter.

It must have been with a sense of increasing frustration, then, that a weary Cairine Wilson convened a meeting of the CNCR's executive committee in her office that evening. Well aware of the daunting challenge they faced, the Committee drew up a plan of action. To carry it out, they named the League of Nations Society in Canada's secretariat the new organization's secretariat and designated Constance Hayward of the Society's staff as its executive secretary. They then formulated a request to individuals and organizations comprising the main committee to provide for an expense fund of $1,000 and made arrangements for the executive committee to become more representative. Senator Wilson and Dr T.H. Leggett were asked to continue as co-chairmen, although the Committee recognized "the great burden which this placed upon them." When Leggett regretfully declined the position of joint chairman, Cairine Wilson found herself shouldering the "great burden" alone. Just how onerous and demanding a responsibility this would prove to be, events would soon reveal.

Part of this responsibility involved publicizing the work of the CNCR and soliciting financial support and cooperation from other organizations. Along with Constance Hayward, Anna (Nan) Cooke, who later became the tireless chairman of the CNCR's Ottawa branch, Mrs Kathleen Price, wife of the Dominion carilloneur, and other dedicated workers, Cairine Wilson mounted many a public platform during the winter of 1938-39.[22] At one point, early in her apprenticeship, she reported in a letter to young Cairine, "Yesterday Miss Hayward spoke at the Women's Guild at St. Andrew's Church on refugee questions, and I was at the meeting of the Knox Church Ladies' Aid. However, I fear I did not do my subject justice for I had very little time for preparation and have not had much experience at discussing the particular aspects of refugee settlement."[23]

One of her first public appearances — made while she was laying the groundwork for the CNCR — was before the Women's Canadian Club of Montreal where, on 28 November, she joined Lord Marley, Deputy Speaker of the House of Lords, on the speakers' dais. A fervent apostle of increased aid to refugees, Lord Marley was in Montreal to publicize the plight of these unfortunates and to enlist the support of sympathetic groups such as the Women's Canadian Club.

During a question period after his address, Lord Marley queried the Senator about what Canada was doing for refugees; to her chagrin Cairine Wilson was forced to concede that what was being done was "lamentably small." By way of explanation, she noted that only a few refugees were being admitted and that these were individuals with capital, agricultural workers of five years' standing, professionals, or entrepreneurs in a position to establish new enterprises. Then, with just that touch of irony that was one of her trademarks, she said that she had asked immigration officials why, since so many refugees with capital had come in, a few with no money should not be admitted. In reply, Lord Marley commented on the good luck of Canada, unlike Britain, in having women in its "House of Lords."[24]

Among the first organizations before which Senator Wilson appeared in her new capacity as CNCR chairman was the Ottawa chapter of Hadassah, the Women's Zionist Organization of America. The occasion was a large dinner which Hadassah staged at the Chateau Laurier on 13 December 1938, a week after the CNCR's first general meeting. Here, before an audience of over 430 members of the local Jewish community, she pledged to continue her interest in the refugee question, declaring, "I would not be worthy of the name of woman were my heart not wrung by the troubles to which your people have been subjected."[25]

According to press reports, this was the first Hadassah dinner Cairine Wilson had ever attended. If this is correct, the occasion was memorable for more than one reason because it was from this platform that prominent Ottawa merchant A. J. Freiman delivered the Canadian Zionist Organization's first official response to certain Jewish resettlement proposals that had been aired at the Evian Conference. The brainchild of Reinhard Heydrich, head of the S.S. Security Service, and other Nazis as well as some non-German Europeans, these proposals — the so-called "Madagascar Plan" — called for the resettlement of millions of European Jews on the French-owned island of Madagascar.[26] Speaking in his capacity as president of the organization, Archibald Freiman declared:

> We don't want the jungles of Africa — we are people, we are human beings. We don't want to hurt anybody, but we have a right as human beings to be on this earth. We are not any better, but certainly not any worse and you cannot show me a time in history when Jews acted towards nations as an alleged civilized nation is treating the Jews in Germany. We don't want the jungles of Africa, we want Palestine.[27]

Of course, what none of his more than four-hundred listeners knew then was that eventually the Madagascar Plan would collapse and that the chemical compound Zyklon B and the Nazi death camps would supplant it as the solution to "the Jewish problem."

Cairine Wilson's closest friend and associate in the work of the CNCR was Constance Hayward, who was in her early thirties when she became involved with the Senator in the refugee cause. A native of Moncton, New Brunswick, Hayward belonged to that small group of Canadian families for whom great wealth is regarded not so much as an avenue to luxury as an opportunity for service. Like Cairine Wilson, she could easily have spent her time in travel and frivolous pursuits. Instead, she, like the Senator, chose to work hard for others and to donate large sums of money to charities and institutions.

To her position as CNCR executive secretary she brought compassion, outstanding administrative ability and intellectual gifts. In 1927, at a time when it was unusual for Canadian women to obtain a college degree, she graduated from Acadia University in Wolfville, Nova Scotia. She then proceeded to the Ontario College of Education and, after three years of teaching at the Scarborough Collegiate Institute, to the London School of Economics. There she took a course in international relations designed principally for men entering the foreign service. Returning to Canada in a "crusading spirit," she began organizing study groups for the League of Nations Society in Canada and giving addresses on the deteriorating situation in Europe. (In the fledgling Department of External Affairs women were not encouraged to apply for foreign postings unless they were secretaries!)[28] It was in this capacity that she had first met Cairine Wilson who, although considerably older, would soon become a good friend. They would remain close friends right up until the Senator's death, by which time Constance Hayward had retired to Wolfville after working ten years for the CNCR and ten years as a senior official for the Department of Citizenship and Immigration.

But all this lay in the distant future when Cairine Wilson and Constance Hayward began marshalling their energies in the winter of 1938-39 to launch the CNCR on its ten-year career. For both of them it was a frenetic winter so demanding were the challenges posed by the establishment of this new organization. There were not only countless addresses to give, there was a membership drive to organize, fund-raising efforts to mastermind, and endless meetings to arrange and conduct. Never could refugees and their plight be far from the Senator's mind as Evelyn Rosenthal, a dedicated worker for the League of Nations Society in Canada and the CNCR, discovered. In 1986, she recalled an unexpected visit that Clifford, the Wilson chauffeur, made to the Rosenthal home one morning. Looming up unannounced, he presented Miss Rosenthal with a box from Cairine Wilson. When Miss Rosenthal opened it, she discovered to her astonishment that it contained a pheasant skin, which was just what she needed for the "fancies" that she made for men's and women's sports hats. "When I phoned the Senator to thank her profusely, she explained that she had attended a dinner the night before where pheasant had been served with a skin over it. Knowing that I used pheasant feathers to make fancies for sale by the refugee committee, she saved the skin for me."[29]

A large number of organizations would endorse the CNCR's aims and provide invaluable support. Chief among these were the Jewish refugee societies, such as the Canadian Jewish Congress refugee committee, which financed the direct and indirect costs of several CNCR projects. Provincial and welfare agencies would also furnish assistance on refugee matters, as well as leading national organizations representing a broad spectrum of interests. Additional help would come from a wide range of other social, educational, religious and professional organizations.

That winter — on 23 February 1939 — Cairine and Norman Wilson celebrated their thirtieth wedding anniversary, if "celebrated" can be used in this sense, for the Wilsons never observed these events with much fanfare. As always, on such occasions, Mackenzie King sent his congratulations and best wishes. In her reply to the punctilious bachelor, the Senator observed, "Although much has happened during the past thirty years, I can hardly imagine that it is so long since we met at Quebec, when Norman and I were first engaged, and so happy to take part with you in the Henry IV court at the tercentennial celebrations."[30]

Because of the demands made on her time by the CNCR, to say nothing of her Senate and other responsibilities, there was little time for reminiscing in the early months of 1939. That March, for example, arrangements had to be completed for the CNCR's second general meeting. Although the Committee was based in Ottawa — sharing office space with the League of Nations Society in Canada at 124 Wellington Street — this second general meeting convened at Toronto's Royal York Hotel. Here, on 20 March, Cairine Wilson chaired the morning's proceedings before hurrying off to a speaking engagement in Hamilton.[31]

As a result of decisions taken at this meeting, a telegram was dispatched to the Prime Minister. Predictably, it urged immediate government action to lower immigration barriers. But it also demanded a clear statement from the Government about Canada's commitment to the Intergovernmental Committee on Refugees and pledged the CNCR to raise large sums of money for the care of refugees, provided that the Government indicated the number to be admitted and the guarantees required. To underline the urgency of the situation, it requested an early meeting with King.[32]

In March Cairine Wilson led another CNCR delegation to see the Prime Minister and once again the Committee was treated to bland platitudes. As Constance Hayward later summarized the meeting, King gave the delegation assurances "that there would be a change in policy in the refugees' favour. But governments move slowly."[33] The following month the Senator again petitioned the Prime Minister, this time regarding an urgent request from the International Commission for the Assistance of Child Refugees in Spain which had asked her to intervene with the Canadian government on its behalf. Writing in her own handwriting, Cairine Wilson said:

> ...The Situation is so dreadful that I hope it will be possible for Canada to send some of the food so sorely needed.

> We are planning to leave tomorrow by motor for a few days in Virginia, which explains the Sunday letter. I hate to be away, but know it will be a good thing to forget for a few hours.[34]

As for the CNCR, it moved quickly to establish a special "campaign committee" with G. Raymond Booth, of the Society of Friends, as secretary. Located in Toronto, it began raising funds to defray the CNCR's administrative expenses and to assist in the settlement of needy refugees who had succeeded in breaching the immigration wall. Later that year the campaign committee would merge with the CNCR's executive committee and the CNCR would move its administrative headquarters to Toronto where a great deal of refugee case work had developed. It was a move that Cairine Wilson must have regarded with mixed emotions. On the one hand, she would have recognized the need for the CNCR's administrative quarters to be where most of the refugees were located, but she must have regretted the prospect of having to spend still more time on business trips away from home and family.

The early months of 1939 found the Senator occupied as never before with refugee matters. From all quarters appeals for assistance poured in, including one from the evangelical-minded temperance leader, author and co-appellant in the *Persons'* case, Nellie McClung. From Regina, which she was then visiting, Mrs. McClung wrote on 6 March 1939:

> Dear Senator Wilson:

> I have a friend in Bielefeld, Germany, a Miss Theresa Henson, and she has written me guarded, but anguished

letters concerning the plight of some of her friends there
— Jewish people. Now I have received letters from them,
and I am at a loss to know what we can do for them. No
doubt you are flooded with similar letters.

Some of them have drawn high quota numbers from
the United States, but want to come here to wait their time.
All of them would like to come to Canada, and stay now.
Have you a better chance of getting permission for them
to come, and stay until they can enter the US?[35]

In a second letter, dated 26 March 1939, Nellie McClung implored the
Senator, even though she knew that she was "simply swamped" with
cases, to give her attention to two families that were of particular interest
to the women's activist from the West. One of these was a German rabbi,
who was serving at a Buffalo, New York synagogue and who wanted to
have his family admitted to the United States. According to Mrs McClung,
the rabbi wanted to see the American immigration agents at Niagara Falls,
Ontario, believing that if he did so, he could obtain permission for his wife
and his children to enter the United States. Kronheim found his plans
thwarted right from the start, however, by the refusal of the Canadian
immigration agent to let him see his American counterpart Continued
Mrs McClung:

Surely there can be no danger in granting this privilege. I will enclose his letter. I have written to Mr Blair,
but a word from you is better than many letters.
With kindest regards and congratulations on the good
fight you are waging on behalf of these poor helpless
people.[36]

Nellie McClung's faith in Cairine Wilson's dedication and powers of
persuasion is certainly touching. It is not known, however, if in this
instance her faith was well placed.

The Senator's friendship with Dr Charley Best was no doubt responsible for her efforts on behalf of Dr Bruno Mendel, a research scientist who
was employed by the University of Toronto's Banting Institute after he
had arrived in this country with his own laboratory equipment, library and
personal assistant. It is not clear what request Dr Mendel made of the
Government (He may have asked it to help finance some of his research),
but on 17 April 1939 an aroused Cairine Wilson wrote to Dr Frederick
Banting, the co-discoverer of insulin:

Many times I have longed to have a talk with you
about the awful problem of refugees and am particularly

pleased that the Society for the Protection of Science and Learning has been formed from the members of the faculties of our universities. Dr R.C. Wallace (Principal of Queen's University) was in Ottawa on Friday when he spoke at the annual meeting of the Victorian Order of Nurses, and I have also had a letter from Dr Huntsman, as well as a few words on the subject from Dr Charley Best.

I was somewhat horrified on Saturday morning when, in conversation with Mr F.C. Blair, he seemed to think that Dr Bruno Mendel was asking a great favour, for Canada had shown such generosity in admitting him and his family. I endeavoured to tell Mr Blair that as far as I understood the matter, Canada was benefitting from Dr Mendel's presence in Canada and that I did not think that they had been the recipients of any generosity from the Goverrnment.

I am exceedingly sorry that this letter is so hurried, for we are leaving Ottawa in a few minutes for a short motor trip to Virginia, and expect to [be] back in eight days. It seems dreadful to go away from all these troubles but I feel that perhaps I shall be able to accomplish more on my return. It is such a help to know that you are interested and I trust that we shall be able to enlist the sympathy of the members of the Leadership League.[37]

On the subject of Dr Mendel, Sir Lyman Duff wrote:

We are leaving this morning for Quebec. I hope I shall see you shortly when I must try to get you to speak more explicitly about Dr Mendel. I have really been very pre-occupied since I saw you last and I am afraid I am getting to be a bit too much of a recluse, or worse. It is impossible to exaggerate the importance of supporting and encouraging men like Dr Mendel. Speaking broadly, their work is simply incalculable in its results. I feel that I am becoming a legal monastic while the real world goes on outside.

I hope you won't mind my saying that you are choosing the higher part in giving your sympathy and support to these people.[38]

While the Senator poured her energies into fighting for the admission of individual refugees and their families, the CNCR under her chairmanship was busy organizing local chapters across the country and lobbying for the admission of more refugees. It also sought to educate the Canadian public about the plight of these people. Often this education program took the form of "educational tours" undertaken by members of the executive Committee and other pro-refugee speakers, who fanned across the country addressing service clubs and community groups. Frequently it embraced pro-refugee articles, such as the piece which Cairine Wilson composed for *The Key*, a newsletter issued by one of Canada's more elitist women's service organizations, the Junior League of Toronto. In the June 1939 issue she wrote:

> The members of the Junior League are tremendously interested in the Humane Society and we know that their efforts have meant much in preventing cruelty towards animals. Among the victims of persecution today are cultured and educated people, including some of the most famous brains of the world, who will die from conditions of labour far harder than we would think fit for a criminal in penal servitude, and under conditions from which any animal would be protected.

> The persecution of the Jewish and non-Aryan population has been so intensified that we are apt to overlook the fact that the refugee question has never been especially Jewish, even in the countries which make anti-Semitism their leading idea. Nobody can be true to ideals of religion, liberty, and democratic principles and exist under a Nazi or Fascist regime. Without a belief in the dignity of man, without indignation against arbitrarily created human suffering, there can be no democratic principles.

> ...The opportunity is ours today which is never likely to occur again, for our country can profit by the admission of political and Jewish refugees.[39]

In a different category altogether were "refugee success" stories destined for public consumption. Usually these were planted in daily newspapers by the energetic Constance Hayward, who never missed an opportunity to publicize the contributions of refugees, particularly when these contributions benefited Canada's war effort.

One refugee, who soon came to the CNCR's attention, and who became an outstanding success in his adopted country, was Thomas Bata, the Czech-born industrialist and later head of the Bata shoemaking empire. In March 1938, just a few days before German troops invaded his homeland, Bata, then aged twenty-four, fled to Switzerland. From there he eventually made his way to England where he sought permission to enter Canada and establish his shoemaking business. When it became apparent that well- orchestrated pressure would have to be exerted on the Canadian government to obtain the necessary permission, the CNCR went to work. In the spring of 1939, for example, a recently established committee in Belleville, Ontario organized representations from assorted boards of trade, county councils, and area MPs on behalf of the Bata Shoe Company, while in Toronto the acting secretary of the CNCR's Toronto branch spearheaded a letter campaign to the press.[40] In due course Thomas Bata and eighty-two of his key Czech workers settled just outside of Frankford, Ontario, where they laid the foundations of a business that would employ over seven hundred workers by the fall of 1940 and become an international success story in the post-war years. In fact, by March 1944, the Bata Shoe Company would be one of at least fifty "refugee" industries established in Canada since 1939.

Another such industry — and again one in which Cairine Wilson and the CNCR took a special interest — was a flourishing glove-making factory that the Czech Jewish entrepreneur, Louis Fischl, had established near Prescott, Ontario. Fischl had been conducting a thriving export business to North America when the storm clouds began to gather over Europe. Realizing that another war was inevitable, he contacted the Canadian government to see if he could transfer his glove-making operations from Czechoslovakia to Canada. As he had capital, equipment and personnel, his application for an immigration permit was granted, and in due course Fischl, his immediate family, and more than one hundred Czechs, some of whom were related to him, settled in and around the small Ontario town of Prescott. Such was the success of this glove-making enterprise that Senator Wilson and members of the CNCR seized on it to illustrate the benefits that could accrue from increased immigration, believing that Fischl's example could not help but further the refugee cause. For Cairine Wilson especially, it was a showcase industry that invited mention in various pleas for a lowering of immigration barriers as, for example, on 18 May 1943 when she noted in the Senate, "Prior to the war England suffered severely from unemployment, yet refugee industries that were set up there brought relief to many distressed areas. And the mayor of one of our smaller municipalities said that, thanks to the glove industry established by a refugee from Czechoslovakia there was no unemployment in the town."[41]

Cairine Wilson was not content just to exploit the public relations potential of the glove factory, however. She also assisted members of the

Fischl family, one of whom was Hanna Fischl Spencer, who, on 19 December 1945, when she was a young housewife in Trail, British Columbia, expressed her gratitude to the Senator on the back of a Christmas card: "Today, your voice came over the radio as if you were in this room. And once again I realized how indebted I am to you for the happiness which I am enjoying now. As one of the many whom you have helped, your words had special meaning for me."[42]

Hanna arrived in Canada in 1939 from England, where she had been employed as a domestic. Although she had a Ph.D. and had taught in Czechoslovakia before fleeing abroad, she had to go to work in her Uncle Louis's glove factory because this had been the condition of her being admitted to Canada. But the young woman yearned to return to teaching and so one day late in 1940 she went to Ottawa to seek the advice of Charles Bowman, Editor of the *Ottawa Citizen*. After dropping in unannounced on Bowman in his office, she explained why she had come and he immediately picked up the phone and called Cairine Wilson. On receiving his call, the Senator promptly invited him and Hanna to tea at the Manor House. They arrived an hour or so later to find themselves surrounded by children of all ages, including British evacuees who were staying with the Wilsons. Shortly afterwards, while the toddlers were climbing all over Hanna, Mrs Buck, the Principal of Elmwood School, arrived, having also been invited. The adults sipped tea and then Hanna returned to Prescott. A few days later, in mid-term, she received a letter from Mrs Buck offering her a job at Elmwood. Hanna began teaching there in January 1941 and only left in July 1942 to marry Elvins Spencer and move to Windsor, Ontario.

Cairine Wilson's involvement in Hanna's life began even before the memorable tea party, although the young woman did not realize it at the time. Her diary reveals that on 1 November 1939 her Uncle Louis returned from Ottawa with the news that F.C. Blair had asked him if he had any objection to Hanna's giving a lecture in the capital. With her uncle's consent, she dutifully addressed the Junior Branch of the League of Nations Society in Canada on 25 November. Before she left Ottawa to return to Prescott she found herself inundated with requests to speak to other organizations: the League of Nations Society in Canada (the adults' section), the Ottawa Teachers College, the Canadian National Committee on Refugees, a church group and a school. When she addressed the Zonta Club of Ottawa the following January, Anna Cooke, who had introduced her, reported that the evening had been "a tremendous success" and that "within forty minutes [Hanna] had won Ottawa ... and converted it for the refugees."[43] Hanna Spencer has since asked herself if Cairine Wilson and her friends ever realized what a snowball effect these initial speaking engagements had. Within two to three months Senator Wilson's protégée addressed some forty-five different groups in the Prescott area, including two in New York State!

Cairine Wilson's and the CNCR's efforts to combat anti-Semitism were another important feature of their continuing education program. These were given a new sense of urgency by the so-called "Voyage of the Damned," an infamous voyage that held up a mirror to mankind.

On 13 May 1939, 936 passengers — 930 of them Jewish refugees — sailed from Hamburg, Germany on the Cuba-bound luxury liner, *St. Louis*. Without exception, all the refugees had been stripped of their possessions and driven from their homes and businesses. Nevertheless, before the Nazi noose tightened completely, each had managed to scrape together the necessary funds for the boat passage to Cuba and to obtain an official landing certificate signed by Cuba's director general of immigration.

When the *St. Louis* docked at Havana on the 27 May, however, only 28 passengers were allowed to leave the ship. Lengthy negotiations were conducted with the Cuban government but in vain, and at the insistence of the Cuban president, the *St. Louis* left Havana harbour on 2 June.

In an attempt to allow more time for negotiations with Cuban authorities and other governments, the ship sailed slowly northward. But all appeals went unanswered. Finally, in a last desperate effort to obtain sanctuary, the distraught passengers sent a telegram to American president Franklin Roosevelt. It went unanswered. Instead, the American authorities sent a coast guard cutter to shadow the liner and to make sure that not a single frantic passenger managed to swim to shore.[44] In Canada, 44 well-known Torontonians, led by Professor George M. Wrong of the University of Toronto, sent a telegram to Mackenzie King urging him to offer the homeless exiles sanctuary in this country. Among the signatories were B.K. Sandwell, the illustrious editor of *Saturday Night* and later honorary chairman of the CNCR, another CNCR board member, Sir Ellsworth Flavelle, the wealthy industrialist son of Sir Joseph Flavelle,[45] and Sir Robert Falconer, past-president of the League of Nations Society in Canada and in 1939 honorary chairman of the CNCR.[46]

The telegram met with a negative response. King, who was in Washington at the time accompanying King George VI and Queen Elizabeth on the final leg of a triumphant North American tour, instructed his advisers in Ottawa to tell Wrong that the question was under consideration. This telegram was followed on 19 June by a letter advising Wrong that it was impossible to admit refugees en bloc to Canada. Once again, Ernest Lapointe and F.C. Blair had intervened to prevent the admission of Jewish refugees.[47] With all appeals rejected, the *St. Louis* had no alternative but to continue its voyage to Europe where almost certain death awaited most of its passengers.

Only one month previously J.S. Woodsworth, founding leader of the Co-operative Commonwealth Federation, had written to Cairine Wilson on the subject of refugees:

I am sure that you must feel half desperate with regard
to the response which has met your efforts along these
lines. I personally feel almost ashamed of our Canadian
smugness and selfishness.

I know that for most Canadians Europe is a long way
off, but it would seem as if on the whole we are quite
content to reap any advantage that may come through our
dealings with a disturbed world, without on the other
hand, being willing to assume any responsibility for the
distress which our neighbours are suffering.[48]

* * * *

On 10 September 1939, while Cairine Wilson was vacationing at her
beloved Clibrig, Canada declared war on Germany. It was just ten years
since the onset of the Great Depression, and Canada, now a nation of
nearly 11 million, was still trying to recover from that ordeal. The war
would spell the end of the Depression, the doubling of the gross national
product, and the creation of new industries that would figure prominently
in the post-war economy. But the costs would be high: 43,000 men and
women lost in combat and a quadrupling of the national debt.

Cairine Wilson did not return to Ottawa for the opening of Parliament
on 7 September 1939. As a result, she was not in the Senate chamber that
afternoon to hear Governor General Lord Tweedsmuir read the Throne
speech before her Senate colleagues and assembled members of the House
of Commons. Not until the middle of the month — after saying good bye
to sculptor Felix de Weldon, who had spent the summer at Clibrig
modelling her portrait in clay — would she and Norman journey back to
the nation's capital.

In no time this small, sedate capital would be swollen by an influx of
civilian and military personnel for, in addition to being the seat of
government and the headquarters for all three armed services, Ottawa was
also the largest air-training centre in Canada and an important recruiting
depot. Among those who took up residence in the capital during these
years were leading Canadians in business and industry who went to work
for the Canadian government and who were known as "Dollar-a-Year
Men," although most of those employed full-time were paid at the going
rate. The new arrivals also included refugees, particularly British children,
who stayed with Ottawa families during the war. Among the refugees was
at least one distinguished royal personage — Crown Princess Juliana,
daughter of Queen Wilhelmina of the Netherlands. Forced to flee Holland
after the Nazis invaded her country, Princess Juliana arrived in Ottawa

with her two daughters, Beatrix and Irene, in June 1940. Like many a less exalted refugee, this unassuming woman would become a friend of Cairine Wilson and a visitor to The Manor House.

After the outbreak of war, Cairine and Norman saw three of their children enlist in the armed services. Angus, after his graduation from Ashbury and a year's pre-medical training at McGill University, joined the Royal Canadian Signals Corps and spent four-and-a-half-years in Europe while Robert spent the years from August 1941 to the conclusion of hostilities as an Observer with the RCAF. Even Peggy joined the services. In December 1941, she was taken on strength as a private in the first group to be accepted into the Canadian Women's Army Corps. After taking a basic training course at Gananoque, she returned to Ottawa where she was attached to the Royal Canadian Ordinance Corps.

The Wilsons' two sons-in-law made notable contributions to the war effort. Chemist Alan Gill, Olive's husband, accompanied General A.G.L. McNaughton to England in 1939 on a Canadian Manufacturers Association mission on armaments. While there he worked with the British Standards Institution on the coordination of British and Canadian standards and specifications for war purposes. On returning to Canada, he took a leave of absence from the National Research Council and went to the Department of Munitions and Supply where he became Assistant Director General of Munitions.[49]

Stockbroker Charles Burns, Janet's husband, joined the RCAF after the outbreak of war and rose eventually to the rank of wing commander. In his new role he organized the flying control for Eastern Air Command, an organization which saved at least a hundred airmen from a watery grave in the Atlantic off the shores of the Maritimes, Newfoundland and Labrador.

The war also had an impact on the CNCR's work. When it was founded, the organization had assigned high priority to lobbying for a liberalization of Canada's immigration policy. The outbreak of hostilities, however, forced a change in tactics. After all, a government that had been decidedly opposed to refugee immigration before the outbreak of the war could hardly be expected to devote more time and attention to refugee questions now that thousands of men and women had to be mobilized and outfitted for the armed forces and all kinds of new industries created. The CNCR therefore stopped pressing for immediate legislative changes in immigration policy and instead began to concentrate on trying to obtain the admission of individuals and single family units; providing the Government with guarantees of financial assistance for refugees and aiding them in establishing themselves in Canada.

With her quiet determination, unflagging persistence and compassion, Cairine Wilson was ideally suited to this task. Not one to give in to despair, she went on badgering government officials, pleading individual cases before cabinet ministers, and unravelling reams of government red tape in her attempts to get individual refugees into Canada. Many of them never learned the identity of their benefactor until they arrived in this country, if ever.

A case in point is that of a Czechoslovakian tool designer and his wife who fled their native country after it had been invaded by Germany and finally made their way to Lisbon. The tool designer wrote numerous letters from Portugal in an attempt to obtain an American visa, but in vain. With his meagre resources shrinking rapidly and the Portuguese government considering the establishment of concentration camps for foreigners, the man became desperate. It was then that he chanced to flip through his address book and discover Sir Robert Falconer's address. He had recorded it some months previously after reading an article about the CNCR in a Paris newspaper. He wrote immediately to Sir Robert who turned the letter over to Cairine Wilson with the poignant comment, "So many of these and we can do nothing".[50]

The Senator thought differently. She got in touch with her old friend, Layton Ralston, the Minister of Defence, and he contacted two or three other parties. Eventually the Director of Immigration told her, in despair, that if the couple could pass the medical examination, they could come to Canada. They passed the exam and finally made their way to this country via Havana and New York. In April 1941, in Ottawa, the Czech tool designer met the Senator for the first time.

The war may have discouraged attempts to press for legislative changes in government immigration policy, but it did not deter Cairine Wilson and the CNCR from continuing to exert pressure on the Government to admit more refugees. As part of this non-stop campaign the Committee, in 1943, organized a nation-wide petition urging Ottawa to admit victims of political or religious persecution without regard to race, creed, or financial condition. Reflecting the CNCR's realistic appraisal of the situation, the petition did not seek permanent changes in the Immigration Act or unrestricted immigration. Instead, it merely requested the waiving of certain restrictions to allow more victims of Nazi persecution, particularly those living in neutral countries such as Spain and Portugal, to enter Canada. To make the appeal more palatable to the Government, the CNCR gave assurances that it would help to support all refugees who might be admitted to Canada, except those looked after by the United Jewish Refugee and War Relief Agencies or individual sponsors.

Coincidental with the launching of the CNCR petition — the autumn of 1943 — the Government finalized arrangements to admit 200 refugee families from the Iberian Peninsula. On 2 November 1943, Mackenzie

King announced details of the timid scheme to the press, without mentioning that a limit of 200 families had been placed on the movement. Immediately a storm of protest went up from the anti-refugee interests who, fearing the worst, anticipated an unchecked flow of immigrants to Canada and the Government's surrender to pressure from the Jewish lobby.

Among the most vocal and cynical opponents of the project was Maurice Duplessis, leader of the Union Nationale opposition in Quebec and provincial premier before his party's defeat in the 1939 provincial election. At a rousing pre-election political meeting he charged that federal and provincial Liberals would allow the "International Zionist Brotherhood" to settle 100,000 Jewish refugees in Quebec in return for election financing.[51] The organization that he named was a pure invention and the allegation a pernicious falsehood. But such was Duplessis's performance and the anti-Jewish climate in Quebec that the charge struck a responsive chord. In no time at all the issue was enlivened by charges, countercharges and denials. And shortly thereafter the charismatic politician was re-elected premier of Quebec. But not before Cairine Wilson and the leaders of other refugee organizations had entered the fray. Determined to expose the politician's fraud, the Senator observed in an interview:

> It [Duplessis's allegation] will do more good than
> harm because his statements are so patently absurd. It is
> a direct political move. He is trying to build up his own
> political position on racial prejudice.[52]

Notwithstanding Duplessis's charges and the general anti-refugee clamour, refugees from the Iberian Peninsula were admitted to Canada in the spring of 1944. Of these, the CNCR helped to locate and support twenty-two families: fourteen in Toronto, four in Montreal, one in Hamilton and three in Winnipeg.

As for the CNCR petition, it met with only limited success despite the organization's vigorous four-year education program. But if Cairine Wilson was disappointed by this development, she was even more upset by the failure of the CNCR's valiant attempts to bring refugee children from Europe to Canada. In fact, the Senator confessed to a Senate Immigration and Labour Committee hearing in 1948 that the failure of their efforts in this connection represented one of her "most heartbreaking experiences".[53]

By the spring of 1939, more than 9,000 refugee children, many of them orphans, had made their way by various means from the Continent to

Britain. Most of these youngsters were Jewish and they came mainly from Germany, Austria, Poland, Czechoslovakia, and Spain.

When Senator Wilson and the CNCR became aware of these children, they lobbied the Canadian government to have one hundred of them admitted to Canada for adoption or guaranteed hospitality under the auspices of the CNCR. Ottawa finally gave its permission for such a scheme, but stipulated, among its three pages of regulations, that the children must be between three and thirteen years of age and either orphans or semi-orphans, i.e., children with one parent living but from whom a release had to be obtained.[54]

The CNCR executive hired a social worker to examine prospective candidates in Britain and spent many days in the winter of 1939-40 discussing arrangements with the federal and provincial governments, the Immigration Branch of the Department of Mines and Resources and various social agencies. On 16 May 1940, when the refugee situation was desperate, Cairine Wilson even wrote personally to the Prime Minister in an attempt to prod the Government into taking emergency action on behalf of such children.[55]

Her letter was followed the next day by a telegram signed by the Senator and Constance Hayward; still later a small CNCR delegation visited King. However, despite these and related efforts, the Government refused to waive any of its stringent regulations, in particular the one requiring that all children considered for the project have a signed release from a parent. As a result, only two children were admitted under the scheme and they were sent to British Columbia because an Englishwoman who was living there had asked for them some months, if not years, previously.[56]

Although she was very upset by the outcome of this project, Cairine Wilson had to admit that her efforts and those of the CNCR were not altogether wasted because the knowledge that they gained of all the regulations stood her in good stead when she served as a member of a government-appointed body involved in the evacuation of British children from the United Kingdom and Northern Ireland to Canada. Known as the National Advisory Committee for Children from Overseas, it was established by an order-in-council on 9 July 1940 in response to a growing demand for the Canadian government to evacuate endangered British children. In the government-assisted scheme which came into being, a British-appointed board (the Children's Overseas Reception Board) received applications, examined individual cases, classified the children and arranged for their transportation and assistance on the voyage, the costs of the crossing being defrayed by the British government. Then, at the Canadian port, the children were received by Immigration Branch officials who arranged for their transportation to provincial clearing centres. Here, provincial authorities took charge, and through the Children's Aid or other child welfare organizations, placed the youngsters in carefully selected homes.

As a member of the committee, Senator Wilson worked closely with Dr R.C. Wallace, its chairman and principal of Queen's University, and other committee members, such as Charlotte Whitton and her old friends, Fred Bronson and Ken Greene, to ensure the success of the evacuation movement. Thanks to their dedication to the cause and close cooperation among committees and governments at all levels, some 1,500 children were brought to Canada under government sponsorship during the summer of 1940. Then the program was abruptly terminated because of the sinking on 17 September 1940 of the S.S.*City of Benares* with the loss of 73 children and the difficulty of obtaining warships for convoy duty.[57]

Ironically, Sir Lyman Duff, had written to her just two weeks before the sinking of the S.S. *City of Benares*:

> I hope that you will not allow yourself to be completely overwhelmed by your concern about the refugees. For my own part, I have always doubted whether the risk of remaining in England was as great as the risk of attempting to cross the Atlantic. I shall be surprised if the migration of the children is not discontinued for a time at least. This, of course, is of no great comfort to you who have had the responsibility thrust upon you.[58]

Among the children who survived a treacherous crossing in the summer of 1940 were Michael, David and Judith Marshall, distant connections of Cairine Wilson's friends, Senator Adrian Knatchbull Hugessen and his wife, Margaret, who was very active in the CNCR's Montreal committee. The Marshall youngsters stayed with the Wilsons before returning to the U.K. in the winter of 1942-43. By the time the evacuation program came to an end, Cairine Wilson could take pride in the fact that she had played no small role in arranging for a sizable number of British children to spend the remaining war years in Canadian homes, far removed from the terrors of German bombing raids. She could also rejoice in the knowledge that the CNCR was now firmly on its feet; but it had been slow work. For a long time the Committee had been "Senator Wilson's Committee," always running out of money and always being saved by a cheque from the Senator.[59] Thanks to her determined efforts the CNCR had become a creditable national body with a growing reputation. With the taking on of a new role — the rendering of assistance to internment camp inmates — this reputation would be further enhanced and Cairine Wilson's title, "Mother of the Refugees," would take on new meaning.

10

SIR HERBERT EMERSON'S REPRESENTATIVE

When Cairine Wilson took up the refugee cause in 1938 she could not have imagined that one day she would become deeply involved in helping hundreds of hapless refugees who came to this country by accident rather than design. They were the approximately 2,500 Austrian, German and Italian refugees who had been transported from Britain to Canada in the dark days of June and July 1940 and then interned in Canadian camps under conditions suitable for the incarceration of dangerous prisoners-of-war and political subversives. The role that the Senator and her colleagues played in ameliorating conditions in these camps and in securing the release of individual internees came close to eclipsing everything else that the Canadian National Committee on Refugees accomplished.

Canada's involvement with the United Kingdom internees was anticipated by developments on the war front in the spring of 1940. That May Nazi forces swept through the Netherlands, Belgium and France and the British government, fearing an imminent assault on its shores, began rounding up thousands of Austrian and German nationals who might pose a threat to British security. Many were refugees who had fled Nazi oppression in their homelands while others were students enrolled in British schools and universities when the war broke out. No matter what their status, however, all had been previously declared good or relatively good security risks by one-man judicial tribunals established in the fall of

1939 after England declared war on Germany. Using dossiers supplied by the Home Office, these officials classified the thousands of enemy aliens who appeared before them as either "refugees from Nazi oppression" or as members of one of three categories:

A. Those men and women who were to be interned immediately;

B. Those who were to remain at liberty, but subject to restrictions;

C. Those German and Austrian nationals allowed to remain at liberty without restrictions.

The tribunals began their work in October 1939 and completed it six months later, by which time they had decreed internment for only one percent of the more than 73,000 cases that they had examined. And there the matter might have rested but for the German invasion of Norway and Denmark on 9 April 1940 and the development of war hysteria in Great Britain. As the German forces advanced southward, this hysteria mounted as did demands for the internment of larger numbers of enemy aliens. The demands met with a quick response for shortly after Winston Churchill replaced Neville Chamberlain as prime minister — on 10 May 1940 — the new government designated certain areas of the east and south coasts of the British Isles "protected areas" and decreed that all male Austrian and German nationals between the ages of 16 and 60 living in these regions be interned immediately.

When Hitler's armies swept into France and the German war machine was poised for an assault on England's shores, the internment criteria were widened to include individuals that the tribunals had earlier allowed to remain at liberty without any restrictions whatsoever. With Italy's entry into the war, on 10 June, it was decided to intern all Italians who had lived in England for less than twenty years.

It was against this backdrop of mounting panic that Vincent Massey, the Canadian high commissioner in London, cabled Ottawa on 30 May 1940 to ask whether in principle the Canadian government would be prepared to assist the hard-pressed British by receiving a number of enemy aliens who were "potentially dangerous." Ottawa cabled London that it was prepared to consider the question of interned enemy aliens, but was not in a position to "undertake acceptance." In reply, the United Kingdom government stated, on 7 June, that the situation was urgent because pro-Nazi civilians and German prisoners-of-war would be dangerous in the event of parachute landings in Britain or invasion by sea. It was hoped that Canada would accept almost 4,000 interned civilians and some 3,000 prisoners of war; the U.K. would defray their transportation and custody costs. This was followed by another cable three days later asking the Canadian government to accept just under 4,500 people, not the previous number of 7,000. By a strange quirk of fate, however, this cable never made it to the cabinet table before the Canadian government finally decided, on 10 June, to come to Britain's aid. As a result, Canada agreed to accept custody of nearly 7,000 male internees and POWs, not 4,500. On learning of this, British authorities decided to make up the difference in numbers with approximately 2,500 civilian internees from categories B and C. Later it would be discovered that about 75 precent of them were either Jewish or partly Jewish and violently anti-Nazi.

From that date the wheels of bureaucracy turned swiftly, so fast, in fact, that in less than two weeks the first shipload of civilian male internees and prisoners-of-war was on its way to Canada.[1] Before the summer of 1940 was over, close to five thousand German, Austrian and Italian internees and almost two thousand prisoners-of-war were packed into prison ships and transported across the submarine-infested Atlantic to Canada, where they were distributed among heavily guarded internment camps in the eastern part of the country.

The Canadian authorities had been led to believe that they were accepting custody of highly dangerous enemy aliens. They were some-what taken back, therefore, to find a motley assortment of teen-age school boys, university students, professors, priests, and rabbis among the prisoners who stepped ashore at Quebec. One of the officials who was most surprised and puzzled by these developments was General Edouard de B. Panet, who had been appointed the Director of Internment Operations in 1939. He was so sure that a gross blunder had been committed and that these civilian internees were not in the least risky that he suggested to the Canadian government that all guards be removed from their camps and that the camps themselves be reconstituted as refugee republics. The Secretary of State, Pierre Casgrain, the husband of Cairine Wilson's friend, Thérèse Casgrain, was all in favour of such a move, but the Senator's old friend, Layton Ralston, the Minister of Defence and the other cabinet member responsible for internment camps, was not. He noted that the internees had been labelled dangerous by the Home government and that responsibility for their safekeeping had been delegated to the Canadian government. Under no circumstances, he said, would he agree to a relaxation of internment conditions unless the British government provided assurances that these men and boys did not pose a threat to security. He then suggested that Ottawa ask Britain to send out a responsible official to advise the Canadian government on the degree of risk of the various categories of internees.[2]

This suggestion was taken up and in November 1940 the British Home Office sent out Alexander Paterson, a commissioner of prisons who had achieved prominence for his reforming zeal and his role in establishing boys' clubs in East End London. During his seven-and-a-half-month sojourn in Canada, this engaging civil servant visited the five camps where categories B and C aliens were interned to consider the cases of individual internees and to recommend which of them should be allowed to return to Britain or to emigrate to the United States. In the course of his work he met with leading Canadians active in the prisoners' welfare: Saul Hayes, a

Canadian Jewish Congress Archives

Saul Hayes taken in the 1940s.

young Montreal lawyer, who worked tirelessly on behalf of the Jewish internees; Ann Cowan, a prominent member of the CNCR's Toronto branch; Margaret Hugessen, the wife of the Montreal Liberal senator, Knatchbull Hugessen; another leading CNCR member, Canon Judd from the Anglican Church headquarters in Toronto; Constance Hayward, the CNCR's executive secretary; and, of course, Senator Wilson.

In the highly readable report that he wrote before leaving Canada, Alexander Paterson recorded his impressions of the Senator:

> We were exceptionally fortunate to secure Senator R. Cairine Wilson (*sic*), the only woman Senator in Canada, as the Chairman of the Committee [Central Committee for Interned Refugees]. Throughout the Dominion she is known as a woman of wide human sympathy, and she enjoys considerable influence with all the ranks in the administration. When she was named a Senator, some legal doubt arose as to whether the word "person" in the British North America Act could be held to include a woman. The point was referred to the Privy Council, who decided that Senator Wilson was a "person." They were right.[3]

Admittedly this short excerpt contains a few errors: the misplacement of the initial R in the Senator's name; a reference to Cairine Wilson being the only Canadian woman senator when in fact Iva Fallis had been appointed to the Senate in 1935; and some confusion regarding the sequence of events leading up to Cairine Wilson's appointment to the Senate in 1930. Still, these errors are minor. What really counts is the accuracy of Paterson's pungent assessment of the Senator. The Senator for her part probably thought very highly of Paterson because after his death, in 1947, she sent his widow, Lady Paterson, a letter of condolences and a parcel containing some cheese.

Cairine Wilson's involvement with interned refugees began in the late summer of 1940, at a time when their plight had yet to excite the widespread attention of the Canadian press. The Senator was probably alerted to their existence by her friend Constance Hayward, who first became aware of these unfortunate victims earlier in the summer when corresponding with Bloomsbury House (the British headquarters of the principal organizations concerned with the welfare of German and Austrian refugees). Although she would normally be vacationing at Clibrig in late August, Cairine Wilson called a meeting of the CNCR executive committee for the twenty-seventh of the month to discuss this latest development in the unfolding refugee saga. Little could she have realized that the committee's deliberations, held at the Chateau Laurier, would have far-reaching consequences for both herself and the CNCR.

Besides the Senator and Connie Hayward, there were seven others present: the Senator's good friend Beatrice Belcourt, Anna Cooke, Isabel Cummings, a fellow member of the Zonta Club of Ottawa who worked for the Bell Telephone Company, Robert Inch, the secretary of the League of Nations Society in Canada, Canon Judd, Dean D. L. Ritchie, a vice-chairman of the CNCR's Montreal branch, and Cairine Wilson's friend Dr Henry Marshall Tory. As a result of their discussions — gently, but firmly, guided, no doubt, by the Senator — the committee agreed that it would be glad to render assistance to the interned refugees. Having made this all-important decision, it then asked that redoubtable and beloved scientist and educator, Dr Tory, to see what sort of educational facilities were available in the camps and to report back to the committee the kind of educational assistance that was required. The committee also made several recommendations, the key one being that the national organization help the 544 non-Jewish internees among the 2,290 non-dangerous prisoners sent to Canada that fateful summer.[4] Jewish refugees, the committee felt, would be well looked after by Jewish refugee organizations. As it turned out, however, Cairine Wilson and her CNCR colleagues would provide invaluable assistance to both groups.

In the dying days of the summer, then, Senator Wilson found herself caught up not only in the many organizational details associated with the evacuation of British children to Canada but also in the carving out of a new role for the CNCR and herself. To establish how the Committee could best assist interned refugees, she consulted with government officials such as Colonel H. Stetham, who had succeeded General Panet as Director of Internment Operations in the fall of 1940, and with YMCA officials involved in refugee work.[5] The outcome of these investigations and a suggestion made by Bloomsbury House was the establishment, in January 1941, of a new committee to aid the interned refugees by formulating general policy and delegating most of the detailed work to members of its two constituent organizations.

Known as The Central Committee for Interned Refugees, or simply as "The Committee," it was composed of representatives of the CNCR and the Montreal-based national organization, The United Jewish Refugee and War Relief Agencies, a federation of Jewish relief and community agencies formed in 1939 to deal with refugees. The Senator was appointed chairman, Saul Hayes and Constance Hayward joint secretaries, Stanley Goldner, a Montreal lawyer, liaison officer, and Charles Raphael, a young Jewish scholar from London, England, coordinating officer. In her new role, Cairine Wilson would interview refugees in the camps, advise them by mail, seek improvements in their welfare and obtain sponsors for those being considered for release. Much of this would involve her in what had become second nature to her: badgering civil service bureaucrats and petitioning the Government.

Her closest associate in this work was Constance Hayward, who was frequently sent into the camps as her emissary. William Heckscher, a former internee, reminiscences quite uninhibitedly about the first visit that the executive secretary, who became known as "The Angel," made to the Farnham camp where Heckscher was an inmate:

> ...Then came the day that Constance Hayward visited our prison camp as an emissary of Senator Wilson. I was on such occasions called out to the commandant's barracks — guided by a Canadian soldier — wearing my necktie and standing as was the custom outside the commandant's office. I suddenly realized that there was a woman with Col. Kippen and that I had to admonish myself to keep my mind in order and that if I fainted to faint in such a way that I would fall on her lap.

> This wasn't necessary. Constance Hayward sat without looking at me, seemingly taking notes on a writing pad, when I noticed that she was just as nervous as I was. The commandant allowed me for the first time to sit down in his presence and this was when I learned of the existence of Cairine Wilson. Constance Hayward explained to me why she was there. That Senator Wilson, whose aide she was, had sent her to find out if there might be some kind of modality by which Canadians might provide financial guarantees for young students, thereby obtaining their release. Those were immensely moving moments — perhaps because of the sudden and unexpected awareness that there was someone of influence outside our camp who saw the situation of "innocence incarcerated" clearly.[6]

Another close associate in this work was Saul Hayes, the leading spokesman for the United Jewish and War Relief Agencies. As soon as he learned of the Jewish internees' plight, in August 1940, Hayes made the first of countless trips to the nation's capital to plead for the right of observant Jews to have Kosher food and a work-free Sabbath, for inmates to be allowed newspapers, radios, and magazines, for movies to be shown in the camps, for recognition of the internees' refugee status, and for the separation of known Nazis from the refugees. Along with other members of the Central Committee, he also visited the camps.[7]

One of these other members was Cairine Wilson. According to Eric Kippen, a one-time camp commandant, she began visiting internment camps as early as the fall of 1940.[8] Unlike Colonel Stetham and his officers, who avoided the camps, the Senator undertook to find out at first hand what conditions were like and what could be done for internees in the B and C categories.

When the Canadian journalist and author Gladys Arnold looks back on those early war years, she recalls visiting Cairine Wilson in her office and talking about the internees. Well over four decades after these chats, Miss Arnold has distinct recollections of the Senator saying, "It's very important for the Government to realize that we must fulfill the Geneva Convention to the letter. We should see that these people are occupied and have books and games. They have to be treated as human beings, because after the war they will be a witness to our treatment of them."[9]

Among the first camps the Senator toured was the one at Ile Aux Noix, an island in the Richelieu River one mile southeast of the village of Saint Paul-de-l'Ile-aux-Noix. Ile Aux Noix (or Camp I as it was also called) was not a modern facility like the camps at Farnham, Quebec and Fredericton, New Brunswick, which had been designed to house people, but was an aged military fortification, Fort Lennox, which had been built between 1819 and 1828 and vacated in 1880. Converted with lightning speed in the opening weeks of July 1940, it housed some 270 refugees, the majority of whom were Jews.

To visit such a camp must have been a daunting experience for a shy and compassionate woman like Cairine Wilson for Ile Aux Noix, like its counterparts elsewhere in eastern Canada, was a self-contained male world with all the outward trappings of a maximum security prison: barbed wire (three circles some eight to nine feet high with a cape facing towards the prisoners' compound); a catwalk patrolled by armed sentries; a manned guard tower at each of the four corners of the compound; and internees wearing a degrading prison uniform.[10]

Since there are no accounts of how the Senator reacted to this experience, we can only speculate on how she felt. It is probably safe to say, though, that she was saddened by the spectacle of innocent young boys and men incarcerated under such conditions and outraged by the absurdity of it all. And no doubt her discomfiture was only increased by the realization that she was viewed by officials in Ottawa as a nuisance to be barely tolerated. Indeed, the military, in its preoccupation with security, distrusted all voluntary agencies, regarding volunteers as traffickers and smugglers who were a threat to order and security.

The camp commandant who received her on this, her first visit to Ile Aux Noix, was Major Eric Kippen, an investment dealer who had been a prisoner in a German POW camp in World War I and who would serve as a commandant of six different Canadian internment camps before the end of World War II. A man of great judiciousness and integrity, he sought whenever possible to find solutions to the inmates' difficulties, perhaps because of his own experiences as a POW. When he was in his mid-eighties, he could still remember the Senator's first tour of Ile Aux Noix. She came over to the island by ferry and, after being received by Major Kippen, was turned over to Sergeant-Major J. Breslin, a "front-line soldier," whose booming voice could shake Fort Lennox's very foundations.

After she had toured the prisoners' compound with Sergeant-Major Breslin, Senator Wilson returned to the commandant's office, where she had what would be the first of several meetings with Kippen over the years. On this first encounter, he was impressed by her charm, her compassion and her determination:

> She felt very sorry for these poor fellows behind the wire and I remember saying to her, 'Senator, these chaps don't know how lucky they are. I have two sons who are in the service and they are probably going overseas. For all I know, these fellows will be out of danger's way for a long time to come.

> After her tour of the enclosure, she remarked that she had the impression that a lot of the internees shouldn't be there. And I replied, 'You're probably quite right, Senator, but it's not for me to say who should or shouldn't be here.

> And then she said, "I'm going to try to do something about the situation. If it can be proven that they are all right, I'm quite willing to put up bonds for them so that they won't become a charge on the state."[11]

Unfortunately, the Senator could not act immediately to secure the release of individual refugees. She would have to wait until the Canadian cabinet's decision, on 13 May 1941, which allowed for the release of individual internees provided that sponsors could be found to guarantee their maintenance.[12] Meanwhile, she and her committee could and would achieve notable results in another area — the furnishing of education assistance to interned youths.

This was where Cairine Wilson's friend, Dr Tory, entered the picture. In the course of carrying out the instructions that he had received from the CNCR's executive committee, he visited the Eastern Townships in the autumn of 1940. There, on one dark, foggy night, he accidentally made a visit to the Farnham internment camp that would have important consequences.

That fall Tory was seventy-six, still a vigorous worker for the League of Nations Society in Canada, and a veteran educator, who had headed the Khaki University, an educational institution which conducted classes for Canadian troops in Britain during and after World War I. Later he became founder and first president of the University of Alberta and president of the National Research Council. On this particular night he had been en route to a nearby military camp when his taxi blundered through the fog into the Farnham internment camp. There he met Major Kippen, the newly installed commandant, and in his office the two began discussing attempts which were then under way to establish a school at the camp, which would allow the young internees to resume their interrupted education and to put their lives in order.

The driving force behind these efforts was William Heckscher, an outstanding teacher and art historian whose grandfather had taught French prisoners-of-war in Germany during World War I. When Tory arrived unannounced at Farnham, Heckscher was fast asleep on his bunk. But not for long because a guard soon loomed up with the news that the commandant wanted to see him in his office. Heckscher recalls the evening:

> I was called out to join this meeting and Tory with his splendid mind immediately saw that we were in need of books and writing material and that we had to be informed about the requirements of the McGill University exams. He acted with marvellous speed and soon our educational work had a more meaningful direction.[13]

Dr Tory was indeed heaven-sent for he had a wide network of excellent academic contacts. One of these was Thomas Matthews, registrar of McGill University, where Tory had once taught mathematics. Matthews's help was enlisted and, at his instigation, arrangements were made for students from all the camps to sit for the McGill matriculation exams at the internment camp on St Helen's Island, off Montreal.

Among those who passed the junior matriculation exams in June 1941 were forty-two students from the Farnham camp, some of whom had mastered English only recently. One of them even managed to obtain the highest marks in the province of Quebec.

Before the students in this unique experiment sat for their exams, however, they had to have books and paper because the camps, although rich in academic talent, lacked vital teaching aids. To the rescue came Dale Brown of the YMCA, who was the Canadian representative of the European Student Relief Fund. He supplied books, paper and pencils ("very important: my early notes, on toilet paper, did not hold together very well," recalls a Farnham camp school graduate[14]) and visited the camps, sometimes in Cairine Wilson's company, to ascertain what was needed and to provide encouragement. He was often joined by Constance Hayward, as well as by numerous individuals from other voluntary organizations.

Since the Senator was keenly interested in education, she did whatever she could to aid the cause of the camp schools and universities, even going to the trouble of locating unexpected sources of books and forwarding requested texts and periodicals to inmates. Writing to an internee at the Sherbrooke camp, for example, she said:

Dear Dr Koller,

Under separate cover, I am today forwarding two or three pamphlets and my copy of "Winston Churchill" by René Kraus, which you may add to the Camp library.

On Saturday I was pleased to have a visit from Mr Dale Brown, who was then on his way to the Camps and I expect you have already had an opportunity to talk with him. While he was here, I suggested that he look through the books which have been brought to the large room under the Senate Chamber, for Mrs Read — who is in charge — said I might have some of them. Mr Brown discovered that there were many which would be useful to the Matriculation students and I am hoping to send them forward very soon... [15]

Eric Kippen was one camp commandant who took an active interest in his camp school and did whatever he could to assist its progress. He clearly realized the importance of keeping those in his charge occupied as much as possible, noting in the camp commandant's diary for 7 November 1940:

A Camp University has been organized and it is really amazing the number of applicants who are interested in joining it. There are some very good professors and teachers among the internees, so there will be no trouble in this regard, although books will be probably hard to secure. The idea behind this is to give internees as much mental activity as possible, as it takes their minds off their many worries and makes them that much easier to control.[16]

Cairine Wilson viewed the camp schools from a somewhat different perspective. As one who was deeply concerned about the welfare of the three hundred or so refugees of student age, she regarded the schools as instruments for enhancing the lives of impressionable youths and salvaging interrupted educations. She also saw them as possible avenues for release from imprisonment. Here she was prophetic, because after the Canadian cabinet's landmark decision of 13 May 1941, students were indeed one of the first categories of internees to be given priority for release. In fact, as a result of a meeting Alexander Paterson had with Mr Crerar, the minister in charge of immigration, and his advisers, it was agreed that about one hundred school boys and students under the age of twenty-one should be released in Canada.[17]

The first students were given their liberty in the summer of 1941 after sponsors had been found to assume guardianship of them, which entailed paying for their maintenance and education. If there were deserving students under twenty-one who could not name sponsors, Cairine Wilson and her colleagues found sponsors for them or provided financial assistance from the Committee's limited funds. To supplement these funds, the Senator frequently appealed to members from her own circle of friends and acquaintances to make donations for tuition and living expenses.

Fortunately she often met with success. Such was the case when she solicited financial assistance for a very talented young student, Charles Wasserman, who went on to become a well-known journalist, broadcaster, novelist and film-maker before his untimely death in 1978. His mother Marta was so grateful to Cairine Wilson for what she had done for her son that after the Senator's death she wrote to young Cairine:

> ... For almost twenty years, or even more I have carried in my heart a warm and very deep feeling of gratitude towards Senator Wilson. For I was indebted to her for an unforgettable moment of happiness amidst a world of sorrow and suffering: That was the day when my son descended from the train in Montreal, a free young man after ten months of captivity, while I had tried incessantly but in vain to obtain his entry to Canada from a very unwilling Director of Immigration in Ottawa! I

know I am only one among thousands who owed so much
to the courage, perseverance and devotion of your mother.
But I do want you to know that as long as I am alive I will
not forget. I will treasure her memory.[18]

Charles Wasserman was lucky in that he was one of the first students
to be discharged from camp. Many of these young men would have to wait
much longer for their freedom. Nevertheless, by February 1943 the Senator
and other CNCR members would be successful in obtaining the release of
230 students — 122 to universities, and the remainder to secondary schools
and rabbinical seminaries.[19] Among those released was at least one
internee for whom the Senator personally accepted sponsorship. He
graduated with honours from the University of Toronto.[20]

The British government had already released well over 17,000 internees before the Canadian breakthrough. Even so, another important development would have to take place before refugees of all descriptions could
be freed on a large scale: the reclassification of Prisoners-of-War Class 2
(the designation given civilian internees of B and C categories) to that of
refugees.

This important step — the result of groundwork laid by Alexander
Paterson, Saul Hayes, and Cairine Wilson — was finally taken on 25 June
1941 when by P.C. 4568 provision was made for reclassifying civilian
internees of B and C categories as refugees and for designating three
internment camps (Farnham, Sherbrooke, and Ile Aux Noix) as refugee
camps. Appointed commissioner of the camps was Colonel R.W.S.
Fordham, a camp commandant who had been a prisoner-of-war in World
War I and a distinguished lawyer in Niagara Falls between the wars.

Fordham had been suggested for the appointment by Alexander
Paterson, who had been impressed by his wide sympathy, strong character
and charming personality. In his new position, however, little of this "wide
sympathy" would make itself felt, for although he accepted Paterson's
recommendations for improving conditions in the camps, Fordham retained much of their military character.

In the months ahead he would often have occasion to meet with the
Senator, who sometimes accompanied him on visits to the camps under his
jurisdiction. Although not given to making disparaging remarks about
other people, Cairine Wilson is known to have commented upon the
Commissioner's rigidity and military cast of mind. Certainly Fordham did
not have much use for representatives of voluntary agencies — at least if
the contents of a memo he prepared on the handling of refugees is any
guide. Written on 17 August 1944 for Norman Robertson, the Under-
Secretary of State for External Affairs, the memo advocates the censoring
of all refugee mail and the stringent rationing of visits by outsiders.

5. Visitors should be allowed to visit the camp by appointment only and for short periods at a time. The kind of visitors most to be avoided are those filled with good intentions, but entirely lacking in any practical knowledge of organization and administration. This type are guided entirely by their sympathies rather than by logic and good sense. Members of refugee and similar organizations frequently fall within this category, unfortunately.[21]

That spring steps were also taken to invest Cairine Wilson with a new office: that of the representative in Canada of Sir Herbert Emerson, the League of Nations High Commissioner for Refugees. This development resulted from the refusal of the German internees to recognize the Swiss consul as their representative and their written request to "The Committee" to designate an independent authority in Canada as Sir Herbert's deputy.[22]

Upon learning of their concerns, Alexander Paterson recommended that Sir Herbert be named official representative of the refugees interned in Canada and that he delegate his powers to Senator Wilson as chairman of The Central Committee for Interned Refugees. The Canadian government approved of the plan and in June, when the British government confirmed the appointment, the Senator became the High Commissioner's official deputy. In this capacity she would promote the legitimate interests of the interned refugees and deal with their elected spokesmen. Some three years after her appointment she met Sir Herbert when he visited Canada and addressed a meeting of the CNCR national executive on 28 May 1944. Whether on this or on another occasion, the two refugee lobbyists were photographed together and the photo later ran in the 17 September 1944 issue of the *Daily Hebrew Journal*. In the caption the Senator is described as "devoted friend of Jewish war victims."

Dr Bruno Weinberg, an experienced international lawyer who was interned at Farnham and who was in the habit of firing off letters on a variety of legal questions to Senator Wilson and Constance Hayward, wrote requesting particulars about the appointment. In reply, the CNCR's executive secretary observed:

Senator Wilson was appointed to represent Sir Herbert Emerson in Canada with the approval of the Canadian government, although it has not ratified the Conventions of 1933 and 1938. I should think that her position is somewhat stronger than would be indicated by the purely legal basis of the appointment.[23]

As Sir Herbert's representative in Canada and as chairman of The Central Committee for Interned Refugees, Cairine Wilson made repeated visits to the three refugee camps, sometimes alone, but usually in the company of other members of the committee. With her deep-seated feeling for style she made her rounds impeccably dressed or, as one former inmate, Karl Renner, has recounted, wearing elegant clothes, diamond rings and a pearl necklace. He, for one, found it surprising and even flattering that a woman of her station would show her respect for the inmates by dressing in such a fashion. It must have been extremely tiring work if Kippen's diary entry for 1 September 1941 describes a typical tour. On that occasion the Senator, accompanied by lawyer Benjamin Robinson and Toronto stock broker and philanthapist Samuel Zacks of "The Committee," spent about six hours touring the Farnham camp, inspecting accommodation, the kitchen, recreational and educational facilities, and then interviewing refugees.

It was Kippen's view that the party was on the whole "pleased with what they saw".[24] But the reality was somewhat different, because three days after the visit an incensed Benjamin Robinson wrote to the Senator from his Montreal law office:

> Since my return to Montreal from the visit that we had to the Refugee Camp in Farnham, I have given considerable thought to the various incidents that transpired while we were there. I had hoped that my indignation at the manner in which we were treated would have subsided by now, but as the events of the day pass through my mind, I find myself unable to justify the attitude towards us. It may be that we were treated strictly in accordance with the regulations. If so, the regulations should certainly be changed.
>
> As chairman of the Central Committee and as the representative in Canada of the High Commissioner for Refugees under the protection of the League of Nations, I really feel that you should have been given every opportunity to discover for yourself the actual conditions that exist in that particular camp... [25]

Whether Cairine Wilson shared Benjamin Robinson's outrage at the way she was treated by military officialdom is not known. In any event, when The Central Committee for Interned Refugees next met — on 10 September 1941 — it asked the Senator to see her friend Layton Ralston to explain her position and seek a better understanding of the situation.

The Senator's reaction to her treatment at Farnham is open to conjecture, but her view of her role as chairman of "The Committee" is not. As its head, she expected to be kept fully informed of the Committee's activities and to be consulted about any important step contemplated by Saul Hayes and his close associates. If she thought that she had been kept in the dark about any developments, she could, albeit uncharacteristically, express her feelings in no uncertain terms. This happened on 11 July 1942 when, from Clibrig, she wrote a highly indignant letter to Saul Hayes, then holding down the fort at the Committee's headquarters in Montreal.

> The tone of your letter of July 8th[26] was scarcely what I might have expected and apparently you personally have little confidence in my discretion or in my sympathy with the Refugees. I feel that as Chairman of the Central Committee I am entitled to some consideration and, if the United Jewish and War Relief Agency [sic] has not faith in me, I shall gladly resign. Otherwise, I should prefer to be consulted before letters are written to government officials which arouse resentment. I am perfectly aware of the nature of our Immigration Rules for it has required great patience and endless hours of my time to obtain even minor concessions.[27]

Saul Hayes obviously had no idea what was upsetting Cairine Wilson, because he replied on 14 July expressing amazement at her letter. Then three days later he wrote to Constance Hayward reporting that he was flabbergasted by a "rather peculiar" letter that he had received from the Senator.[28] Well he might have been, because Cairine Wilson rarely vented her anger on anyone, let alone a colleague like Hayes whom she repected highly.

Senator Wilson managed to fit in at least one tour of each refugee camp in the early autumn of 1941. Nevertheless, for some refugee leaders this was not enough. They wanted her to make more frequent visits, feeling that if this could be arranged, the way would be paved for more privileges and more releases. Now that they had been converted by the stroke of a pen, so to speak, from prisoners-of-war to refugees, the internees entertained high hopes of receiving more privileges than the authorities were prepared to grant. Not content with being allowed to wear civilian clothes, write letters on ordinary stationery, and receive outside visitors, they began to agitate for additional freedom and for their plight to be more widely publicized. Demands for more frequent visits from Sir Herbert Emerson's representative in Canada were no doubt a reflection of this restlessness, a restlessness that was exacerbated by the refusal of the

United States to accept released refugees and by the slowness with which the release process proceeded.

Cairine Wilson and "The Committee" did all they could to speed up the process by finding employers and sponsors, keeping in mind the three categories of refugees assigned top priority for release in Canada: students and individuals qualified to do agricultural work or war work (which gradually came to denote any employment in industry or business). The process itself was an involved one, requiring authorization from the Home Office in Britain as well as permission from various Canadian authorities. Ultimately, however, Charles Frederick Blair had the final say in who could be freed. And since he faithfully observed all regulations to the letter, there were often roadblocks to release. As a result, Cairine Wilson, Constance Hayward, and Saul Hayes frequently had to intervene on behalf of individual applicants in an effort to get the overly zealous bureaucrat to change his stand and grant an internee his freedom.

Among those internees that the Senator took a special interest in was Dr Fritz Rothberger, an Austrian mathematician who had written numerous works on the theory of sets. He had escaped from Austria on a visa obtained for him by the Society for the Protection of Science and Learning and had gone to Britain where he continued his research at Cambridge and Oxford. Despite his impressive academic credentials, however, no Canadian university offered to hire him after his discharge from internment. Using her influence, Cairine Wilson arranged for him to teach at tiny Acadia University, to which she contributed funds to pay for his first year.[29]

Senator Wilson was involved not only in attempts to secure the release of individual internees, but also in efforts to obtain better treatment for them on the outside. Writing on behalf of the CNCR and "The Committee," she bombarded the Prime Minister and the Government with letters urging that discharged refugees be accorded immigrant status, that discrimination in the assignment of jobs in war industries be eliminated, and that RCMP surveillance of freed internees be reduced.

For many a refugee, whether on the inside or the outside, the Senator was a beacon of hope in a confusing and contradictory world. As a matter of fact, the widespread perception of her as a worker of near miracles involved her in innumerable encounters with officialdom on behalf of refugees seeking the redress of grievances, immigrant status, and enlistment in the Canadian armed forces. As the war drew to a close, she went to great lengths to persuade the Government to hasten the process of naturalization for those refugees who were in Canada on only temporary permits. Among those who did not enjoy permanent status were most of the onetime internees, hundreds of whom wished to remain in this country after the conclusion of hostilities. Fearing that they would be deported after the war, many contacted The Central Committee's headquarters seeking help in becoming permanent residents. Acting on their behalf as well as that of other concerned refugees, Cairine Wilson wrote to her friend Mackenzie King beseeching the Government to hasten the process of naturalization. Concluding a letter to the Prime Minister on 26 June 1945, she noted:

> ...The General Election naturally caused this question [the naturalization issue] to be thrust aside, but it is difficult to realize the anxiety which these people who are now in Canada are suffering. Some with very valuable qualifications cannot secure positions, and others are fearful that they may be deported.[30]

When this letter did not produce the desired results Cairine Wilson wrote to King in August asking if he would receive a delegation representing the various refugee committees who wished to discuss the naturalization question. Jack Pickersgill, who was then serving as a private secretary to the Prime Minister, tried to deflect her in her aims by suggesting that it would suffice for her to see Paul Martin, newly appointed Secretary of State, and J.A. Glen, newly appointed Minister of Mines and Resources. The Senator, however, refused to settle for anybody but King, who replied that he could not fit in a delegation until after Parliament reconvened.[31] In any event, that October Canada reclassified its former prisoners as "Interned Refugees" (Friendly Aliens) from the United Kingdom and invited them to become Canadian citizens. Nine hundred and seventy-two chose to do so.[32]

Often, but certainly not always, Cairine Wilson was able, thanks to her far-flung network of contacts and her dogged persistence, to bring about the results that she was seeking. Such was the outcome of the Walter Loevinsohn case, a case that illustrates perfectly how she operated.

Walter Loevinsohn, who became a senior engineering executive with a Montreal firm, was a youth of eighteen when he fled Nazi Germany for England in the spring of 1939. There he tried to enlist in the British army, but because he was an enemy alien, he was turned down. He therefore became an instructor with the Jewish Volunteer Committee, an organization that furnished military training without weapons to Jewish refugees planning to enlist in the British army when war broke out or to emigrate to Palestine. Because of this activity he was labelled a "militant Zionist and dangerous troublemaker" and, in 1939, when regional advisory committees were established to review the cases of all enemy aliens, he was classified as Category A (to be interned for the duration of the war).

In the summer of 1940, he was interned in Canada where he subsequently developed tuberculosis of the hip-joint. Eventually, however, he was released in the custody of the Canadian Jewish Congress so that he could be hospitalized in a civilian sanatorium, Mount Sinai, at Ste Agathe in the Laurentians. When the war ended he was still in the sanatorium although by now he had recovered to the point where he could walk and work as a clerk-bookkeeper in the office of the medical superintendent.[33]

One day when he was alone in the medical superintendent's office, Loevinsohn learned some startling news. As he recalls that memorable day:

> The phone rang and the person at the other end of the line identified himself as a military official from Military District 4 in Montreal. He didn't ask who I was, he just enquired if we had a prisoner by the name of Loevinsohn. I replied "yes" without adding that I was the man in question. Then the other party mentioned the names of three other refugees and reported that a military escort was being dispatched immediately to Ste Agathe to fetch us as we were to be shipped back to England that night. I immediately replied, "Okay, Sir, I'll make sure that they're here."

> As soon as I put down the phone, I called Senator Wilson whom I had met earlier in the war. She wasn't in her office, but her secretary, Sybil Wright, was and she contacted the Senator. Mrs Wilson in turn phoned Major-General Walford, who was then Adjutant General of the Canadian army, and asked him to stop all this nonsense because she couldn't see why, since the war was over, Canada should be in such a hurry to send us back to Britain where we didn't want to go and where presumably we wouldn't receive the best of treatment as convalescents. Besides, she wasn't at all sure that Britain's intentions in one or two of our cases were all that honourable.

> Walford for some reason gave orders to "hold it." In about an hour-and-a-half another call came from MD4 asking if the escort had arrived. When I replied "no," the other party gave instructions for the escort captain to call him as soon as they arrived. Well, the escort arrived a few minutes later — one sedan for the escort and a van for the prisoners. When the captain marched in I gave him the

telephone message and he immediately phoned Montreal. It was then he learned that he and his men were to
return empty-handed to Montreal. We were saved.

I was very glad that the Senator acted instantly and
where it mattered. This distinguished her from many
other people who mouth pious platitudes, but who don't
have the knack for translating them into effective action.[34]

When Loevinsohn was ready to obtain his medical discharge from the
sanatorium, Cairine Wilson asked him to come to Ottawa. There she took
him to see Escott Reid, who was then Under-Secretary of State for
External Affairs. In the course of the interview she told Reid that she
expected his department to raise no objections if Britain changed its
position and gave permission for the refugees to remain in Canada. She
then wrote to her old friend, Vincent Massey, Canadian High Commissioner in London, and asked him to intervene with the Home Office on
Loevinsohn's behalf. Massey, who disliked Jews*, agreed to do so.
Putting aside principles in favour of personal connections, he went to the
Home Office and argued in support of Loevinsohn's staying in Canada. He
must have argued very persuasively because after two hours the officials
threw up their hands and said, "If you want him that badly, you can have
him!"
    In 1947, Loevinsohn's wife-to-be arrived from Britain and one of the
first things the young couple did was go to Ottawa to meet the ex-
internee's fairy godmother. They met the Senator in her office and she
asked them if they were free that afternoon to have tea at The Manor
House. They accepted the invitation and later attended a reception for
Cairine Wilson's friend Lotta Hitschmanova, then executive director of
the Unitarian Service Committee.[35] At this mammoth tea there were over
a hundred women and Walter Loevinsohn.
    It was typical of Cairine Wilson that she would ask the young couple
to tea because such was her compassion for the less fortunate and the
lonely that she frequently extended hospitality to those refugees that she
personally assisted. The Senator also entertained groups of refugees, one
being a trio of former internees who donated their services to a money-
raising concert staged by the CNCR's Ottawa branch at the Ottawa

---

* Claude Bissell in his biography, *The Young Vincent Massey*, p. 162, reports that
although Massey was attracted to individual Jews, because of their intellectual and
artistic gifts, he was not favourably disposed to Jews in general.

Technical High School on 17 November 1942. Two of the artists who performed that evening later became well-known figures on the Canadian musical scene — Johnny Newmark, the pianist, and Helmuth Blume, one-time dean of McGill University's faculty of music. They were joined by Gerhard Kander, who would carve out a career for himself as a stockbroker, but who, on this occasion, earned plaudits as an accomplished violinist. After the concert they and other guests were entertained at the Manor House.[36]

Sometimes when she could not preside over such a function herself, Cairine Wilson would ask her marvellous secretary, Sybil Wright, to act for her. English-born Sybil was one of those rare beings: a politically conscious Canadian who was a CCF partisan. She was also one with a real grasp and understanding of the refugee situation. One occasion when Sybil Wright acted for the Senator was a dinner that Cairine Wilson had arranged for about fifteen released internees at the Chateau Laurier Hotel. Herman Nathan, who attended the dinner, recalls that Sybil Wright not only hosted the function but also helped him to open up a charge account at a local department store, assuring him that the Senator would guarantee purchases up to $150.00.[37]

The end of the war brought to a close Cairine Wilson's heaviest involvement with refugee concerns. But it certainly did not spell the end of her refugee work. As she soon discovered, the immediate post-war years posed a new set of daunting challenges.

11

OLD AND NEW CHALLENGES

For years Cairine Wilson cherished the dream of a greater Canada: a Canada of vibrant cities, new industries and a standard of living that would be the envy of the world; a land of hope and opportunity for Europe's war-weary and oppressed. When World War II ended it seemed that the premise on which this dream was founded — a more liberal immigration policy — might soon become a reality. For one thing, the socio-economic climate in the country had changed dramatically since the Great Depression. Canadians were no longer haunted by the profound feelings of economic insecurity that had plagued them during that dreary decade. The war with its voracious appetite for skilled and unskilled labour had dispelled the worst of their fears about unemployment. Then too, the Canadian government was demonstrating an interest in refugees and displaced persons to the extent of donating substantial funds to agencies involved in postwar rehabilitation and reconstruction in war-ravaged Europe, notably the United Nations Relief and Rehabilitation Administration (UNRRA) and the United Nations Children's Emergency Fund (UNICEF). Both these developments seemed to augur well for an almost immediate lowering of Canada's immigration barriers and the entry of many homeless Europeans seeking to rebuild shattered lives.

Cairine Wilson and the CNCR soon realized, however, that a more enlightened immigration policy was not just around the corner and that, in fact, Mackenzie King's government was still resolutely opposed to an increase in immigration. When asked to justify this position, government spokesmen invariably cited the possibility of a postwar economic recession such as the one that had followed World War I and the lack of ships to transport people from Europe to Canada. A shortage of shipping made it imperative that first priority be assigned to returning servicemen and their dependents who were still overseas, and reintegrating them into Canadian society. It was an argument that would be raised even when its validity was questionable.

The whole question of Canada's restrictive immigration policy was thrown into sharp relief by the presence of well over a million refugees and displaced persons in European camps maintained by United Nations agencies. The most significant in terms of numbers were the so-called displaced persons who had been uprooted from their homelands or displaced in their own countries by the war. Their ranks included thousands of concentration camp survivors as well as individuals who had been sent to slave labour camps in Austria and Germany. Among those who had been forced from their homelands were many who refused to be repatriated. Refugees, by strict definition, were all those people who had fled totalitarian regimes before the outbreak of World War II and those who, starting in the second half of 1945, had left East European countries which had come under the Communist yoke.[1] Irrespective of label, however, all these abject souls were virtually refugees without a country, home, material goods or future. In the words of B.K. Sandwell, the distinquished editor of *Saturday Night*, who was then an honorary chairman of the CNCR, they were like prisoners in "a great, dark, airless room which [had] fifty different doors, the doors of admission to fifty different countries where they could build their lives afresh; but every door [was] locked, barred and bolted."[2]

The desperate plight of these camp inmates affected Cairine Wilson deeply and she seized every possible opportunity to sensitize Canadian public opinion and the Government to their predicament. Addressing the women's guild of St. Andrew's, Ottawa, she described "displaced persons," by which she meant all refugees, as a "potential cause of war" and a "challenge to Christianity."[3] Four months later, on 13 March 1947, she rose in the Senate and painted a heart-rending picture of their circumstances:

> I expect that most of us listened to President Truman when he spoke over the radio last night. I was struck by his specific mention of the importance of strengthening the causes of democracy in Europe. Canada has, I fear, been very negligent for at the present time, about two years after the close of the war, these people who showed

their opposition to Nazism, Fascism and Communism are
still languishing in displaced persons camps in Europe, or
wandering from country to country, asking merely for an
opportunity to rebuild their shattered lives. People of the
type now in D.P. camps are not likely to be available for
immigration later on. I think many Canadians fail to
understand the quality of the people who are eating out
their hearts and deteriorating morally and physically after
two years of waiting. We gave them high hopes for the
future, and now they wonder what to make of our prom-
ises.[4]

With memories of the demoralizing internment operations in the
Eastern Townships still fresh in her mind, the Senator knew whereof she
spoke. But she had also consulted with people who had worked in or
visited the refugee camps scattered throughout Austria, Germany, and
Italy. She would soon update her information about conditions in these
temporary homes as Connie Hayward had left earlier that month for a
whirlwind tour of camps in the British and American zones of Germany
and the British and French zones of Austria. Violet McAlonan Herrington,
who was then Cairine Wilson's private secretary, remembered well some
of the preparations for this fact-finding tour if for no other reason than that
the ever efficient, normally composed Connie was a bundle of nerves
when she visited the Senator's office just before departure time. Recalled
Mrs Herrington:

She was so nervous that she made repeated trips to the
washroom before leaving the office. She needed a lot of
support from Mrs Wilson who coached her in what to do
and say. But she was so preoccupied that she didn't hear
half of what the Senator said. She just kept running from
her office to mine.[5]

Cairine Wilson and the CNCR did not confine themselves to fact-
finding and publicizing the lot of these refugees. They also made direct
appeals to members of the Government. As she had done so often in years
past, Cairine Wilson made the rounds of cabinet ministers and bureaucrats, arguing the case for changes in prevailing policy. Sometimes she
was accompanied by fellow members of the CNCR, as on 30 November
1945, when she led a delegation of national executive colleagues that met
with the newly installed minister of Mines and Resources, J. A. Glen.
Speaking for the group, Saul Hayes requested the admission of 1,000
refugee children and approximately 1,000 individuals who had survived

concentration camps and who already had relatives in Canada. Compelling as the delegation's arguments were, however, Glen could give only a non-commital response.[6] But then this was to be expected given the Government's prevailing views on immigration and Glen's own predisposition to leave things as they were.

Cairine Wilson followed up this visit with a letter to the Minister reiterating the Committee's request that displaced persons and refugees with relatives in Canada be admitted. When she had received no reply by 18 March of the following year, she consoled herself with the thought that Glen could not make a commitment because of a shortage of shipping. She also took comfort in the fact that she had detected signs of a more sympathetic attitude on the part of the Government towards refugees.[7] However, just to be sure that the Government was getting the message, she wrote to King on 30 April 1946, enclosing a resolution of the CNCR calling on Canada to admit immediately " a quota of refugees and displaced persons of not less than 10,000 from the 75,000 now in Europe who are the responsibility of the Intergovernmental Committee."[8]

In reponse to public pressure and labour market requirements, the Government began slowly but surely to open Canada's doors to Europe's homeless. Nevertheless, the refugee picture was not as rosy as that painted by Glen in a Winnipeg speech the following January. In that address the Minister was so ill-informed or foolhardy as to boast that "Canada had "already done more than any other country so far in assuming responsibility of taking refugees from Europe." The inaccuracy of this pronouncement was so egregious that Cairine Wilson immediately wrote to the Prime Minister to set the record straight, but in typical fashion she mixed praise with implied criticism and concluded on a positive note.[9]

Demands for a more humane immigration policy were increasing as more and more Canadians, moved by the plight of the refugees, called for the prompt admission of them on the grounds of simple human decency. Responding to the appeals of their constituents, many of whom represented ethnic organizations, Members of Parliament began urging the Government to open Canada's doors to Europe's homeless. Even the Senate was getting into the act. Eager to examine the different views on immigration, it reconstituted its lapsed Standing Committee on Immigration and Labour in 1946. The motion to re-establish the committee was made not by Cairine Wilson, though, but by Senator Arthur Roebuck, that zealous defender of the interests of Japanese Canadians and a staunch proponent of a liberalized immigration policy.

Cairine Wilson became a leading member of that committee and eventually its chairman. Before taking on that demanding post, though, she appeared before the committee as a witness. This took place in 1946, when representing the CNCR, she presented a brief that called on the

Government to: admit substantial numbers of "displaced persons and refugees;" send immigration officers to camps to interview and process prospective immigrants; and exempt persons described as "refugees" by the International Refugee Organization from ordinary restrictions on immigration into Canada. It is significant that, in replying to questions posed by committee members, she observed:

> The few refugees admitted to Canada have in a short time made such a splendid contribution to Canadian life in the cultural, scientific and industrial fields, as well as to the more widely publicized war effort that I trust Senators may be convinced that this Committee on Immigration and Labour should advocate the adoption of a more generous policy by our Government and bear in mind Mr Cameron's* quotation,"Where there is no vision, the people perish."[10]

In the widely circulated report which it prepared, the Senate Committee on Immigration and Labour referred to the government's "non-immigration policy" and recommended the introduction of a new act in Parliament to meet Canada's postwar immigration requirements, the reopening of Canadian immigration offices in Europe as soon as possible, and the admission of as many displaced persons as Canada could absorb successfully.[11]

The widespread approval that the report generated in the Canadian press together with the growing dismay expressed by many MPs over government inaction on immigration made it inevitable that Mackenzie King and his cabinet would have to move on the question. And move they did in the spring of 1947. On 1 May, the Prime Minister read in the House of Commons a statement on immigration. Somewhat progressive in tone, it proposed the enouragement of such numbers of immigrants as the Canadian economy could absorb advantageously. However, to pacify those who had qualms about increased immigration, there was a warning that immigration must be related to "absorbtive capacity," which would change from year to year. Canada's right to discriminate was also defended, although it was accompanied by the assertion that this country was prepared to enter into international agreements based on full equality. Applicants from the "old" Commonwealth countries and the United States were to be given special consideration. Finally came the real breakthrough that Cairine Wilson and other advocates of a more humane immigration

---

* Cameron was a CPR colonization official.

policy had been waiting for: "During the depression and the war immigration was inevitably restricted; now the categories of admissible persons have been considerably widened. Special steps will also be taken to provide for the admission of carefully selected immigrants from among the Displaced Persons of Europe."[12]

While the Government was unfolding its new immigration policy, Cairine Wilson was dispatching a steady stream of letters to Connie Hayward, who was then on an exhausting speaking tour of western Canada to rouse interest in displaced persons' immigration. Writing on 19 May, the Senator remarked:

> ... I fear that it must have been difficult to repeat the same story at each stopping place and to find that despite all your efforts Canadian people are still so ill-informed regarding the displaced persons.
>
> You will be among friends at Winnipeg and if you see Mrs MacWilliams, please give her my remembrances and tell her that we hope for her continued interest in the Princess Alice Foundation Fund*.[13]

With indications that the Government would soon be acting on its declarations regarding displaced persons, Cairine Wilson wrote excitedly in her own handwriting to Constance on 24 May 1947:

> There are many things which I should be doing at the present moment, but I cannot resist writing to let you know that the outlook for our d.p.'s looks much better. This afternoon, at the Czechoslovak Legation, I met Dr Hugh Keenleyside, who asked 'Have you any cases?' He then said by the middle of next week there will be an important pronouncement, with which you will be pleased. Cabinet ministers are vying with each other to make applications for those not present admissible.[14]

Sure enough, an order-in-council was issued in early June permitting the admission of a number of displaced persons. It and two other orders-

---

*The Princess Alice Foundation Fund encouraged the training and development of young people by awarding scholarships to promising youth leaders. Senator Wilson, its first president, spearheaded the fund's establishment in 1945 by launching a campaign to raise $50,000.

in-council, dated 18 July and 1 October 1947, would make provision for the admission of a total of 20,000 displaced perons, not including those with close relatives in Canada.

The going had been slow and the results of their campaign frequently discouraging, but Senator Wilson and the Committee had persevered, always hoping for an improvement in the situation. Now it appeared that the Government was finally acceding to some of their requests and moving in the right direction with regard to immigration policy. It was a time for quiet rejoicing and grateful thanks. So on 1 October 1947, the date of the third order-in-council, the Senator, accompanied by lawyer Evan Gray, another member of the CNCR executive, and Connie Hayward, called on Dr Keenleyside to let him know how pleased they were with the recent changes in government immigration policy. In reply the Deputy Minister of Mines and Resources credited the Committee with helping to bring about the new turn of events, noting that it had played a significant role in influencing public opinion and government attitudes towards immigration.[15]

If Keenleyside had elaborated, he might have remarked that Cairine Wilson's stature in political circles and quiet diplomacy had a lot to do with this influence. But the Committee's cause was also aided by the urbane deputy minister, who was genuinely eager to participate in the search for at least a partial solution to the dilemma of refugees and displaced persons. The Senator acknowledged this when, in a letter to Connie Hayward, she observed, "It is very encouraging that Dr Keenleyside takes such an interest in our committee and Mr Jerry Riddell [an official with the Department of External Affairs] mentioned last evening that he thought we could take considerable credit for the change in Government policy."[16]

In this one sentence Cairine Wilson throws into sharp focus the difference in attitude between Keenleyside and the unaccommodating, obdurate Blair, who did not believe in immigration and fought her and the Committee at every turn. Working with Blair had been a trial, demanding the utmost in persistence, determination, and occasionally guile. By constrast, working with Keenleyside and Blair's highly competent, but humane, successor, A. L. Jolliffe, was a real pleasure. Cairine Wilson's delight in this new, fruitful relationship shines through in an article written for *The Presbyterian Record* in which she recounts the role that she and Keenleyside played in arranging for the admission to Canada of an English pediatrician, her Austrian husband and their family.[17]

The fall of 1947 was a pivotal one in the history of the CNCR because rapidly dwindling financial resources required it to make some hard decisions about its future. In short, it had to decide whether or not its task had been completed and, if work remained to be done, whether the CNCR was the organization best equipped to undertake it. On 21 November members of the national executive met at the Chateau Laurier to find answers to these questions.

Two themes dominated the discussions: the value of the CNCR's work and the worsening financial situation. Senator Wilson observed that the attitude of the Deputy Minister and of officials of the Department of External Affairs testified to the importance that they attached to the Committee's work while Saul Hayes stressed the valuable role played by the CNCR in pointing out weaknesses and inequities in Canadian immigration cases. Committee members, he observed, recognized just how much the Chairman did along these lines.

Other Committee members advanced the case for an experienced, non-sectarian body like the CNCR to assist other refugee organizations in the future. Everybody recognized, however, that unless the nagging problem of inadequate funds could be overcome, there was no future for their group. Finally the Committee passed two key resolutions. The most important one called for the CNCR to carry on for another year, continuing with its "propaganda work" and stressing the practical applications of Canadian immigration law. The other one provided for the establishment of a finance committee made up of Cairine Wilson, B.K. Sandwell and Mrs A.K. Hugesssen.[18]

The precariousness of the CNCR's financial condition was later underscored by Senator Wilson who wrote, in a letter to Connie Hayward, "I must get busy myself and see if I cannot gather a few dollars in order that the committee may continue to function."[19] Despite the Senator's and the finance committee's efforts, however, the financial situation did not improve markedly and the stage was set for a further winding down of the CNCR's operations. In May 1948, Connie Hayward left to join the Citizenship Branch of the Secretary of State and was replaced on a part-time basis by Ellen Buzek, the wife of Karel Buzek, a CNCR executive committee member. Then, on 27 October 1948, Cairine Wilson and other members of the executive committee convened in Toronto for what would turn out to be their last formal meeting. Among the issues raised on that sad occasion was the CNCR's continuing obligation to a tuberculosis patient whom they had been supporting because his illness prevented him from obtaining a landing permit and employment. The committee knew full well that he risked being deported unless he received continuing financial assistance, but reluctantly decided that it could not take any action on his case because the CNCR might soon be terminating its activities.[20] Given the circumstances, this was the only decision that could be made. For shortly after this meeting the CNCR ceased to function as a formally constituted national organization. Some of its activities did continue on a vastly reduced scale, however, one being the support of the

TB patient. Somehow or other the means were found to send a monthly cheque to him and when funds were not immediately forthcoming Cairine Wilson dipped into her own pocket. To the end of her life the Senator took a personal interest in his case. She arranged for CNCR members in Montreal to look in on him, wrote regularly to him and dispatched a steady stream of orders for the leather goods that he made when his health permitted.

The CNCR's virtual dissolution must have produced mixed feelings in Senator Wilson. On the one hand, she could take comfort in the knowledge that "her committee" had achieved its principal goal of exciting public interest in refugees and displaced persons. It was also obvious that the recent establishment of other organizations involved with refugees obviated the need for the CNCR to monopolize centre stage in refugee work. But still, the Senator must have rued the fact that the Committee was fading from the scene at a time when emigration to Canada was just getting under way in earnest and when co-ordination between the growing number of volunteer agancies and government bodies involved in refugee work was becoming essential. If there was one role that a viable CNCR was ideally equipped to play, it was surely in co-ordinating these multiplying services. Unfortunately, it would never perform this valuable function.

Although the CNCR virtually folded as a national body in late 1948, Cairine Wilson did not abandon her involvment with refugees. Far from it. Admittedly the most active phase was now over, but for the rest of her life the Senator would continue to promote their interests. Even as the CNCR was limping to a halt, she became involved once again with Czechoslovak refugees, this time with those who had fled their country after the Communist take-over in 1948 and began arriving in Canada at the end of that year. In response to an invitation from the Czechoslovak community, she took on the chairmanship of a newly created committee designed to aid recently arrived Czechoslovaks until such time as they became self-supporting.[21]

Her role as chairman of the Canadian Fund for Czechoslovak Refugees may have been largely an honorary one, but nevertheless Senator Wilson devoted considerable time and effort to assisting it and its sponsoring body, the Czechoslovak National Alliance in Canada. The work that she did for Czechoslovaks both in Canada and abroad was deeply appreciated by the Alliance whose officials visited Parliament Hill in May 1950 to thank the Senator, on behalf of Czechoslovak refugees in exile, for all that she had done to promote their interests. In thanking Mrs Wilson, Ota Hora, Chairman of the Ottawa Branch of the Alliance, said, "The Czechoslovak [sic] acquired, during the hard times of the first and second exiles, many good friends who, by their deeds, stepped into the history of our country. We are pleased to say, that as one of these friends, your name will never be forgotten."[22]

Far more demanding was the chairmanship of the Senate Committee on Immigration and Labour, which Senator Wilson "finally" agreed to take on in the closing weeks of 1947. The chairmanship would prove to be challenging and time-consuming. But such was her interest in immigration that the Senator would preside in this capacity from January 1948 until the end of 1961, shortly before her death.

A little over six months after the last recorded meeting of the CNCR, Cairine Wilson took on still another refugee-related role, one that took her right into the very forum where the most important refugee questions of the day were being discussed: the United Nations. The new post was announced by a phone call from Prime Minister Louis St. Laurent (Mackenzie King's successor) on Monday, 15 August 1949 asking the Senator if she would become a member of the Canadian delegation to the fourth General Assembly of the United Nations when it met that fall at Lake Success, New York and Flushing Meadow, New York. When she received the call, she and Norman were at Clibrig where the Senator was nursing an injured back, the result of a fall that she had taken in a Montreal hospital in April. Such was her eagerness to accept the appointment, however, that in two days' time Cairine Wilson was writing to St. Laurent:

> ... In the first place I regret that I must write in long hand for I am constantly told that my script is illegible, but stenographic service is not available. I was tremendously flattered by your telephone call last Monday but pleased that I should be chosen as a member of the Canadian Delegation to the next meeting of the United Nations at Lake Success.
>
> I feared that there might be some objection on the part of the doctors, who have had a good deal to say with regard to my movements since I injured my back last April. I could not reach Dr George Armstrong, but I spoke to Dr C. Laidlaw in Prince Edward Island who thought that I could undertake the assignment. I am feeling so much better that I trust nothing will interfere with my going to Lake Success and that I shall form a moderately satisfactory representation.[23]

In the early days of the United Nations, appointments to Canada's prestigious UN delegation made news and none was more newsworthy than Cairine Wilson's. It attracted special attention because, although MP Cora T. Casselman had played an important role in the San Francisco Conference when the UN Charter was drafted, the Senator was the first woman to be appointed to a Canadian delegation to the General Assembly, the UN's deliberative body. Her appointment, in fact, heralded further recognition for women during the St Laurent regime because four years later the courtly prime minister appointed three women to the Senate: Muriel McQueen Fergusson (New Brunswick), Marianne Beauchamp Jodoin (Quebec) and Nancy Hodges (British Columbia).

Cairine Wilson was one of five senior delegates on a Canadian delegation headed by affable Lester B. Pearson, then Minister of External Affairs and a rising star in the UN firmament. The others in order of seniority were Paul Martin, Minister of National Health and Welfare, who boasted an impressive background in international studies and law, but who was often viewed as just a canny, ward-heeling politician, and General The Hon. A.G.L. McNaughton, then Canada's permanent delegate to the United nations. A man of strong views and a passionate Canadian nationalist, General McNaughton had distinguished himself as one of Canada's outstanding army commanders in both world wars and during the inter-war period. Now at the United Nations, this eminent soldier, scientist and public servant would become noted for hard work and a remarkable talent for keeping a lot of balls in the air at the same time. The Senator was next in order of seniority, followed by Conservative René Norbert Jutras, MP for Provencher, Manitoba.

If Cairine Wilson was thrilled at the thought of serving her country at the UN, women's groups were no less elated. One such organization was Montreal's Local Council of Women whose president Mrs W.S. Edgar wrote to Louis St. Laurent on 19 October expressing the Council's enthusiastic appreciation of the appointment and adding:

> The Council notes with pride the favourable impression that Senator Wilson's skill in debate in the Third (Social) Committee has already produced and trusts that not only will future delegations to the United Nations General Assembly contain one or more women reresentatives but that each suceeding year will see an increase in the Government's appointment of Canadian women to the various bodies comprising the United Nations organizations.[24]

The Third Committee to which the Senator was assigned was one of the six principal committees of the United Nations to which the plenary session of the General Assembly referred issues for study and action.

Because it dealt with social, humanitarian and cultural questions, Committee Three, as it was also called, did not enjoy the same prestige as, for example, the First Committee (Political and Security) which elected Pearson chairman. Agnes Macphail had been incensed at an attempt to place her on the Third Committee at the League of Nations in 1929. "That's the committee where they stow women away," she had snorted and promptly countered with a request that she be placed on the committee dealing with disarmament. She succeeded in having her way.[25] Eleanor Roosevelt, who represented the United States on the Third Committee during Cairine Wilson's UN stint, had similar misgivings about being appointed to that committee. After briefings and talks with officials, however, she concluded that it might turn out to be much more important than she had expected it to be. Developments proved her correct.[26] Cairine Wilson would also discover the importance of the Third Committee, but then it is highly unlikely that she had any reservations about being appointed to it so closely did its mandate coincide with her particular interests and expertise. At any rate, on 24 December 1950 she told an audience in Timmins, Ontario that she had been delighted with her appointment to the Third Committee because its assignments produced none of the disappointments associated with the work of the Political Committee or some of the other committees.[27]

The Canadian delegation flew from Ottawa to New York on the evening of 18 September to allow time for its members to settle in at the Biltmore Hotel and to get their bearings before the General Assembly met. For over two months Cairine Wilson's home away from the Manor House would be this comfortable, if undistinguished, commercial hostelry located on Forty-third Street, across from a Schrafft's restaurant and just a few steps away from the Hotel Roosevelt grill, where Guy Lombardo and his Royal Canadians serenaded fans with "the sweetest music this side of heaven."

When the fourth session of the General Assembly convened on 20 September, the Canadians discovered that the atmosphere, although not one of rosy optimism, was certainly one of brisk efficiency and realism. In previous years the opening formalities had taken many days, but this September the officers were chosen, the agenda was agreed upon and the general debate was launched within four days.[28] It seemed as if there was a widespread wish to get on with the job of tackling some of the sixty-nine items on the Assembly's agenda and contributing in any way to the lessening of international tension. For already there was growing antagonism between the Western powers and the Soviet Union which, backed by its armies, had succeeded in imposing satellite regimes on a wide swath of neighbouring states. Just one year earlier, in 1948, a full-blown crisis had erupted when the Soviet authorities had imposed traffic restrictions which had reduced West Berlin, located in the Russian-occupied zone of Germany, to a state of near-seige. Only when the Western powers had responded with an "airlift" which flew in supplies had the threat of open warfare been averted. Nevertheless, the very real threat of a new war hung over the deliberations of the General Assembly when it met in Paris in 1948. Now, on Friday, 23 September, 1949 shortly after the opening of the fourth session of the General Assembly, had come U.S. President Harry Truman's dramatic announcement of an atomic explosion in the USSR.

Despite these disquieting developments and the failure of the United Nations to resolve such troublesome and dangerous issues as Palestine, Kashmir and Indonesia, many people shared Cairine Wilson's view that the world organization represented the best hope for preserving peace and security in the world. True, the veto power possessed by each of the five permanent members of the Security Council inhibited that body from taking effective action against an aggressor state. Nevertheless, there was still an enormous fund of enthusiasm for the United Nations and that year the various items on its agenda attracted a lot of American press coverage. So did delegates like Cairine Wilson, who found that she was not the only one of her sex among the top delegates. Besides Eleanor Roosevelt, who sat near the Senator on the Third Committee, there were also such notables as Third Committee member Barbara Castle, British MP and parliamentary secretary to the president of the Board of Trade, and Mme Vijaya Lakshmi Pandit, sister of Jawaharlal Nehru, India's Prime Minister.

The UN's permanent headquarters had yet to be built on the seventeen and a half-acre site that John D. Rockefeller had donated for this purpose on the East River in New York City. As a result, the General Assembly met in the world's fair buildings at Flushing Meadow, New York and committees in the former Sperry Gyroscope plant at Lake Success on Long Island, a tedious forty-five minute drive from congested Manhattan. In the next couple of months Cairine Wilson would spend countless hours and cover hundreds of miles driving back and forth between the two centres and New York.

Interviewed at Lake Success just after her arrival at the UN, the Senator put her hand to her back and remarked, smiling, " I hope people here won't think all Canadians are deformed because of my recently injured back. I still have to wear a brace."[29] She did not allow her back injury to interfere with any of her UN activities. It may have prevented her from wearing a favourite evening dress to one of the UN's numerous social functions, but that was probably all that it succeeded in doing. With her customary dedication she met her new job head on, striving to master details quickly and to meet as many delegates from the other fifty-eight delegations as she could.

Among those who watched the Senator taking up her duties at the United Nations was Basil Robinson, onetime Under-Secretary of External Affairs. He has recalled "a warm, friendly, gracious" woman, who was serious about her work, in short, a representative who was "a great asset to the Canadian delegation."[30]

The world to which Cairine Wilson, the UN neophyte, had to adapt was fast-paced and exhilarating. It was also tiring. Shortly after breakfast each weekday morning, the Senator, along with fellow members of the Canadian delegation, their advisors, and other government officials, met at the Biltmore for half to three-quarters of an hour to review the previous day's developments in the UN committees and to take stock of where Canada was in a given committee. After the meeting Cairine Wilson drove in a delegation limousine to Lake Success, usually in the company of her advisor, George Grande, with whom she discussed freely what she was going to say in the Third Committee if it convened that day. For its meetings she was often armed with a speech that Grande had drafted the night before. But even if she did not anticipate addressing her fellow delegates, she would be conversant with the details of the issues under discussion, having assiduously studied her briefing papers.

On days that she and her fellow Third Committee delegates met at Lake Success, the Senator might return to New York for a meal. This meant that she invariably faced two round-trips to Lake Success in the same day. Irrespective of where she lunched, Cairine Wilson still put in a long day, working from early in the morning to late in the evening. If the Third Committee's agenda dictated a rare weekend session, she might also find herself at Lake Success on a Saturday. But if nothing was planned for the weekend, she might journey back to Ottawa for a brief respite at the Manor House with Norman, young Cairine and Peggy.

Caught up as she was in the rhythm of this frenetic lifestyle, Cairine Wilson soon became a seasoned player. But before she mastered the ropes, observed Basil Robinson, she was "modest and tentative." This assessment is supported by George Grande, who remembered that the Senator was at first reluctant to make ad hoc interventions in meetings, "but if she decided to say something she said it well." So grateful was she to have an advisor and so pleased was she with his assistance that after his return to Ottawa Cairine Wilson invited George Grande and his wife to the Manor House for a "fabulous," old-style tea party. Decades after the event, Grande recalled the impressive silver tea service, the tea-pourer, the table groaning with goodies and the host of political celebrities, deputy ministers, bankers and leading clergymen "floating around" the palatial Manor House. There was also a tour of the greenhouse conducted by the Senator herself, who wanted to impress on Grande just how much she appreciated his help when she was at the United Nations. "She was very warm-hearted, intelligent and loyal," commented the former External Affairs official.[31]

The Third Committee meetings where Cairine Wilson put in so many hours during that eventful autumn assembled in a spacious room where delegates from some thirty to thirty-five states sat around a huge, round table. In sessions that often pitted East against West, they discussed and debated items that had been referred to their attention by the General Assembly. These included such issues as assistance to Palestine refugees; a convention on freedom of information; the discrimination practised by certain states against immigrant labour; refugees and stateless persons; and much to Cairine Wilson's discomforture, a draft convention on prostitution. Undoubtedly the last thing that the Senator had expected to debate in this committee was an international agreement to control prostitution and so she was taken aback when informed she would have to speak on the question. "George I don't think I can talk about this!," she protested. George Grande assured the Senator that she could and, of course she obliged. She delivered an address that he had written and that she had reviewed and edited. As her onetime advisor tells it, "She was a real brick. She read the speech and participated nobly in the debate. But I think she never forgot that."[32]

Refugees and stateless persons was a subject that Cairine Wilson was much more knowledgeable about and comfortable discussing. It is ironic that this issue, which generated so much political heat over the years, was handled by the so-called "unimportant" committee to which the Senator and most of the other women delegates to the UN had been appointed. The topic owed its contentiousness to the fact that the Soviet Union and its Communist allies regarded any displaced Ukranians, Poles, Byelorussians, Czechoslovaks, Lithuanians, Estonians and others who did not return home to live under Communist rule as traitors and quislings who should be forced to do so. The Western members of the UN argued, of course, that these displaced persons were neither traitors nor quislings and that they should be guaranteed the right to choose whether or not to return to their country of origin. The Third Committee spent countless hours trying to frame a resolution on which everybody could agree, but failed. Finally it presented a majority report to the General Assembly, which voted for it despite a formidable challenge mounted by the USSR.[33]

Victory for the Western position meant that the West would be concerned with the ultimate fate of refugees and stateless persons for years to come as Cairine Wilson discovered when she made her debut in the Third Committee. That autumn, however, this most troubling and perplexing of issues assumed a new urgency because the International Refugee Organization (IRO), a UN body, was scheduled to cease operations in

1951 and the General Assembly had to decide what should succeed it. To the Third committee was delegated the task of recommending the form that the replacement should take and the terms of reference that it should adopt.[34]

Such a seemingly innocuous assignment could hardly be expected to further embitter relations between East and West. But since the Cold War was now a grim reality, this is just what happened in some of the Third Committee debates on the problems of refugees and stateless persons. Two of the more stormy sessions that pitted East against West occurred on 4 and 8 November 1949 and drew Cairine Wilson into the fray. The opening salvo was fired on the afternoon of 4 November when in the midst of a discussion on stateless persons and a High Commissioner's mandate, the Polish delegate accused Canada of kidnapping 123 Polish children, who had recently arrived in this country from a refugee camp in Tanganyika.[35]

When it came time for Cairine Wilson to speak she quickly refuted, with all the force that she could muster, the Polish delegate's irresponsible and unfounded charges against Canada. Kidnapping, she pointed out, was a serious crime, with two components: abduction and ransom. It was absurd to level such accusations against the Canadian government when its actions were dictated solely by humanitarian feelings and a desire to aid certain unfortunates without any thought of advantage for itself. "Perhaps the representative of Poland cannot understand why a Government does something for no other reason than that of kindness and pity and an impelling desire to help without the thought of gain," she said. The Polish children in question formed part of a convoy of refugees that had been evacuated from the USSR through the Middle East following agreement with the Soviet government. Canada had welcomed the children on the recommendation of the IRO and after being assured that they were all orphans. If the Polish government had any doubts on this score, it should take the matter up with the IRO.[36]

Not content with this explanation, the Polish delegation renewed its attack against Canada on 8 November. Only this time it also raised the question of the Polish art collection that had been brought to Canada in 1940 for safekeeping but had not been returned to Poland. Summary records of the Third Committee proceedings note that the committee chairman had to intervene at this point and admonish members for making digressions and "offensive personal allusions." Just what insults were hurled is not indicated but in all likelihood the reference relates in part to aspersions cast on Cairine Wilson. For, after her return to Ottawa, the Senator gave an interview in which she noted that a committee member from one of the satellite countries had ascribed her views on the kidnapping of children to a lack of maternal feeling; the implication was that Cairine Wilson either had no children or too few to qualify her for the title of "mother"![37]

Before the Third Committee completed its work in late November, the Senator made a general statement before it in which she endorsed the appointment of a High Comissioner for Refugees who would report to the General Assembly through the Economic and Social Council and whose office would be a constant reminder to UN members of the importance of the refugee problem. This position was later adopted by the Committee and then by the General Assembly, which decided on 3 December to establish just such an office as of 1 January 1951. For her part Cairine Wilson was exceedingly sorry to see the winding up of the International Refugee Organization and the appointment of a High Commissioner of Refugees to replace it. In her view such an official would never command the necessary resources to deal with the staggering refugee problem, a point that she emphasized, when addressing the Senate four years later, she touched on the UN. In that debate she noted sadly, "This international commissioner has never had a satisfactory budget and has constantly been harassed by seeing the need and being unable to place people properly."[38]

When she completed her assignment at the UN, Cairine Wilson could look back on a job well done and take pride in the inscribed scroll that had been presented to her that autumn in the name of the world body's Secretary General, Trygve Lie. It represented his recognition and appreciation of the work that she had performed the previous year as vice-chairman of the National Council for the United Nations Appeal for Children. The Senator could also rejoice in an unanticipated byproduct of her UN stint: improved health. It seems that the long hours and the politically charged atmosphere at the world body had not tired her unduly. The whole experience had been so exhilarating, in fact, that it had recharged her batteries. Certainly this is the impression gleaned from a letter that the Senator wrote to Mackenzie King on 16 December in which she reported, "Mr St Laurent was surprised when I declared that he had given me a health cure, but I am pleased to report that I returned to Ottawa in good physical condition."[39] In that same letter she also mentioned that she had been entertained in New York by one of King's old flames, Beatrix Henderson Robb, a divorcée whom King first met in Europe in 1928 and with whom he would invariably dine when he was in New York.

With the colourful cosmopolitanism and electric atmosphere of the United Nations behind her, Cairine Wilson returned to her ceaseless round of activities in Ottawa. Canada's national capital was still a staid, largely English Canadian city in these years, its Ontario small town character yet to be diluted by sizable influxes of immigrants and the burgeoning of new ethnic restaurants, art galleries and theatres. This transformation would not really get under way until after the Senator's death but it was certainly one she anticipated with her long-held recognition of just how much Canada could be enriched by the skills and cultural gifts of many of Europe's homeless. Whenever she occupied her small cream-coloured Senate office she could not help but be reminded of this because arrayed here and there were hand-crafted gifts that grateful refugees had given to her: book ends, ceramic figures of skiers and skaters, and hand-tooled telephone covers, their edges beautifully braided. In the years ahead she would take inspiration and comfort from these touching reminders of her long crusade on behalf of legions of Europe's refugees.

She continued to promote their cause to the end of her life, frequently speaking out on the continuing injustices in Canada's immigration law and the tendency of Canadian professional associations to attack the immigration of members of their own professions. Thus in an address to Kydd Memorial Church in Montreal on 15 October 1950, she observed:

> It is a reflection upon Canada today that whereas a manual labourer may be readily admitted the intellectuals who have much to contribute are still left to eat their hearts out in Refugee camps. I had always hoped that our Presbyterian Church would lend a helping hand to some of these people for whom Mr Allard, the Chief of Mission, Canada, IRO, has appealed to Rotary Clubs. Unfortunately there is a great reluctance on the part of professional groups to encourage other members of their particular line of work. Each thinks the other association should show the generous spirit.[40]

The injustices in Canadian immigration law to which she alluded derived from the 1931 order-in-council which outlined the stringent terms governing admission of prospective immigrants to Canada. In a wide-ranging speech to the Zonta Club of Ottawa on 25 February 1959, the Senator would deplore the fact that this policy was still in effect and that as a consequence only first-degree relatives of people already in Canada, bona-fide agricultural settlers and people possessing substantial capital qualified as immigrants.[41] In notes prepared for another speech, she would chastise those governments that provided homes for only robust, healthy and skilled refugees and refused to admit the aged and the sick.

As chairman of the Senate Immigration and Labour Committee, Cairine Wilson spelled out clearly just how many immigrants she thought Canada should admit annually. She had occasion to do this on 15 March 1950 when she moved a motion that her committee conduct an all-out enquiry into every phase of Canada's immigration policy. Reported the Senator:

> Many estimates have been made of the the number of immigrants which Canada can satisfactorily absorb in any one year. I think that a fairly reasonable annual figure would be about 200,000, or one and a half percent of the existing population. The highest figure, 125,414, was reached in the calendar year 1948.[42]

To her dismay, the Senator would see immigration of this magnitude only once — in 1957 when the postwar record for immigration was set with the arrival of some 280,000 persons on Canadian shores.[43] The sharp upward swing in immigration that occurred that year and that would never again be repeated in her lifetime was attributable in part to the Suez Crisis and the Hungarian uprising of 1956.

In moving that same motion, Cairine Wilson took great pleasure in reporting the fulfillment of one of her longstanding dreams: the Government's decision in January of that year to recognize the importance of immigration by establishing a separate Department of Citizenship and Immigration. She could pride herself on the fact that she and the now defunct CNCR as well as the Senate Committee on Immigration and Labour under her chairmanship had played no small role in arousing public opinion and the Government to a recognition of the need for this type of service.

If the slim, quiet-speaking senator had wanted to, she could also have basked in the praise of Senator John Haig, Leader of the Opposition in the Senate. After she had spoken to her motion, Senator Haig informed his colleagues, "For two or more sessions [Cairine Wilson] has been Chairman of the Committee on Immigration, of which I had the honour to be a member, and she handled the committee's work well, better than most men would have done. She knows the subject of immigration, and has a very sympathetic heart towards it."[44] Coming from an elderly male senator that was praise indeed!

Quite a different honour was paid to Cairine Wilson that May by the National Council of Women. It chose her as Canada's representative to receive an award from the American Mothers Committee of New York, an organization that sought to promote the cause of peace through the women of the world. "She's top 'Momma' is Senator Cairine Wilson" proclaimed *Toronto Saturday Night* in its 30 May edition. No less enthusiastic but much more dignified were the tributes of Cairine Wilson's fellow senators who, on 8 May, rose in the Senate to acclaim her as Canada's first "Mother of the Year." Replying to their congratulations, she observed, "The congratulations of this body are a refreshing change from the accusation made last October, while I was attending the United Nations, that I was devoid of a mother's feelings about the kidnapping of children." [45]

A few days later the Senator journeyed to New York to receive her award at a ceremony staged by the American Mothers Committee at the Waldorf Astoria Hotel. In a news photograph, which shows her with recipients from five other UN member states, she sports a large-brimmed black hat, a tailored grey suit and a somewhat pensive look.

Another and deeply treasured honour came her way later that year when she was presented with the Cross of the Knight of the Legion of Honour (the lowest of the award's five classes). The Senator had arrived home from Clibrig on the 25th July to attend Mackenzie King's funeral to find a letter from the French ambassador Hubert Guerin announcing the news of her award. Reported the Ambassador:

> I have great pleasure in informing you that, upon my request, the President of the French Republic has awarded you the Cross of Chevalier de la Légion d'Honneur. It is particularly gratifying to me that the French Government should pay tribute to the outstanding services you have rendered to France during the war years.[46]

Photo by NEWTON, Ottawa

Cairine Wilson receiving the Legion of Honour from French Ambassador Hubert Guerin on 31 October 1950. Looking on is Dr Gustave Lanctôt, former Dominion Archivist.

That autumn, on the 31 October, the Ambassador pinned the small medal's scarlet ribbon on her in a brief ceremony at the French Embassy. Looking on was Dr Gustave Lanctôt, former Dominion Archivist, who was also decorated with the Legion of Honour, and a small group of family and friends. Upon learning of the Senator's latest recognition, the journalist, soldier and diplomat, Victor Odlum, who was then Canada's ambassador to Turkey, wrote from Ankara congratulating her on her achievement and adding:

> I am delighted. You have been serving Canada in a specialized field for a long time and you have done it with distinction.

> I will never forget the kindnesses you have shown me from time to time when I have been in Ottawa. I will always bear in memory pictures of the luncheons in your home and of the delightful surroundings and personalities which made a visit there a definite "event."[47]

In her own quiet way, Cairine Wilson was thrilled to receive this honour because it represented tangible recognition of all that she had done for French refugees. It was also a tribute to her deep affection for France and her sympathy for the Free French cause during the Second War. But overshadowing the news of the award was the death of Norman's and her old friend Mackenzie King, who had died at his country estate at Kingsmere, Quebec. The aging bachelor had retired from the Liberal leadership only two years earlier in failing health and seemingly content to leave the office of prime minister to the courtly Quebec corporation lawyer Louis St Laurent. Now after a heart attack in late December 1949 and pneumonia in July, King was dead at seventy-five.

During his two quiet years of retirement, however, the elderly bachelor had continued to play a role in Wilson family affairs and to exchange letters and birthday greetings with the Senator. In fact, in May 1949, he had attended the wedding of the Wilsons' "baby girl," Norma, who was married to career air force officer Jim Davies. Following the wedding the Senator wrote to King:

> It was very good of you to write to me, and we did appreciate your presence at the wedding and also your short speech about which there have been many favourable comments. My colleague, Norman Lambert, did not give me an opportunity to reply, for you gave me two or

three openings — one, that "Laurier House" had been more successful in Wilson matrimonial matters than those of the present owner; and that Lady Laurier always said she had a large family by proxy.[48]

Interestingly enough, the Senator had thrown her inborn reticience to the winds and employed the intimate salutation "My dear Rex" for the first time a month earlier when replying to a letter from her old friend. King had suggested many years ago that she use this distinctive nickname that had been bestowed on him at university and that was employed only by his close friends when addressing him. However, until her letter of 4 May 1949 the Senator had refrained from doing so, contenting herself in the 1930s and the 1940s with "My dear Chief" or occasionally with "My dear Mr King."

King, for his part, addressed the Senator as "My dear Cairine" from late 1930 until the final months of his life. Certainly this was the salutation that he used in a letter dated 25 January 1950 thanking her for the beautiful azalea plant and kind note that she had sent to him. Both, he averred, "[brought], with them, a note of the new life which comes with thoughts of Spring."[49] With this poignant, almost lyrical, reference and a comment on the Senator's health, King brought to a close what was probably the last letter that he dispatched to Cairine Wilson, although he did, as was his custom, telegraph birthday greetings to her the following month.

On 26 July, Cairine Wilson joined hundreds of mourners in a long funeral procession that made its way from the Parliament Buildings, where King's body lay in state in the Hall of Fame, to nearby St Andrew's Presbyterian Church, the former prime minister's place of worship for almost fifty years. Ahead of her, advancing slowly to the beat of muffled drums and funeral music, was an escort provided by the three services and the limousine bearing Mr King's body. Then followed top-hatted, morning-coated honorary pallbearers led by Sir Lyman Duff, and Royal Canadian Mounted Police pallbearers resplendent in their dazzling scarlet coats. Close behind were diplomats from nations accredited to Canada, senior government officials, members of Parliament like herself and old friends. Surrounded as she was by men, the Senator really stood out: a slim figure in a simple black dress who held herself very erect and walked with great dignity.[50] As she advanced slowly forward in the bright July sun past the dense crowds lining Wellington Street, Cairine Wilson no doubt reflected on a similar role that she had played on 8 February 1947. On that memorable occasion she had been one of the mourners in the funeral procession of another good friend, Dr. Henry Marshall Tory.

Memories of another important funeral that she had attended, that of her friend, Sir Wilfred Laurier, probably also came flooding back. It had taken place on a February day back in 1919 when the Senator was a newcomer to Ottawa and a young wife and mother still immersed in domestic pursuits. Unlike King's, Laurier's body had been attired in a Windsor uniform and had lain in state in the Victoria museum, which was then serving as a substitute parliament building. The Laurier funeral procession also contrasted sharply with the bachelor prime minister's in that it was almost 100 percent horse-drawn. Some of the horses had even galloped when they got behind and were whipped by inexperienced riders.

The contrasts between the King and Laurier funerals symbolized in a way the dramatic changes that had occurred in Cairine Wilson's own life over the years. Two of these developments — her appointment to the Senate and the founding of the Canadian National Committee on Refugees — were so momentous that they altered her life irrevocably. Apart from the death of her beloved Norman in 1956 and her own deteriorating health, however, there would be few dramatic changes in the years ahead. Life would continue along well trod paths, full and eventful, but not veering off in radically new directions.

In the Senate the Senator continued to identify with progressive thinking. On 21 March 1951, for example, when her colleagues were debating the establishment of a committee to inquire into and report upon how the Upper House could "make its maximum contribution to the welfare of the Canadian people," she rose in her seat to give her whole-hearted support to Senate reform proposals outlined earlier by her friend, Senator A.K. Hugessen. In doing so she spoke out in favour of a mandatory retirement age for senators and for "some provision for nominations from the provinces" for Senate appointments.[51]

The Senate's navel-gazing produced a torrent of speeches and a great deal of heated discussion, but, as was to be expected, no action, for on 24 May the motion which had started it all (the resolution introduced by Senator Wishart McL. Robertson on 12 February 1951) was withdrawn. Not until 1965 would legislation be enacted imposing a compulsory retirement age for senators. That age was seventy-five and applied to all senators appointed after the passage of the bill. As for the suggestion of Cairine Wilson and some of her colleagues that some provision should be made for "nominations from the provinces,[52] it would not attract widespread attention until the publication of the report of the Task Force on Canadian Unity in 1979.

Senator Wilson took up the cause of liberalized divorce again in 1955 when she voted for a bill that was almost an exact replica of the one passed by the Senate on 18 May 1938. When speaking to the bill, she remarked, "Personally, I am among the fortunate ones who enjoy a very happy married life. However, that does not prevent me understanding the misery which others have endured. Also, honourable senators, I have seen many happy second marriages.[53]

When she had made that observation Cairine Wilson had been married for forty-six years and had just celebrated her twenty-fifth anniversary as a senator. Interviewed shortly after that anniversary, she informed Shirley Gillespie of the *Ottawa Journal* that notwithstanding her long time in the Senate she still received mail addressed "Dear Sir." Then, when asked to explain the small number of women MPs, the Senator said, "It is probably because we, as women, expect a great deal more of our women representatives." This, she speculated, was probably one reason why women had difficulty getting nominated. She then remarked, as she had frequently over the years, how disappointed she was that Canadian women did not take a greater interest in the affairs of government.[54]

Because the Senate was not sitting on the twenty-fifth anniversary of Cairine Wilson's appointment, her fellow senators had to delay their tribute to her. This took place on 8 March when Senator Ross Macdonald, Solicitor General and Government Leader in the Senate, rose in his seat to deliver the first accolade. After her fellow senators had their say, Cairine Wilson, in typically modest fashion, noted, "I confess that this year I was rather pleased that both my birthday and the anniversary of my appointment to this chamber fell on days when the Senate was adjourned for a long weekend; however, I apparently did not go unnoticed."[55]

Cairine Wilson not only contributed to Senate debates in these years she also assumed the duties of a Deputy Speaker on several occasions. She even made parliamentary history on the evening of Tuesday, 3 May 1955 when she became the first woman ever to take the Speaker's chair in the ornate red chamber. Because there has never been any provision either in law or in the rules of the Senate for the appointment of a permanent Deputy Speaker, the Senate appoints a temporary Speaker when the permanent one is unavoidably absent for a sitting. This is what happened on the evening of 3 May when the Senators, on convening for their first sitting after an Easter holiday, found themselves without the services of Speaker Wishart Robertson, who was away ill. Using a procedure similiar to that employed in the House of Commons, the Leader of the Government in the Senate, Solicitor-General Ross Macdonald, nominated Cairine Wilson to deputize. The acting Leader of the Opposition, Senator Walter Aseltine, seconded the motion and the assembled senators passed it unanimously.

After being ceremoniously escorted to the chair, Cairine Wilson led the Senators in Prayers, employing a "flawless" French accent. It so happened that Tuesday was an evening when prayers were said in French, the Senate alternating betweeen prayers in English and French. These formalities out of the way, the Senator proceeded to call the business of the

Senate. This was no light task as Parliament had recessed for almost a month and there were numerous pieces of legislation that had been passed by the Commons and that had to be put on the record. Cairine Wilson, however, handled matters in her usual quiet, efficient manner. Perhaps because she acquitted herself so well, she was called on later in the year, on 26, 27, and 28 July, to once again deputize for the Speaker.

Although these later years brought increasing recognition of the Senator's acheivements and many a reason to celebrate, they also introduced the frustration and sorrow born of serious illness and death. Both would figure prominently in Cairine Wilson's final years and test to the utmost her deep religious faith.

12

THE TWILIGHT YEARS

A n outside observer watching the busy Senator in action in these years would not have guessed that her serene demeanor masked a growing concern about her husband's rapidly deteriorating health. Norman had developed diabetes in the early 1930s, when he was in his fifties, and now, in his declining years, he was also suffering from Parkinson's disease and hardening of the arteries in the brain. Towards the end, cancer would also be involved. One of the Senator's most striking gifts was her ability to accept such unfortunate developments with stoicism and grace. It was not in her nature, for example, to hide the fact that her beloved husband was becoming increasingly confused. Notwithstanding his mental condition, he was always welcomed among his wife's guests at Manor House functions. And no matter how trying he might be, Cairine Wilson was invariably patient and good with him. Still, she could not refrain from hinting at some of her frustration and worry in a letter to her old friend, Lyman Duff. Writing to the eighty-eight-year-old jurist on 12 August 1953, the Senator observed:

> We have had very fine weather for the most part, and I am pleased to report that my own health is very much better than for a long time past. I cannot give such a good report on Norman, however, for although his physical condition is no worse, he is increasingly confused in mind. I reply to the same question three or four times within ten or fifteen minutes.[1]

On 14 July 1956, Norman died in the Ottawa Civic Hospital. In the years, prior to the onslaught of serious illness, he had played his part as the kind, large-hearted host, putting guests to the Manor House at ease. It was a job that he had performed well. Because he was basically a shy man, however, he had really been at his best in the midst of his family: the devoted husband, the loving father, and then, in more recent years, the affectionate grandfather. Now he was gone. With his death, a great void opened up in Cairine Wilson's life which neither her large family, most of whose members were now raising families of their own, and many friends nor her innumerable outside pursuits could fill. Despite all these interests she would become a lonely woman in the years that lay ahead.

The Mackay family ranks were shrinking too. In 1942, her brother Hugh, who had been in deteriorating health, had succumbed to the after-effects of a severe sunstroke suffered two months earlier. He left behind a wife, Isabel Greenshields, from whom he had been separated for years, three adult children and a reputation as a highly regarded corporation lawyer. Then, in 1954, Cairine Wilson's sole surviving brother, Edward, had died, a lonely, embittered man with a mere handful of friends and an only son whom he repudiated. When they were growing up Edward and Cairine had been very close to each other. However, the years had taken their toll of this relationship, largely because of a longstanding feud that had developed between Edward and sister, Anna, who lived opposite his large mansion on Montreal's McGregor Street. Cairine Wilson lost all patience with her brother when he steadfastly rejected Anna's repeated attempts at reconciliation. As a result there there was little, if any, communication between Cairine and Edward in later years. But then Edward associated with few people towards the end of his life. After the untimely death of his attractive wife, Jean, in 1944, he slid into the lifestyle of a millionaire recluse, who looked for all the world like a derelict when he plodded along exclusive residential streets in a tattered overcoat accompanied by his Pekingese.

Edward's death left Cairine and Anna, who had been invalided by a series of strokes, the sole survivors of nine children. Until her own death, two years before that of Anna, Cairine Wilson would make repeated trips to Montreal to visit the sister, with whom she was so close, sometimes spending a night on a cot at the Montreal General Hospital in order to be near her when there was a medical crisis.

While the Mackay family ranks were thinning, close friends were also fading from the scene. One of these was Sir Lyman Duff, who died on 26 April 1955 at the age of ninety. In a letter written to young Cairine some five years earlier, the Senator provides a touching portrait of the aging, grey-haired jurist with the Van Dyke beard. Describing a visit that she and

Peggy made to Duff, when he was living in the book-filled house that he owned on Clemow Avenue, Cairine Wilson said:

> At Sir Lyman's we found him sitting in the room to the right of the door with his feet encased in felt slippers, and his heating pad. He appeared delighted to see us, however — in fact talked so much we found difficulty in getting away. I came away supplied with a volume by James Russell Lowell and another, which I have for the moment forgotten, while Peggy was given a French story, which she promised to read. Unfortunately Sir Lyman appears to think that I have read more widely than is the case![2]

The Senator was, of course, an avid reader but her tastes did not run the gamut of Sir Lyman's. Her friend had a voracious appetite for books, which he not only bought in large quantities but read. And unlike his friend's, his library represented just about every field imaginable, from novels by Disraeli, detective stories and cookbooks to medical journals, scientific works and tomes on economics.[3] Cairine Wilson read mostly international newspapers, such as The *Christian Science Monitor*, which she subscribed to, *The Manchester Guardian*, *The New York Times* and the local papers. She liked biographies and serious magazines, especially *Saturday Night*, and disdained anything that could be considered "wasting time," in which category she placed most fiction. Idleness, it goes without saying, was abhorrent to the Senator, who could not see the point of just sitting and doing nothing. Time had to be employed in what she regarded as meaningful activity and so when she found herself relaxing indoors with family and friends she often busied herself with knitting.

Unfortunately for the Senator, ill health forced months of comparative inactivity on her in the last decade of her life. In August 1951, less than two years after the lengthy siege with her back, for example, she was ordered to spend three weeks in bed at Clibrig because of an overstrained heart. The degree of chagrin and frustration that she experienced can well be imagined because this was probably the first time in her life that Cairine Wilson was confronted by a potentially serious health problem and forced to rein herself in severely. Writing on 27 December 1951 to Gordon Wallace, the administrator of the Mackay estate, she remarked:

> Of late I appear to have been particularly busy and cannot do all that I should wish. I am thankful to report that after a long period of inactivity I am feeling very much better and have been able to take up a good part of

my former work. I have been advised to avoid all public
speaking, however, and I have not ventured to raise my
voice in the Senate but a long time ago agreed to speak in
Montreal on 11th February.[4]

Some two years before her death, the Senator developed uterine
cancer. From the uterus it eventually spread throughtout her body,
combining with osteoporosis to weaken her bone structure. From now on
she suffered repeated setbacks in health. One even prevented her from
journeying to Toronto to receive an award on 27 November 1960 from the
B'nai B'rith Women of Toronto who had chosen her Woman of the Year.
Young Cairine dutifully made the trip and accepted the award in her
mother's absence. In thanking Charles Clay on 10 December for his letter
of congratulations, the Senator mentioned that she had been on the inactive
list since October but that she hoped that she would be able to resume work
after the first of February.

As was her wont, Cairine Wilson devoted much of her time and energy
before this latest illness to promoting the cause of refugees. She did so
within the context of World Refugee Year which had been proclaimed by
the United Nations to spotlight the plight of the world's refugees. World
Refugee Year, which ran from 1 June 1959 to 30 June 1960, saw some
seventy nations intensify their longstanding campaign to close down
refugee camps around the world and to rehabilitate thousands upon
thousands of despairing people without a country. As one of the par-
ticpating nations, Canada admitted in excess of 3,500 refugees, including
more than 200 tubercular patients and their families, in 1959-1960.[5] This
country also raised funds for the relief of refugees living in United
Nations' camps, one of these being a camp near Linz, Austria, which was
adopted by the Ottawa Committee for World Refugee Year, of which the
Senator was honorary chairman. Cairine Wilson was delighted with
Canada's decision to admit tubercular refugees. Writing to Saul Hayes on
16 June 1960, she said:

> I expect that you also are pleased with the appoint-
> ment of Dr George Davidson as Deputy Minister of
> Citizenship and Immigration but fear that he will be
> confronted with many problems. It is encouraging,
> however, that the government is undertaking to admit a
> further 100 families with one or more members suffering
> from tuberculosis.[6]

The movement to empty the refugee camps got off to a slow start in
Canada, but eventually gained momentum, thanks in large measure to the

drive of a young Englishman and civil servant, Peter Casson, who was sent to Canada to publicize the campaign by the UN High Commissioner for Refugees. Casson crisscrossed the country addressing meetings and helping to organize committees. Cairine Wilson, who was now in her mid-seventies and in failing health, no longer had the stamina to embark on such an undertaking but nevertheless she threw herself into the forefront of Canada's campaign, pleading the cause of the refugees at every conceivable opportunity. Such an occasion was presented by the annual meeting of the National Council of Women, held at Wasagaming, Manitoba in June 1960. There, on 13 June, only five days after the mammoth party in her own garden to raise funds for World Refugee Year, she told 125 delegates about the "appalling conditions" that existed in refugee camps and deplored the fact that until recently Canada had given little support to the long-range plan to close them down.

Back in Ottawa, she wrote one week later to Leonard Brockington, a lawyer friend, who had served as a special assistant in Mackenzie King's office before becoming first chairman of the Broadcasting Commission (later to become the Canadian Broadcasting Corporation):

> I continue to miss the opportunities I had for calling upon you at the P.M.'s office when I was pleased to ask advice on many subjects. So much is happening that it is scarcely surprising that our minds are confused and I wonder what the state of the world will be in the years to come.

> The present government [John Diefenbaker's Conservative goverment] is certainly going very far ahead in social legislation and I see many troubles before us with the amendments to the Old Age Security Act which was passed so easily last week. The retirement age for the Judges places the Senate in an awkward postion for there is no doubt that the people of Canada would favour retirement age. I feel, however, that it is a great mistake to ask Parliament at Westminister to change the B.N.A. Act. This could easily become a second constitutional crisis.[7]

The following year, on 22 May, the Senator fell in the Senate building and broke her right hip. After five weeks in hospital, she returned home, where, on 5 July, she slid off a chair onto the floor and broke her left hip. Just before leaving hospital after her first fall Cairine Wilson wrote to the Czech-born artist, Hella Moravec Street, to thank her for a magnificent vase of deep red roses and to say how much she regretted not having been able to journey to New York to see her friend's recent exhibition. Then, in a postscript that she had penned herself, the Senator added that she had returned to the Manor House and was overjoyed to welcome home young Cairine, who, in her capacity as president of the Canadian Save the Children Fund, had returned the previous evening from an overseas trip that had taken her to Geneva for the annual meeting of the International Council for Child Welfare and to Israel, where she had seen much of the work being carried on by the Canadian Hadassah. In a departure from normal procedure, the Senator signed herself "Cairine 1."[8]

The end of the year brought further health setbacks. On 30 December, when retiring for the night, the Senator pulled a stubborn bedroom door, which promptly flew open, sending her to the floor, As a result of her tumble, she sustained a broken right shoulder. She was taken to the Civic Hospital the next morning, where she remained until 11 January 1962. The next month she was again admitted to the Civic, this time suffering from a recurrence of cancer and complications resulting from her hip fractures of the previous spring. It was during these final weeks of her life that her friend, art historian Bill Heckscher, saw her for the last time. When he visited her the onetime internee found a serene Cairine Wilson, who spoke of her ebbing life with remarkable detachment and with that typical smile of hers "that would do honor to a Roman stoical philosopher such as Marcus Aurelius."[9]

Cairine Wilson died suddenly on Saturday 3 March at the Civic while making plans to have lunch with her old friend Elizabeth Smellie. Her body was taken to the Manor House, where it lay in an open casket, and later to St. Andrew's Presbyterian Church for the funeral on Tuesday 6 March. People from all walks of life packed the old mahogany pews in the downstairs and the balcony. Her friend Ian Burnett, returned, at the family's invitation, to deliver a fulsome eulogy. After the service, her body was taken to the small cemetery on the eastern outskirts of Cumberland, Ontario, Dales Cemetery, to be laid beside her husband Norman. There it rests not far from a stand of evergreens, with only an austere granite gravestone and two small junipers to mark the place of burial. The reticient inscription reads simply:

Wilson
Norman Frank Wilson
1876-1956

His Wife
Cairine Reay Mackay
1885-1962
Appointed to the Senate 1930

Men and women from across the land mourned the Senator and newspapers both in Canada and overseas carried lengthy tributes to her life and work. Her legacy was perhaps best summed up, however, by two pithy sentences contained in a short poem. Composed by the late Theresa E. Thomson, then executive secretary-treasurer of the Canadian Writers' Foundation, they read:

> I cannot write of her in enigmatic phrases: /she served the artisan and erudite/ with equal fervor,/ leaving each a vast inheritance.[10]

When the Senate convened on the evening of 13 March eleven senators rose to pay tribute to their late colleague. Among them was Cairine Wilson's good friend Muriel McQ. Fergusson, who quoted the above exerpt from the Thomson poem and later observed:

> Through all her thirty-two years in the Senate, Cairine Wilson carried the honour of being a senator — as well as many other honours which she subsequently won for herself — with dignity and distinction. She also won deep respect for her conscientious and scrupulous observance of her Senate duties and responsibilities. Again, to quote from the poem I referred to earlier: "The halls that heard her footsteps were respectful in her presence and behind her back."

> Senator Wilson not only won respect for herself and a place in Canadian history but, by her example, she helped to make a respected place for women in public life in this country. Canadian women, who are saddened by her death, will long remember and pay tribute to her.[11]

These tributes of Mrs Thomson's and Senator Fergusson's along with some of the simple, but heartfelt, letters of sympathy written to members of the family by onetime refugees speak eloquently of Cairine Wilson and her greatest achievements. They describe a compassionate, deeply committed woman, who by her example, sparked an interest and then an urge in many members of her sex to play an active role in the politics of their community and country. They reveal a great humanitarian, who in her own quiet way, was one of the greatest practical idealists of her time.

At her death Cairine Wilson left an estate valued at $2,012, 724.49.[12] There were probably more than a few observers who were surprised that the estate was not considerably larger, but the fact remains that the Senator gave away a lot of money during her lifetime to individuals and causes. Some of these causes benefited handsomely in her will, namely the Mackay Institute for the Deaf; the Presbyterian Church in Canada; The Presbyterian College, Montreal; Acadia University; Carleton College (now Carleton University); the Young Women's Christian Association of Canada; and the Victorian Order of Nurses.[13]

The Senator's proudest legacy — her children — all survived their mother. Young Cairine, who remained unmarried but who emulated her mother's involvement in community organizations, served for many years as president of the Canadian Save the Children Fund. She died in July 1987, just two months before her brother Ralph, who maintained the farm at Clibrig up until his death. Angus, the other farmer in the family, continues to operate the old Wilson farm at Cumberland, Ontario where he and his wife Alice raised three children. His brother Robert, who had four children by his first wife, Dorothy, lives at Cumberland and sells real estate. Olive, the oldest daughter, died in January 1981 after moving to Ottawa from Vancouver, where the Gills had been living prior to Alan Gill's death in 1972. Their daughter, Margaret Gilliam, C.F.A., who inherited her grandmother's aptitude for financial management, is Vice-president, Research, The First Boston Corporation, New York City. Anna (Peggy) died in October 1981, leaving a husband Alan Thistle. Of the two surviving daughters, Norma (Mrs James Davies) lives in Rockcliffe Park with her husband Jim. Their four children are now all adults. Janet, following the death of her stock broker husband, Charles Burns, in 1982, took over the management of Kingfield Foundation which directs money to education and medical services. She and her husband Charles had three children, one of whom, Michael, is president of Crownx and chairman of Crown Life Insurance Company.

NOTES

Chapter One

1. Cairine Wilson to Margaret Wherry, 20 June 1960, Cairine Wilson papers, vol 4, file 29.
2. Interview with Kathleen Ryan, 3 August 1983.
3. Letter from Myra Punnett to the author, 8 June 1983.
4. Cairine Wilson to Henry Marshall Tory, 18 July 1939, Tory papers, vol. 21, League of Nations folder.
5. Interview with Felix de Weldon, 30 September 1983.
6. Interview with Mrs Isabel Percival, 10 August 1983.
7. Letter from Ellen Fairclough to the author, 15 December 1983.
8. Interview with Kathleen Ryan, 3 August 1983.
9. Interview with Felix de Weldon, 30 September 1983.
10. Canada, The Senate, *Debates*, 14 June 1960, Appendix, p. 804.
11. Ibid.
12. Ibid., pp. 804-805.
13. Ibid., p. 805.

Chapter Two

1. Edgar Andrew Collard, *Call Back Yesterdays* (Don Mills: Longmans Canada Ltd., 1965), p. 203.
2. Agnes Muir Mackenzie, *Scotland in Modern Times* (London and Edinburgh: W. and R. Chambers, 1942), p. 111.
3. John Prebble, *The Highland Clearances* (London: Secker and Warburg, 1963), p. 111.
4. Gravestone, Mid-Clyth Cemetery, Caithness.
5. Joseph Mackay and family papers, vol. 1, file 5.
6. Ibid.
7. Unidentified document in possession of Valerie Knowles.
8. Rolls of Evaluation for St. Antoine Ward, cadastral number 1744.
9. Edgar Andrew Collard, "Sleighs, Hussars and Joseph Mackay," *The* [Montreal] *Gazette*, 10 April 1976.
10. Interview with Anna Cundill, 13 January 1983.
11. *Dictionary of Canadian Biography, 1881-1890* (Toronto: University of Toronto Press, 1982), vol. X1, p. 560.
12. L. Haworth, *A History of the Mackay School for the Deaf*. M.A. dissertation, McGill University, 1960, p. 26.
13. Sermon preached by A. B. Mackay on the death of Joseph Mackay. Joseph Mackay and family papers, vol. 1, file 5.
14. *Dictionary of Canadian Biography, 1881-1890*, vol. XI, p. 560.
15. Sermon preached by A.B. Mackay on the death of Joseph Mackay.
16. Robert Mackay to George Munroe, 18 May 1858, Joseph Mackay and family papers, vol 1, file 15.
17. Robert Mackay to Catherine Macdonald, n.d., Joseph Mackay and family papers, vol.1, file 22.

18. *The Lethbridge Daily Herald*, 6 November 1924.
19. Henry James Morgan, *The Canadian Men and Women of the Time*, 2nd edition (Toronto: William Briggs, 1912), p. 698.
20. *Canadian Dictionary of Biography 1871-1880* (Toronto: University of Toronto Press, 1972), vol. X, pp. 32-34.
21. Jane Mackay to Robert Mackay, 5 June 1879, Joseph Mackay and family papers, vol. 1, file 16.
22. Kathleen Jenkins, *Montreal* (Garden City, New York: Doubleday & Company, 1966), pp. 418-419.
23. Norma Phillips Muir, "Senator Cairine Wilson — Woman," *Canadian Home Journal*, June, 1930, p.6.
24. Diary, 20 August 1904, Cairine Wilson papers, vol. 4.
25. *New York Herald*, 29 May 1892.
26. W. Stanford Reid, editor, *The Scottish Tradition in Canada* (Toronto: McClelland and Stewart, 1976), p. 120.
27. *The Storied Province of Quebec* (Toronto: The Dominion Publishing Company, 1932), vol. 5, p. 762.
28. *The* [Montreal] *Gazette*, 5 November 1983.
29. Ibid.
30. Edgar Andrew Collard, *Call Back Yesterdays* (Don Mills: Longmans Canada Ltd., 1965), p.180.
31. [Montreal] *Star*, 24 November 1930.
32. *Trafalgar Echoes*, June, 1930, p. 17.
33. Ibid., June 1932.
34. Information supplied by Jean Harvie, Montreal.
35. Ibid.
36. Letter from Lawrence McDougall to the author, 13 October 1986.
37. The Diary, Cairine Wilson Papers, vol. 4.
38. *Sunday Sun*, 11 October 1903.
39. R.W.B. Lewis, *Edith Wharton* (Toronto: Fitzhenry & Whiteside Ltd., 1975), pp. 174-175.
40. Cairine Wilson papers, vol. 4.
41. Speech to the University Women's Club, December 1948, Cairine Wilson papers, vol. 6, file 6.2.
42. Diary, Cairine Wilson papers, vol. 4.
43. Cairine Wilson papers, vol. 2, file 12.
44. Cairine Wilson papers, vol.12.
45. Robert MacRay to Sir Wilfrid Laurier, 21 August 1896, vol. 17, pp. 6490A-6490B, Laurier papers.
46. *Montreal Daily Herald*, 19 October 1900.
47. John Scott, "Our New Woman Senator," *Maclean's Magazine*, 1 April 1930.
48. Radio address by Cairine Wilson, Laurier papers, vol. 810.

Chapter Three

1. Norma Phillips Muir, "Senator Cairine Wilson - Woman," *Canadian Home Journal*, June 1930, p. 6 and notes for an unidentified speech in the Cairine Wilson papers, vol 5.

2. Ibid.
3. The Canadian *Parliamentary Guide* (Ottawa: Queen's Printer, 1908), p. 139.
4. Cairine Wilson papers, vol.13, file 13.1.
5. Norma Phillips Muir, loc. cit., p. 6.
6. Cairine Wilson to Mackenzie King, 25 February 1939, King Personal correspondence, MG 26, J8, vol. 41, folder 3.
7. Letter from Janet Burns to the author, 12 March 1984.
8. Cairine Wilson papers, vol. 7, file 7. 3.
9. Serge Béland and Vianney Laporte, *La Petite Histoire de Rockland* (Published by the Municipality of Rockland, 1982.) pages 49-50.
10. C.H. Little, *Rideau Curling Club Ottawa. A Short History 1888-1978* (Privately published), p. 80.
11. Cairine Wilson papers, vol. 1, file 1.7.
12. Visitors' book in the possession of the Wilson family.
13. Information supplied to the author by Cairine Wilson, Jr.
14. Anna Loring to Cairine Wilson, 18 March 1915. Letter in possession of the Wilson family.
15. Robert Mackay will, Joseph Mackay and family papers, vol. 2, file 3.
16. Memorandum prepared by the Thiel Detective Service Company for Hugh Mackay. In possession of Valerie Knowles.
17. William Cameron Edwards will. Registry Office, Ottawa-Carleton.
18. Catherine Margaret Edwards will. Registry Office, Ottawa-Carleton.
19. Letter from Anna Loring to Cairine Wilson, 7 September 1922. Letter in possession of the Wilson family.
20. Letter from Anna Loring to Cairine Wilson, n.d. Letter in possession of the Wilson family.
21. *Ottawa Journal*, 11 November 1918.
22. Interview with Betty Hurdman and Helen Clayton, 3 November 1983.
23. Interview with Norma Davies, 8 January 1983.
24. Interview with Anne Carver, 13 October 1983.
25. Cairine Wilson, "Home and Love Life's Boons," *Canadian Home Journal*, May 1931.
26. Cairine Wilson papers, vol. 7, folder 7.4.
27. Cairine Wilson, *Canadian Home Journal*, May 1931.
28. Cairine Wilson to Mackenzie King, 18 December 1927, Mackenzie King Personal Correspondence, MG 26, J8, vol. 41, file 3.
29. Cairine Wilson to Mackenzie King, 25 February 1922, King Personal Correspondence, MG 26, J8, vol. 41, file 3.
30. Cairine Wilson to Mackenzie King, 16 December 1928, King Personal Correspondence, vol. 41, file 3.
31. Alexander Smith papers, vol. 1.
32. Helen Doherty to Mackenzie King, 15 February 1928, King Primary Correspondence, MG 26, J1, vol. 151, p. 129104.
33. *Ottawa Evening Journal*, 18 April 1928.
34. *Ottawa Evening Journal*, 19 April 1928.
35. *Ottawa Evening Citizen*, 19 April 1928.
36. Pamphlet published by the National Federation of Liberal Women of Canada.
37. *The Beaver-Canada First*, 1 July 1930.

38. Proceedings of the First National Convention of the Twentieth Century Liberal Association of Canada, p. 19.
39. Interview with Helen Campell, 14 November 1984.
40. Interview with George McIlraith, 7 June 1983.
41. Interview with Kathleen Ryan, 3 August 1983.

Chapter Four

1. Catherine L. Cleverdon, *The Woman Suffrage Movement In Canada*.(Toronto: University of Toronto Press, 1974), p. 142.
2. Ibid.
3. Eleanor Harman, "Five Persons From Alberta," *The Clear Spirit*. Edited by Mary Innis. (Toronto: University of Toronto Press, 1967), p. 164.
4. Ibid., p. 165.
5. David Ricardo Williams, *Duff: A Life In The Law* (Vancouver: University of British Columbia Press, 1984), p. 145.
6. Ibid.
7. Ibid.
8. Canada, The Senate, *Debates*, 8 March 1955, p. 256.
9. *Ottawa Citizen*, 21 April 1958.
10. Eleanor Harman, "Five Persons From Alberta," *The Clear Spirit*. Edited by Mary Innis. (Toronto: University of Toronto Press, 1967), pp. 174-175.
11. Ibid., p. 175.
12. Williams, *Duff: A Life In The Law*, p. 148.
13. *Christian Science Monitor*, 26 June 1940.
14. Senator Andrew Haydon was a friend of King's and a loyal Liberal fund-raiser.
15. King diary, 14 February 1930.
16. A prominent Liberal from Ottawa who chaired the first national assembly of the Liberal Women of Canada.
17. King diary, 14 February 1930.
18. Ibid., 15 February 1930.
19. Cairine Wilson to Janet Wilson, 18 February 1930. Letter in possession of Janet Burns.
20. Ibid.
21. Azilda Dumais to Mackenzie King, 17 February 1930, King Primary Correspondence, MG 26, J1, vol 173, p. 147646.
22. Canada, The Senate, *Debates*, 8 March 1955, p. 256.
23. Ibid.
24. Letter from Janet Wilson Burns to the author, 14 August 1984.
25. Letter from Olive Wilson to Janet Wilson. Undated. In possession of Janet Burns.
26. *Saturday Night*, 1 March 1930.
27. Canada, The Senate, *Journals*, vol. LXV11, 20 February 1930.
28. *Toronto Star*, 21 February 1930.
29. Cairine Wilson, "The Biggest Moment of My Life," *Chatelaine*, August 1933.
30. *Detroit News*, 21 February 1930.
31. *Revised Statutes of Canada*, 1927, vol. 3, p. 2924.
32. *Toronto Star*, 21 February 1930.

33. Letter from Olive Wilson to Janet Wilson. Undated. In possession of Janet Burns.
34. Mackenzie King diary, 21 February 1930.
35. Norman Wilson to Janet Wilson, 22 February 1930. Letter in possession of Janet Burns.
36. Cairine Wilson to Janet Wilson, 2 March 1930. Letter in possession of Janet Burns.
37. Ibid.
38. Canada, The Senate, *Debates*, 25 February 1930, p. 8.
39. Ibid.
40. Cairine Wilson to Janet Wilson, 2 March 1930. Letter in possession of Janet Burns.
41. Norman Wilson to Janet Wilson, 26 February 1930. Letter in possession of Janet Burns.
42. Norman Wilson to Janet Wilson, 28 February 1930. Letter in possession of Janet Burns.
43. *Toronto Mail and Empire*, 5 March 1930.
44. The inclusion of the Skeltons was certainly politic. For Dr Skelton, as Under-Secretary of State for External Affairs and King's closest adviser on both foreign and domestic issues, would prove an invaluable contact in government circles.
45. Norma Phillips Muir, "Senator Cairine Wilson - Woman," *Canadian Home Journal*, June 1930, p. 96.
46. Local Architectural Conservation Advisory Committee, *Walking In The Village of Rockcliffe Park* (Village of Rockcliffe Park, 1982), pp. 17-19.
47. Cairine Wilson to John Ames, 13 February 1930, Cairine Wilson papers, vol. 2, folder 14.
48. *Brantford Times*, 21 March 1930.
49. *Ottawa Journal*, 23 February 1955 and Mackenzie King's diary, 16 February 1931.

Chapter Five

1. Canada, The Senate, *Debates*, 11 January 1955, p. 10.
2. Cairine Wilson to Mackenzie King, 20 March 1930, Mackenzie King Personal Correspondence, MG 26, J8, vol. 41, file 3.
3. *Lindsay Post*, 20 March 1930.
4. Cairine Wilson to Mackenzie King, 24 September 1930, MG26, J8, vol. 41, file 3.
5. *Toronto Mail and Empire*, 6 June 1930.
6. *Proceedings of the First National Convention of the Twentieth Century Liberal Association of Canada*, pp. 19-20.
7. *Encyclopedia Canadiana* (Toronto: Grolier of Canada, 1977), vol. 8, p. 239C.
8. Letter in Wilson family scrapbook.
9. Cairine Wilson to Mackenzie King, 15 December 1948, Mackenzie King papers, Personal Correspondence, MG 26, J8, vol. 41, file 3.
10. King diary, vol 53, 31 October 1930.
11. King diary, vol 53, 11 November 1930.

12. Interview with the author, 17 July 1987.
13. Cairine Wilson, "The Present Status of Women," *The Canadian Bar Review*, April 1932, vol X, no. 4, p. 221.
14. Speech to St James Literary Society of Montreal, 5 January 1932, Cairine Wilson papers, vol 5, file 5.2.
15. Cairine Wilson papers, vol. 6, folder 6.1.
16. Ibid.
17. *Daily Mail and Empire*, 24 November 1930.
18. Carrie Carmichael to Mackenzie King, 11 August 1933, King Primary Correspondence, MG 26, J1, vol. 195, pp. 165497-165499.
19. King papers, MG 26, J 6, vol 223.
20. Mackenzie King to Carrie Carmichael, 29 September 1933, King Primary Correspondence, vol 195, p. 165501.
21. Canada, The Senate, *Debates*, 3 May 1932, p. 394.
22. Mrs A. H. Askanasy to Kathleen Ryan, 23 May 1960, Cairine Wilson papers, vol 4, Red book.
23. Interview with the author, 25 February 1987.
24. Mackenzie King Primary Correspondence, MG 26, J1, vol 230, p.197417
25. *The Canadian Encyclopedia* (Edmonton: Hurtig Publishers, 1985), vol. 2, p. 1094.
26. *Mail and Empire*, n.d. In Wilson family scrapbook.
27. Myra Punnett in a letter to the author, 8 June 1983.
28. Cairine Wilson to daughters Cairine and Olive, 16 April 1935, Cairine Wilson papers, vol. 4, file 4.7.
29. Brigitte Kitchen, "The Marsh Report Revisited," *Journal of Canadian Studies*, vol. 2, no. 2, pp. 38-47 and Paul Martin, *A Very Public Life* (Ottawa: Deneau Publishing, 1984), vol 1, pp. 315-318.
30. Canada, The Senate, *Debates*, 5 March 1943, p. 93.
31. Address to the Ontario Liberal Women's Association, 1945, Cairine Wilson papers, vol 6, folder 6.1.
32. Canada, The Senate, *Debates*, 3 February 1944, p. 36.
33. Ibid., p. 38.
34. Ibid., p. 39.
35. Ann Sunahara, *The Politics of Racism: The Uprooting of Japanese Canadians During the Second World War* (Toronto: James Lorimer and Company, 1981), pp. 116-117.
36. Canada, The Senate, *Debates*, 28 June 1944, p. 246.
37. Ian Mulgrew, "Time to Acknowledge Injustice?," *The Globe and Mail*, 12 October 1983.
38. *Toronto Daily Star*, 11 January 1946.
39. Ibid.
40. Canada, The Senate, *Debates*, 13 March 1962, p. 287.
41. Cairine Wilson to Mackenzie King, 30 December 1946, King Primary Correspondence, MG 26, J1, vol. 419, p. 390237.
42. Figure supplied by Gabrielle Nishiguishi.
43. Interview with the author, 3 October 1984.
44. Interview with the author, 26 August 1987.
45. As reported by The Hon. Florence Bird in an interview with the author, 24 May 1984.

46. Canada, The Senate, *Debates*, 5 April 1962, p. 455.
47. Dr O.J. Firestone in a letter to the author, 12 January 1987.
48. Address on behalf of the League for Women's Rights, 9 March 1934, Cairine Wilson papers, vol 5, file 5.2.
49. *Ottawa Citizen*, 5 May 1932.
50. Thérèse Casgrain, *A Woman in a Man's World* (Toronto: McClelland and Stewart, 1972), p. 51.
51. Ibid., p. 74.
52. Patricia Myers, " 'A Noble Effort:' The National Federation of Liberal Women of Canada, 1945-1973." M.A. Thesis, University of Waterloo, 1980, p. 25.
53. *Ottawa Journal*, 1 June 1932.
54. King diary, 3 June 1933.
55. Interview with the author, 22 September 1984.
56. Interview with the author, 3 August 1983.
57. Interview with the author, 10 April 1986.
58. *Ottawa Journal*, 29 November 1934.
59. King diary, King Papers, vol. 64, 27 November 1934, p. 492.
60. *Halifax Herald*, 29 May 1941.

Chapter Six

1. Norma Phillips Muir, "Senator Cairine Wilson — Woman," *Canadian Home Journal*, June, 1930, pp. 6-7.
2. Cairine Wilson to Mackenzie King, 17 December 1932, King Personal Correspondence, MG 26, J8, vol. 41, file 3.
3. Interview with Norma and Jim Davies, 8 January 1983.
4. Cairine Wilson papers, vol. 4, folder 4.7.
5. Interview with Norma and Jim Davies, 8 January 1983.
6. Interview with Cairine Wilson and Joanna Wilson, 15 September 1987.
7. Letter from Janet Burns to the author, 27 July 1984.
8. *Toronto Globe*, 25 April 1932.
9. John Leslie Scott, "Our New Woman Senator," *Macleans Magazine*, 1 April 1930.
10. Interview with Dr Bliss Pugsley, 29 June 1983.
11. *Ottawa Journal*, 5 June 1950.
12. Interview with Alixe Carter, 15 January 1987.
13. From a print-out of a diary kept by Eric Newton while on a North American lecture tour in 1937.
14. Cairine Wilson papers, vol. 4, folder 4.7.
15. Donald Creighton, *The Forked Road Canada 1939-1957*.(Toronto: McClelland and Stewart, 1976), pp. 93-95.
16. Interview with Odette Lapointe Ouimet, 16 March 1984.
17. Cairine Wilson to Mackenzie King, 4 May 1949, King Personal Correspondence, MG 26, J8, vol. 41, file 3.
18. Letter from William Heckscher to the author, 22 May 1983.
19. Eric Koch, *Deemed Suspect* (Agincourt, Ontario: Methuen Publications, 1980), pp. 205-206.
20. Interview with Gladys Arnold, 21 June 1984.

21. Cairine Wilson to Sir Lyman Duff, 2 November 1928, Duff papers, vol. 5, file W.
22. Cairine Wilson to Sir Lyman Duff, 11 June 1934, Duff papers, vol. 5, file W.
23. David Ricardo Williams, *Duff A Life In The Law* (Vancouver: University of British Columbia Press in association with the Osgoode Society, 1984), pp. 156-163.
24. Cairine Wilson to Annie Duff, 2 April 1935, Duff papers, vol 7, folder 7.
25. Interview with Violet Herrington, 25 February 1987.
26. Letter from Myra Punnett to the author, 8 June 1983.
27. Cairine Wilson to her daughter Cairine, 4 November 1935, Cairine Wilson papers, vol. 4, file 4.7.
28. Letter from Lawrence McDougall to the author, 13 October 1986.
29. Letter from F.H. Grimner K.C. to A. McLean, 26 February 1918. In possession of the Wilson family.
30. Letter from Anna Loring to Cairine Wilson, 6 June 1922. In possession of the Wilson family.
31. Eulogy delivered 21 December 1916 by the Rev. R.W. Dickie at Crescent Street Church, Montreal. Joseph Mackay and family papers, vol. 1, file 5.
32. Interview with K. McKinney, 29 July 1984 and letter from Myra Punnett to the author, 8 June 1983.
33. Interview with Margaret Doran, 11 November 1986.
34. Cairine Wilson to her daughter, Cairine, 17 September 1938, Cairine Wilson papers, vol. 4, file 4.7.
35. "Happy Birthday Toronto 1834-1984." Pamphlet issued by Cedarvale Tree and Landscape Services.
36. Interview with Janet Burns, 4 July 1984.
37. Interview with Willa Magee Walker, 12 September 1986.
38. Cairine Wilson to Mackenzie King, 9 July 1933, Mackenzie King Personal Correspondence, MG 26, J8, vol. 41, file 3.
39. Mackenzie King to Cairine Wilson, 1 September 1932, Cairine Wilson papers, vol 2, file 2.2.
40. *Halifax Daily Mail*, 26 November 1934.

Chapter Seven

1. Norma Phillips Muir, "Senator Cairine Wilson - Woman," *Canadian Home Journal*, June 1930, pp. 96-97.
2. Notes for a speech to St John's Church, Cornwall, Cairine Wilson papers, vol. 6, file 6.2.
3. *The Story of St Andrew's Cumberland, Ontario* (Privately published), p. 12.
4. Cairine Wilson will, Ontario Archives, #38139/62.
5. O. Mary Hill, *Fifty Years At St Andrew's 1928-1978* (Privately Published), p. 10.
6. Interview with the Hon. Paul Martin, 19 January 1983.
7. O. Mary Hill, *Fifty Years at Andrew's 1928-1978*, p. 22.
8. Cairine Wilson to Mackenzie King, 7 February 1950, King Personal Correspondence, J8, vol 41, file 3.
9. Canada, The Senate, *Debates*, 13 March 1962, p. 283.

10. Cairine Wilson papers, vol. 2, file 2.6.

11. Proceedings of the 28th biennial convention of the Ontario Association of the Deaf, 25-29 June 1948. Cairine Wilson papers, vol. 2, file 2.6.

12. From research undertaken for the VON by Doris Shackleton.

13. Pamphlet on Shernfold School, Canadian Council on Social Development papers, vol 48, file 431.

14. Extract from minutes of the Board of Governors of the Canadian Welfare Council, 10 April 1962.

15. Cairine Wilson to Mary Craig McGeachy, 23 March 1940, Cairine Wilson papers, vol 2, file 2.4.

16. Cairine Wilson to young Cairine, 20 September 1945, Cairine Wilson papers, vol 4, file 4.7.

17. Interview with Dorothy Bishop, 26 November 1983, Interview with Gladys Arnold, 21 June 1984, and the Canadian-American Women's Committee papers.

18. Clyde Sanger, *Lotta and the Unitarian Service Committee Story* (Toronto: Stoddart Publishing Company, Ltd., 1986), p. 43.

19. Ibid., p. 44.

Chapter Eight

1. Cairine Wilson to Ernest Lapointe, 25 October 1933, Ernest Lapointe papers, vol 5, p. 002516.

2. Roger Sarty and Brereton Greenhous, "The Great War," *Horizon Canada*, vol. 8, no. 85, p. 201.

3. *London Advertiser*, 26 November 1931.

4. Canada, The Senate, *Debates*, 16 November 1932, p. 143.

5. Byrne Hope Sanders, *Emily Murphy Crusader* (Toronto: The Macmillan Company of Canada, 1945), p. 206.

6. Canada, The Senate, *Debates*, 23 November 1932, p. 154.

7. Ibid.

8. Ibid.

9. Canada, The Senate, *Debates*, 1 February, 1934, p. 45.

10. Ibid., 16 May 1934, p. 393.

11. Ibid., p. 394.

12. Interview with Dr John Robbins, 10 October 1985.

13. Ibid.

14. John Thompson and Allen Seager, *Canada, 1922-1939* (Toronto: McClelland and Stewart Ltd., 1985), p. 309.

15. Ibid., p. 311.

16. Donald Herperger, The League of Nations Society in Canada in the 1930s, University of Regina M.A. thesis, 1978, p. 90.

17. Dafoe to Cairine Wilson, 23 April 1941, Dafoe papers, M-79.

18. *Interdependence*, vol. 12, no. 4, 1935, pp. 64-65.

19. Robert Inch papers, vol 1, folder 14.

20. Information supplied by Dr Donald Page.

21. Cairine Wilson to Robert Inch, 7 June 1935, vol. 8, file 3641, Robert Inch papers.

22. Address given by Cairine Wilson to the Annual Meeting of the national League of Nations Society in Canada, 30 May 1942, Cairine Wilson papers, vol. 5, file 5.1.

23. Annual Report, 1937-38, League of Nations Society in Canada, Robert Inch papers, vol. 1, folder 9.

24. Inch's address to the annual meeting of the national council, 31 May 1942, vol. 1, folder 14, Robert Inch papers.

25. Ibid.

26. Herperger, The League of Nations Society in Canada in the 1930s, pp. 140-141.

27. Discussion at national executive meeting of the League of Nations Society in Canada, 26 October 1942, p. 4, folder 13, vol. 1, Robert Inch papers.

28. Mackenzie King diary, 29 September 1939, p. 739.

29. Donald Page, "The Institute's 'Popular Arm': The League of Nations Society in Canada," *International Journal*, vol 33, no. 1, p. 64.

30. Interview with George McIlraith, 7 June 1983.

31. Letter from Myra Punnett to the author, 8 June 1983.

32. Robert Inch's statement to a meeting of the national executive committee of the League of Nations Society in Canada on 26 October 1942, Robert Inch papers, vol. 1, folder 13.

33. Letter from Dr James Gibson to the author, 4 December 1986.

34. Mackenzie King diary, 4 October 1938, p. 761.

35. Cairine Wilson papers, vol. 2, file 2.13.

36. Cairine Wilson to J. Napier, 11 October 1938, Cairine Wilson papers, vol. 2, folder 2.13.

37. Cairine Wilson to Sir Lyman Duff, 11 October 1938, Sir Lyman Duff papers, vol. 5, file W.

38. Paul Martin in a letter to the author, February 1983.

39. As reported to the author by Anna Cundill.

40. Chapter 4, *Canada in World Affairs The Pre-war Years* (Toronto: University of Toronto Press, 1941), p. 117.

41. Ernest Lapointe papers, vol. 59, file 87.

42. Inch's Resignation Statement, 26 October 1942, p. 9, file 13, vol. 1, Robert Inch papers.

43. Ibid., pp. 170-171.

44. John A. McLeish, *A Canadian For All Seasons* (Toronto: Lester and Orphen, 1978), p. 112.

Chapter Nine

1. Robert Domanski, "While Six Million Cried: Canada and the Refugee Question, 1938 - 1941," Master's research essay, Institute of Canadian Studies, Carleton University, 1975, p. 10.

2. Ibid., p. 14.

3. *The Evening Citizen*, 21 March 1938, p. 9.

4. Irving Abella and Harold Troper, *None Is Too Many*, (Toronto: Lester & Orpen Dennys, 1982), p. 22.

5. *Halifax Herald*, 25 October 1940.

6. Ibid.

7. CNCR papers, vol. 1, file 5.

8. Ernest Lapointe papers, vol. 59, file 87.

9. Interview with Hon. George McIlraith, 29 September 1982.

10. MacKenzie to Wilson 24 November 1938, the Cairine Wilson Papers, vol. 1, file 1.8.

11. MacKenzie to Wilson, 3 December 1938, Cairine Wilson Papers, vol. 1, file 1.8.

12. Ibid.

13. Abella and Troper, *None is Too Many*, page 59.

14. Tribute paid in St Andrew's Presbyterian Church to Cairine Wilson on 6 March 1962 by the Rev Dr Ian Burnett. In Wilson family scrapbook.

15. Interview with Mrs Anne Carver, 13 October 1983.

16. Abella and Troper, *None Is Too Many*, p. 122.

17. Interview with Isabel Percival, 10 August 1983 and Letters written by Cairine Wilson to her daughter Cairine, 28 February and 14 March 1939, Cairine Wilson papers, vol. 4, file 4.7.

18. CNCR papers, vol 6, file 24.

19. Ibid.

20. Ibid.

21. Ibid.

22. CNCR papers, vol. 6, folder 31.

23. Cairine Wilson to her daughter, Cairine, 4 March 1939, Cairine Wilson papers, vol. 4, file 4.7.

24. *The* [Montreal] *Gazette*, 29 November 1938.

25. *The Evening Citizen*, 14 December 1938.

26. Raul Hilberg, *The Destruction of the European Jews*, (New York: Harper and Row, 1961), p. 128.

27. *The Evening Citizen*, 14 December 1938.

28. J.R.C. Perkin, "Constance Irene Hayward: A Tribute," 10 April 1982.

29. Interview with Evelyn Rosenthal, 2 August 1986.

30. Cairine Wilson to Mackenzie King, 25 Februrary 1939, King Personal Correspondence, MG 26, J8, vol. 41, folder 3.

31. CNCR papers, vol. 6, folder 25.

32. Ibid.

33. Eric Koch, *Deemed Suspect*, (Toronto: Methuen, 1980) p. 182.

34. Cairine Wilson to Mackenzie King, 16 April 1939, Mackenzie King Primary Correspondence, MG 26, J1, vol. 282, pp. 238434-238435.

35. Cairine Wilson papers, vol. 2, file 2. 18.

36. Ibid.

37. Cairine Wilson papers, vol 1, file 1.2.

38. Duff papers, General Correspondence, vol 5, file W.

39. "The Key," vol. XII, no. 8.

40. CNCR papers, vol.6, file 31.

41. Canada, The Senate, *Debates*, 18 May 1943, p. 242.

42. Cairine Wilson papers, vol. 7, file 7.3.

43. Letter from Hanna Fischl Spencer to the author, 9 February 1987.

44. Eric Koch, *Deemed Suspect*, pp. x-xi.

45. Sir Joseph Flavelle was the millionaire chairman of the Imperial Munitions Board in Canada from 1914 to 1920.

46. Abella and Troper, *None Is Too Many*, p. 64.

47. Ibid.
48. J.S. Woodsworth to Cairine Wilson, 10 May 1939, Mackenzie King Primary Correspondence, MG 26, J 1, vol. 282, p. 238438.
49. Information supplied by James Gill.
50. Article from *Le Droit* in Cairine Wilson papers, vol.12, file 12.17.
51. Irving Abella and Harold Troper, *None Is Too Many*, p. 162.
52. *The Daily Hebrew Journal*, 10 November 1943. In the Toronto Jewish Congress/Canadian Jewish Congress Ontario Region Archives.
53. Canada, The Senate, Report of the Standing Committee on Immigration and Labour, 1948, p. 11.
54. Robert Domanski, "While Six Million Cried," pp. 51-52.
55. Cairine Wilson to Mackenzie King, 16 May 1940, Mackenzie King Primary Correspondence, MG 26, J1, vol. 298, p. 253341.
56. Canada, The Senate, *Debates*, 18 May 1943, p. 242.
57. RG 76, vol.453, file 693, 670, part 2.
58. Cairine Wilson papers, vol. 1, file 1.6.
59. Article on Cairine Wilson by Carolyn Cox, *Christian Science Monitor*, 26 June 1940.

Chapter Ten

1. Eric Koch, *Deemed Suspect* (Toronto: Methuen, 1980), pp. 29-31.
2. Alexander Paterson, Report on Civilian Internees Sent From the United Kingdom to Canada During the Unusually Fine Summer of 1940, p. 5.
3. Ibid., p. 37.
4. CNCR papers, minutes of the executive committee, vol. 6, file 26.
5. Ibid.
6. Letter from William Heckscher to the author, 7 June 1983.
7. Eric Koch, *Deemed Suspect*, p. 183.
8. Interview with Eric Kippen, 19 June 1983.
9. Interview with Gladys Arnold, 21 June 1984.
10. Camp commandant's diary, RG 24, vol. 15,399, No. 41 Internment Camp, 6 July 1940.
11. Interview with Eric Kippen, 19 June 1983.
12. Eric Koch, *Deemed Suspect*, p. 230.
13. Letter from William Heckscher to the author, 22 May 1983.
14. Letter from Vernon Brooks to The Rev Dr E. Clifford Knowles, 2 April 1983.
15. Cairine Wilson to Dr Philippe A. Koller, 10 March 1942. Letter in the possession of Mrs Philippe Koller.
16. Camp commandant's diary, RG 24, vol. 15397, No. 40 Internment camp, 7 November 1940.
17. Alexander Paterson, Report on Civilian Internees..., p. 34.
18. Marta Wasserman to Cairine Wilson, Jr., 15 March 1962, Cairine Wilson papers, vol. 13, file 13.6.
19. CNCR papers, vol. 6, folder 5.
20. Charles F. Blair to Cairine Wilson, 31 August 1942, CNCR papers, vol 2, folder 4.
21. External Affairs file, 621-B-40.

22. Report of the Central Committee, 2 June 1941, CNCR papers, vol. 6, file 27.
23. Constance Hayward to Dr Bruno Weinberg, 39 August 1941, CNCR papers, vol 6, file 5.
24. Camp Commandant's diary, RG 24, vol. 15397.
25. Benjamin Robinson to Cairine Wilson, 4 September 1941, Canadian Jewish Congress Collection, Series CA, file 154A.
26. A search has failed to turn up a copy of this letter.
27. Cairine Wilson to Saul Hayes, 11 July 1942, Canadian Jewish Congress Collection, Series CA, file 154A.
28. Canadian Jewish Congress Collection, Series CA, file 154A.
29. Paula Draper, "The Accidental Immigrants: Canada and the Interned Refugees." Ph.D. thesis, University of Toronto, 1983, p. 328.
30. Cairine Wilson to Mackenzie King, 26 June 1945, King Primary Correspondence, MG 26, J1, vol. 397, pp. 359533-359534.
31. Ibid., pp. 359536-359537.
32. Peter and Leni Gillman, *'Collar The Lot'!* London: Quartet Books, 1980), p. 276.
33. External Affairs file, 621-B-40.
34. Interview with Walter Loevinsohn, 19 March 1983.
35. Ibid.
36. *Ottawa Citizen*, 18 November 1942.
37. Interview with Herman Nathan, 9 May 1984.

Chapter Eleven

1. Jacques Vernant, *The Refugee In The Post-War World* (London: George Allen & Unwin Ltd., 1953), pp. 30-31.
2. Canada, The Senate, *Report of the Standing Committee on Immigration and Labour 1946*, p. 240.
3. Cairine Wilson papers, vol. 6, file 6.1.
4. Canada, The Senate, *Debates*, 13 March 1947, p. 129.
5. Interview with Violet MacAlonan Herrington, 25 February 1987.
6. CNCR papers, vol. 6, file 20.
7. Ibid., file 29.
8. Cairine Wilson to Mackenzie King, 30 April 1946, King Primary Correspondence, MG 26, J1, vol. 419, p. 380203.
9. Canada, The Senate, *Debates*, 13 March 1947, p. 130.
10. Canada, The Senate, *Report of the Standing Committee on Immigration and Labour 1946*, p. 231.
11. Gerald Dirks, *Canada's Refugee Policy: Indifference or Opportunism?* (Montreal: McGill-Queen's University Press, 1977), p. 133.
12. Canada, House of Commons, *Debates*, 1 May 1947, p. 2675.
13. CNCR papers, vol. 6, file 19.
14. Ibid.
15. CNCR papers, vol 6, file 30.
16. Cairine Wilson to Constance Hayward, 7 November 1947, CNCR papers, vol 6, file 19.

17. Cairine Wilson, "The Cry of the Homeless," *The Presbyterian Record*, December 1948, pp. 321-322.

18. CNCR papers, vol. 6, file 30.

19. Cairine Wilson to Constance Hayward, 30 January 1948, CNCR papers, vol. 6, file 20.

20. Ibid., file 30.

21. Cairine Wilson papers, vol. 1, file 4.

22. *Ottawa Citizen*, 20 May 1950.

23. Dept. of External affairs papers. EA 5475-DW-3-40.

24. Dept. of External affairs papers. EA 5475-DW-3-40.

25. Margaret Stewart and Doris French, *Ask No Quarter*, (Toronto: Longmans, Green and Company, 1959), p.159.

26. Eleanor Roosevelt, *The Autobiography of Eleanor Roosevelt* (New York: Harper & Brothers Publishers, 1961), p. 303.

27. Address to the Porcupine Inter-University Association, 24 December 1950, Cairine Wilson papers, vol. 6, file 6.2.

28. Text of a broadcast by Lester Pearson on the CBC, 25 September 1949, Department of External Affairs, Statements and Speeches.

29. Lipla Van Zandt in an identified newspaper article in Wilson family scrapbook.

30. Interview with the author, 18 October 1983.

31. Interview with the author, 12 October 1983.

32. Ibid.

33. Eleanor Roosevelt, *The Autobiography of Eleanor Roosevelt*, pp. 307-308.

34. UN General Assembly, Summary Records and Annexes, 4th Session, Third Committee, vol. 3, 4 November 1949, p. 104.

35. Ibid., p. 106.

36. Ibid., and External Affairs file 10. 5475-EA-40, 4 November 1949.

37. Helen Gordon McPherson, "Canadian Woman Heads 'Firsts,' " *Christian Science Monitor*, 26 April 1950.

38. Canada, The Senate, *Debates*, 14 December 1953, p. 144.

39. Cairine Wilson to Mackenzie King, 16 December 1949, King Personal Correspondence, MG 26, J8, vol. 41, file 3.

40. Address to Kydd Memorial Church, 15 October 1950, Cairine Wilson papers, vol. 6, file 6.2.

41. Address to the Zonta Club of Ottawa, 25 February 1959, Cairine Wilson papers, vol. 6, file 6.2.

42. Canada, The Senate, *Debates*, 15 March 1950, p. 61.

43. Dominion Bureau of Statistics, *Canada 1958* (Ottawa, 1958), p. 52.

44. Canada, The Senate, *Debates*, 15 March 1950, p. 63.

45. Canada, The Senate, *Debates*, 8 May 1950, p. 266.

46. Hubert Guerin to Cairine Wilson, 24 July 1950, Cairine Wilson papers, vol. 4, file 4.5.

47. Victor Odlum to Cairine Wilson, 11 August 1950, Victor Odlum papers, vol. 13, file Senator Cairine Wilson.

48. Cairine Wilson to Mackenzie King, 16 June 1949, Mackenzie King Personal Correspondence, MG 26, J8, vol 41, file 3.

49. Cairine Wilson to Mackenzie King, 25 January 1950, King Personal Correspondence, MG 26, J8, vol. 41, file 3.

50. Interview with Florence Bird, 24 May 1984.

51. Canada, The Senate, *Debates*, 21 March 1951, p. 305.
52. *Ibid.*, p. 306.
53. Canada, The Senate, *Debates*, 17 March 1955, p. 316.
54. *Ottawa Journal*, 23 February 1955.
55. Canada, The Senate, *Debates*, 8 March 1955, p. 256.

Chapter Twelve

1. Cairine Wilson to Sir Lyman Duff, 12 August 1953, Cairine Wilson papers, vol. 1, file 6.
2. Cairine Wilson to young Cairine, 4 December 1950, Cairine Wilson papers, vol. 4, file 4.7.
3. David Ricardo Williams, *Duff*, pp. 262-263.
4. Cairine Wilson to Gordon Wallace, 27 December 1951, Cairine Wilson papers, vol. 2, file 14.
5. Dominion Bureau of Statistics, *Canada 1961* (Ottawa, 1961), p. 51.
6. Cairine Wilson to Saul Hayes, 16 June 1960, Cairine Wilson papers, vol 4, file 29.
7. Cairine Wilson to Leonard Brockington, 20 June 1960, Cairine Wilson papers, vol, 4 file 4.2.
8. Cairine Wilson to Hella Moravec Street, 30 June 1961. Letter in possession of Mrs Street.
9. Letter from William Heckscher to the author, 3 March 1983.
10. From the poem entitled "Canada's Chatelaine" by Theresa E. Thomson. Contained in Wilson family scrapbook.
11. Canada, The Senate, *Debates*, 13 March 1962, p. 285.
12. Surrogate Court, The County of Carleton, Non-Contentious Bursaries and Grants Book, June 1961-August 1963, p. 116.
13. Cairine Wilson will, Ontario Archives, Toronto, RG 22, Series 354, #38139/62 Wilson.

LIST OF ILLUSTRATIONS

SOURCES

PUBLIC DOCUMENTS AND RECORDS

Canada, Parliament
    Senate. Debates. 1930 et seq.
    ——Journals. Vol. LXV11.
    ——Reports of the Standing Committee on Immigration and and Labour, 1946
    and 1948.
Department of External Affairs file EA 5475-DW-3-40.
Department of External Affairs file 10. 5475-EA-40.
Department of External Affairs file 621-B-40.

Revised Statutes of Canada 1927.

United Nations General Assembly. Summary Records and Annexes, 4th Session, Third
    Committee.

UNPUBLISHED SOURCES

Abbreviation used: NAC=National Archives of Canada

Domanski, Robert. "While Six Million Cried: Canada and the Refugee Question, 1938-
    1941." Master's research essay, Institute of Canadian Studies, Carleton University,
    1975.
Draper, Paula. "The Accidental Immigrants: Canada and the Interned Refugees." Ph.D
    thesis, University of Toronto, 1983.
Haworth, L.H. "A History of the Mackay School for the Deaf." M.A thesis, McGill
    University, 1960.
Herperger, Donald John. "The League of Nations Society in Canada During the 1930s."
    M.A thesis, University of Regina, 1978.
Myers, Patricia A. " 'A Noble Effort:' The National Federation of Liberal Women of
    Canada, 1945-1973." M.A thesis, University of Waterloo, 1980.
Way, A.R. "From Time to Time in the Queen's Name: The Story of the Honourable
    Cairine Reay Wilson." M.A thesis, Carleton University, 1984.
Canadian-American Women's Committee Papers, NAC.
Canadian Council on Social Development Papers, NAC.
Canadian Jewish Congress Collection, Series CA. Canadian Jewish Congress National
    Archives.
Canadian National Committee on Refugees Papers, NAC.
Chadwick, Ethel, Diaries, NAC.
Clay, Charles, Papers, NAC.
Dafoe, J.W., Papers, NAC.
Duff, Sir Lyman, Papers, NAC.
Inch, Robert, Papers, NAC.
King, William Lyon Mackenzie, Diaries and Papers, NAC.
Lapointe, Ernest, Papers, NAC.

Laurier, Sir Wilfrid, Papers, NAC.
League of Nations Society in Canada Papers, NAC.
Mackay, Joseph and Family Papers, NAC.
Odlum, Victor, Papers, NAC.
Record Group 24 Papers, NAC.
Record Group 76 Papers, NAC.
Smith, Alexander, Papers, NAC.
Spry, Graham, Papers, NAC.
Tory, Henry Marshall, Papers, NAC.
Wilson, Cairine Reay, Papers, NAC.
Paterson, Alexander, *Report on Civilian Internees Sent From the United Kingdom to Canada During the Unusually Fine Summer of 1940.*
Perkin, J.R.C., "Constance Irene Hayward: A Tribute." 10 April 1982.
Proceedings of the First National Convention of the Twentieth Century Liberal Association of Canada.
Diary in possession of Mrs. Hanna Fischl Spencer.
Proceedings of the Second National Convention of the Twentieth Century Liberal Association of Canada.
Letters in the possession of the Wilson family, Mrs Philippe Koller, and Mrs Hella Moravec Street.

PUBLISHED SOURCES

Canada in World Affairs The Pre-War Years. Toronto: University of Toronto Press, 1941.
The Canadian Encyclopedia. Edmonton: Hurtig Publishers, 1985.
The Canadian Parliamentary Guide. Ottawa: Queen's Printer, 1908 et seq.
Dictionary of Canadian Biography, vols. X and X1. Toronto: University of Toronto Press, 1972.
Encyclopedia Canadiana. Toronto: Grolier of Canada, 1977.
"Happy Birthday Toronto 1834-1984." Pamphlet issued by Cedarvale Tree and Landscape Services.
A Standard Dictionary of Canadian Biography. vol 1, 1875-1933. Toronto: Trans-Canada Press, 1934.
The Storied Province of Quebec. vol. 5. Toronto: The Dominion Publishing Company, 1933.
The Story of St Andrew's Cumberland, Ontario. One Hundred and Fiftieth Anniversary 1828-1978.
Abella, Irving and Troper, Harold, *None Is Too Many. Canada and the Jews of Europe 1933-1948.* Toronto: Lester & Orpen Dennys, 1982.
Beland, Serge and Laporte, Vianney, *La Petite Histoire de Rockland.* Muncipality of Rockland, 1982.
Bissell, Claude, *The Young Vincent Massey.* Toronto: University of Toronto Press, 1981.
Bliss, Michael, *A Canadian Millionaire The Life and Times of Sir Joseph Flavelle, Bart. 1858-1939.* Toronto: Macmillan of Canada, 1979.
Brown, Robert Craig and Cook, Ramsay, *Canada 1896-1921.* Toronto: McClelland and Stewart Ltd., 1974.
Cleverdon, Catherine L., *The Woman Suffrage Movement in Canada.* Second Edition. Toronto: University of Toronto Press, 1974.

Collard, Edgar A., *Call Back Yesterdays*. Don Mills, Ontario: Longmans Canada Ltd., 1965.

Creighton, Donald, *The Forked Road. Canada 1939-1957*. Toronto: McClelland and Stewart, 1976.

Cruickshank, J. Evan and Richards, Denis, *The Modern Age, 1760-1955*. Toronto: Longmans, Green and Company, 1957.

De Roquebrune, Robert, *Quartier Saint-Louis*. Montreal: Fides, 1966.

Desbarats, Lilian, *Recollections*. Ottawa: Privately published, 1957.

Dirks, Gerald, *Canada's Refugee Policy: Indifference or Opportunism?* Montreal: McGill-Queen's University Press, 1977.

Gillman, Peter and Leni, *'Collar The Lot!'* London: Quartet Books, 1980.

Glazebrook, G.P. de T., *A History of Canadian External Relations.*, Vol. 2. Revised Edition. The Carleton Library Series. Toronto: McClelland and Stewart, 1966.

Greenhous, Brereton and Sarty, Roger, "The Great War," *Horizon Canada*, vol. 8, no. 85, pp. 2017-2023.

Keenleyside, Hugh, *Memoirs of Hugh Keenleyside*. vol. 2. Toronto: McClelland and Stewart, 19822.

Gwyn, Sandra, *The Private Capital*. Toronto: McClelland and Stewart, 1984.

Heritage Ottawa, *Walking In Sandy Hill, Ottawa*. Published by Heritage Ottawa. No date.

Hilberg, Paul, *The Destruction of the European Jews*. New York: Harper and Row, 1961.

Holt, Simma, *The Other Mrs Diefenbaker*. Toronto: Doubleday Canada Ltd., 1982.

Hubbard, Robert, *Rideau Hall*. Montreal: McGill-Queen's University Press, 1977.

Innis, Mary Q., *The Clear Spirit. Twenty Canadian Women and Their Times*. Toronto: University of Toronto Press, 1967.

Jenkins, Kathleen, *Montreal*. Garden City, New York: Doubleday & Company, 1966.

Kitchen, Brigitte, "The Marsh Report Revisited," *Journal of Canadian Studies*, vol. 2, no. 2, pp. 38-47.

Koch, Eric, *Deemed Suspect. A Wartime Blunder*. Toronto: Methuen, 1980.

L'Esperance, Jeanne, *The Widening Sphere. Women in Canada, 1870-1940*. Ottawa: Public Archives of Canada, 1982.

Lewis, Robert, *Edith Wharton A Biography*. Toronto: Fitzhenry & Whiteside Ltd., 1975.

Little, C.H., *Rideau Curling Club of Ottawa, A Short History 1888-1978*. Privately published.

Local Architectural Conservation Advisory Committee, *Walking in the Village of Rockcliffe Park*. Published by the Village of Rockcliffe Park, 1982.

McCall-Newman, Christina, *Grits. An Intimate Portrait of the Liberal Party*. Toronto: Macmillan of Canada, 1982.

MacKay, Donald, *The Square Mile. Merchant Princes of Montreal*. Toronto: Douglas and McIntyre Ltd., 1987.

McLeish, John A., *A Canadian For All Seasons*. Toronto: Lester and Orphen, 1978.

Martin, Paul, *A Very Public Life*. Ottawa: Deneau Publishing, 1984.

Morgan, Henry J., *The Canadian Men and Women of the Time*. Toronto: William Briggs, 1912.

Muir, Norma P., "Senator Cairine Wilson - Woman," *Canadian Home Journal*, vol. 27, no. 2, June 1930, pp. 6, 7, 96-97.

Neatby, H. Blair, *William Lyon Mackenzie King 1924-1932. The Lonely Heights.* Toronto: University of Toronto Press, 1970.

Newman, Peter C., *The Canadian Establishment.* vol. 1. Toronto: McClelland and Stewart Ltd., 1975.

√ Page, Donald, "The Institute's 'popular arm:' The League of Nations Society in Canada," *International Journal Opinion and Policy.* vol. XXXIII, no. 1, winter 1977-78, pp. 26-65.

Pearson, Lester B., *Mike.* Toronto: University of Toronto Press, 1973.

Prebble, John, *The Highland Clearances.* London: Secker and Warburg, 1963.

Reid, W. Stanford, editor, *The Scottish Tradition in Canada.* Toronto: McClelland and Stewart, 1976.

Roosevelt, Eleanor, *The Autobiography of Eleanor Roosevelt.* New York: Harper and Brothers Publishers, 1961.

Sanders, Byrne, *Emily Murphy Crusader.* Toronto: The Macmillan Company of Canada, 1945.

Sanger, Clyde, *Lotta and the Unitarian Service Committee Story.* Toronto: Stoddart Publishing Company Ltd., 1986.

√ Scott, John Leslie, "Our New Woman Senator," *Macleans Magazine.* 1 April 1930.

Stacey, C.P., *A Very Double Life. The Private World of Mackenzie King.* Toronto: The Macmillan Company of Canada, 1976.

Sunahara, Ann, *The Politics of Racism: The Uprooting of Japanese Canadians During the Second World War.* Toronto: James Lorimer and Company, 1981.

Thompson, John H., and Seager, Allen, *Canada 1922-1939. Decades of Discord.* Toronto: McClelland and Stewart, 1985.

Vernant, Jacques, *The Refugee in the Post-War World.* London: George Allen and Unwin Ltd., 1953.

Williams, David Ricardo, *Duff: A Life in the Law.* Vancouver: University of Vancouver Press in association with Osgoode Hall, 1984.

Woods Jr., Shirley, E., *Ottawa The Capital of Canada.* Toronto: Doubleday Canada Ltd., 1980.

Brantford Times
Christian Science Monitor
Detroit News
Gazette [Montreal]
Hamilton Herald
Mail and Empire [Toronto]
Montreal Daily Herald
Ottawa Evening Citizen
Ottawa Evening Journal
Regina Star
Star [Halifax]
Star [Montreal]
Toronto Daily Star
Toronto Telegram
Vancouver Province

NOTES